DEDICATION

~

Dedicated to the love of our lives,
Alexis, Austin, Amberay & Alaska.

This book is written to guide you in the Way of Life.
The wisdom I pass... is my gift to you.
Isaiah 33:6

~

Your loving Papa

THE DIVINE CODE

A Prophetic Encyclopedia of Numbers, Vol. I

STEVE CIOCCOLANTI

DISCOVER MEDIA

WHAT LEADERS ARE SAYING

"Steve Cioccolanti has written a fascinating book about what different numbers may represent in the Bible and in prophecy. He has assembled an impressive range of prophetic theories about the timing of End Time events. His book is highly readable, carefully researched and provocative. The fact that he is not dogmatic in pushing any one specific prophecy is refreshing. He gives each reader credit for being able to make up their own mind based on the information he has presented."

R. EDWIN SHERMAN
President of Isaac Newton Bible Code Research Society
President of Bible Code Digest
Member of American Academy of Actuaries

"I have been teaching a Biblical view of Creation and science for nearly 50 years. I am still amazed at the newly discovered insights of God's ingenuity. Steve Cioccolanti's *The Divine Code* is another example of an additional 21st-century disclosure that will set the readers heart on fire with the truths he has uncovered.

As someone who has been raised in a family that believes in the supernatural, I commend to you the chapter on numbers and physical healing that isn't New Age but rather the ageless Word of God. If you enjoy God's divine numbers' brain game, you won't want to pass up this enlightening and anointed volume on Biblical numbers code breaker."

DR. DENNIS LINDSAY
President and CEO of Christ For The Nations

"Bible Numerics is a subject that will never be exhausted. The Divine Code by Steve Cioccolanti certainly adds to this amazing and fascinating subject."

KEVIN CONNER
Internationally-Recognized Theologian and Author

"Steve has brilliant insights into numbers and the end times. This is a must read for all connected to the Lord and in tune to the times!"

PASTOR DANIEL FOO
International Faculty of Haggai Institute
Senior Pastor of Bethesda Bedok-Tampines, Singapore

"Over the past several decades many Christian authors have written books on Biblical numbers and their meanings, and some have even taught a complicated and controversial system of numerology. Then a few years ago the Bible Code books caused a sensation, and now we have Jesus codes, Buddha codes, Torah Codes, etc. However much of this is simply speculation focusing on conspiracy theories and strange doctrines that do not edify anyone. They only lead people away from the revelation of the Word of God.

The Divine Code by Steve Cioccolanti is an excellent reference book that is extremely informative, inspirational and practical in every way. Above all the teaching in this book is based on solid Biblical exegesis and accepted and proven evangelical doctrines. Steve has an accepted and proven teaching ministry and deals with many more complicated subjects such as Christianity and postmodern philosophy, evolution and creationism, reconciling Biblical history with science and secular accounts, and many other subjects relevant to 21st-century believers.

This excellent book has reconciled the extremes in doctrines and practices we see all around us, and brings forth the proper balanced Biblical perspective. More than that, the teaching is very practical, and is extremely helpful in the daily lives of the reader. I highly recommend this to every follower of Jesus, and Christian teachers and leaders will find this teaching valuable as they build the church on the foundation of God's Word."

PASTOR DENNIS BALCOMBE

Founder of Revival Chinese Ministries International
Senior Pastor of Revival Christian Church HK
Missionary to Hong Kong and China since 1969

"Steve Cioccolanti's book is both stimulating and thought provoking. It is thoroughly Biblical in its approach and examines issues facing us in our twenty-first century world. I have always been cautious about end times as so many people and churches get sidetracked from the real issues. Steve's book cuts to the core by giving us a solid practical platform to approach this subject. When it comes to addressing the subject of end times, this book focuses on what we need to do, so that we are not caught up in the grip of a world that is under the control of the 'god of this world'. I highly recommend it to all who are seeking to understand end times."

DAVID BOYD

Senior Pastor of Jesus Family Centre, Sydney, Australia
Author of 'You Don't Have to Cross the Ocean to Reach the World

"There is no other book like *The Divine Code*. Most people are scared of numbers and bored by math. But this book will keep you engaged all the way through. Pastor Cioccolanti is the first pastor I know to highlight God's glory in the Bible through numbers in an entertaining way. I don't think Christians appreciate the importance of numbers. They are afraid that they may be dabbling in Kabbalah or the occult, so this book is ground-breaking in educating people that God created numbers to glorify Him. For those who love God's Word, you will find Pastor Cioccolanti's research enlightening. Scholars and lay people will enjoy this thought-provoking book—it will make you think."

LORILYN ROBERTS
Award-Winning Christian Author

"Throughout human history, great minds have recognized that the universe is in essence a mind-boggling mathematical equation. Plato once said, "Mathematics is the language in which the gods speak to people." In *The Divine Code*, Pastor Steve Cioccolanti explores the "divine codes," numbers and patterns in Scripture that reveal the Bible truly is the Word of God. One of the greatest proofs of God is that all is an exquisite symphony composed by a mathematical genius beyond human comprehension. But even more than delving into the mathematical mysteries of life and God, *The Divine Code* is a practical book about numbers and how we can apply them to ourselves to have richer and more meaningful lives."

TROY ANDERSON
Pulitzer Prize-Nominated Journalist
Former Executive Editor of Charisma Magazine
Bestselling Author of Trumpocalypse & the Babylon Code

The Divine Code: *A Biblical Encyclopedia of Numbers, Vol. I*

Published by **Discover Media**

P.O. Box 379, Black Rock

VIC 3193, AUSTRALIA

www.Discover.org.au

Front cover design: Selena Sok

ISBN Digital book: 978-1-922273-03-1

ISBN Paperback: 978-1-922273-07-9

Printed in the U.S.A.

CONTENTS

ACKNOWLEDGMENTS

I wish to thank a few people who helped me with this 20-year project.

Lalaine Villafuerte-Abonal for encouraging me to add number 17, which gave me the impetus to do a massive overhaul of the original version. Many more numbers were thereafter added. Her family also sponsored the first printing.

Dr. Dennis Lindsay who took a personal interest in my project because his father, the late Gordon Lindsay, had been similarly interested in numbers, cycles and codes. Dennis sent me *"God's Plan of the Ages"* which is out-of-print and for which I am grateful. It helped me polish my last chapter which, interestingly enough, was 17 again.

Lorilyn Roberts a top-notch author and speaker in her own right. She credits my end time teaching for inspiring some of her Christian fantasy books. I credit her for inspiring me to add to 666, which I wanted to shorten for this book. (It is still my longest chapter.) If she was not busy doing live broadcast captioning for major television networks, I would have monopolized her amazing literary skills as my full-time editor. She is a constant resource for little tips that make a huge difference.

Selena Sok and **Cathy Wong**, my graphic artists who were on call whenever the need and always came through. Selena's faith in this project can be summed up in her question, "Who wouldn't want to know the number of God and the number of angels?" (She is referring to chapters 7, 26 and '4 Angels'.)

My wife Caren for giving me ideas to improve, laying out this prodigious volume digitally, and asking me to get out of my chair when I was slaving away at finishing this book. She enticed me with walks outside or meals served in front of my computer. I am sorry for missing some meals while they were hot.

My wife is very down-to-earth and spiritually alert at the same time. I have found these two qualities often go together in a person, as they did in Jesus. Given this fact, I pay close attention to reserved and unassuming people when they voice their opinions. Caren thinks every chapter is important in its own right, but her personal favorite is '19 Healings'.

My children. The truth is I wrote this book for you. You are a part of me, and this book is a part of me. I may never write another book quite like this one again. *The Divine Code* is a concentration of my wisdom which I share with you. There is content for every age—every stage of your growth—and my prayer is that as you get older, you will always find more here to appreciate.

∾

This book was released to the public on 17 Nisan—the Day of Victory!

PREFACE

 "In the beginning was the Word [Logos], and the Word [Logos] was with God, and the Word [Logos] was God." (John 1:1)

HOW TO USE THIS BOOK

You can read these chapters in any order. If you are interested in certain numbers, such as those related to your birthday or a number you have seen over and over, then you can flip through this book as a handy reference. You may be interested in studying all the divine codes, then you will enjoy reading this book from cover to cover. My recommended starting point for you is to read this Preface and Introduction first before venturing into your casual read or serious study.

One day Caren (my wife) asked me, "What does 15 mean?" She infrequently poses such questions, so it caught my attention. I suspected God had showed her something intimate. I said, "I have to look it up in my book." When I did, it turned out to be exactly what God had shown her.

This type of experience encourages me that you will be able to use this book to have similar questions answered and confirmations received as we did.

SUMMARY ABOUT THE BOOK

This is a book about numbers—their meanings and patterns in Scripture, nature, history and prophecy. They are 'divine codes' simply because if God did not exist, none of these numbers and patterns would recur in logical fashion at multiple levels of the observable cosmos. God is logical.

Numbers can tell us a lot. While visiting Greece once, a local tour guide informed me that by studying nature, the Greeks believed creation was mathematical. They reasoned that a mind that understands mathematics—a mind similar to ours—created the Universe, because we can understand it on mathematical terms. But of course, they said, his mind must be greater than ours. Furthermore they postulated that he can't be double-minded (or 'bi-polar' we might say), so he can't be many. Through sheer mathematics, they arrived at the conclusion that there must be—behind everything—one single Great God. This is monotheism by mathematics.

This is not a book about mathematics or numerology. It is not too technical nor too theoretical. It is a practical book about numbers, what they tell us, and how we can apply their meanings to have a richer, deeper, more meaningful life.

THE HEART NOT HEAD OF NUMBERS

The Apostle John opens his Gospel with a classic statement: "In the beginning was the Word, and the Word was with God, and the Word was God." Here the Greek word Logos is translated 'Word' in English, but logos means more than just 'word'. The

Greeks actually use lexis to convey 'word'. Some Christians say logos means the 'written word'. But the Greeks use gramma to convey 'written word,' 'writing' or 'letter' (from which we get our English word 'grammar'.)

What does logos really mean? On a cursory look we call tell the Greek logos looks very similar to some of our English words: logic, logical, logistics. Logos can mean word, but it also means: logic, thought, reason, intelligence, planning and carrying out activity, creative power. By extension, one who thinks also utters and speaks. With this understanding, we can read what John was saying, "In the beginning was Logic, and Logic was with God, and the Logic was God." In other words, God is logical.

There is a reason behind everything God does, behind everything He creates, behind every word He writes, behind every number He uses. This is what the world has not understood and what the church has largely forgotten. Our modern services tend to appeal to emotions. Our feel-good sermons skirt the issues and dodge the questions. Christians expect others to accept Bible claims on demand, "Just believe!" Believe in what? And why should one believe?

Paul said "the letter (gramma) kills" (2 Corinthians 3:6). That means you can read a written word or hear a spoken word, but not understand the thought, intent, and heart behind the words. It is possible to hear, know, even obey something that is written or spoken, but not understand the logic of what is being said. This is the crux of tradition and legalism. Religion is not mindless, it is heartless. Skepticism is also not mindless, it is heartless. Neither of them are our friends. Have you ever been in a supermarket or bank where there is no cue, no people standing in line, yet the teller demands that you pull out the waiting ticket with a number? That's someone who knows the gramma or letter of the rule, but not the logos or logic behind the rule.

The written word, the gramma, is the product of the thoughts and intents of God the Logos. We can see things, even believe things, without understanding the reason behind them. I am not speaking about intellectual reasoning, I'm speaking about discovering the spirit of the speaker. As we mature spiritually, God wants us to know Him as the Logos. Without a tender heart to understand the Personal Logos, you cannot logistically walk out what you've heard.

I believe that it was the Greek's fascination with science, numbers and the logic behind them that prepared them for the Gospel that would arrive through Christians. Today, the Church has forgotten logic or even put it down. Some well-meaning Christians tell their skeptical friends to "just believe" without giving any logical reason.

This book is about the logos of numbers. It's about the splendid evidence God intends for us to see. Once you catch the logic, you will also get the logistics of how to apply His wisdom in your life.

NOTES TO THE READERS

We will leave aside the usual convention of writing out numbers (one, two, three) as we have many numbers in this book which will be easier to read as 1, 2, 3, and so on.

I will sometimes refer to the numeric value of a word or its gematria. Turning words into 'geometry' is common among Jewish interpreters and is approved by the New Testament in Revelation 13, which advises us to calculate the number of the Beast's name or 666. How can names be turned into numbers? It is possible only in an alphanumeric system such as Hebrew and Greek.

Jews use 22 letters (all consonants) in their alphabet, and ancient Greeks used 27 letters (both consonants and vowels), but neither had separate symbols for numbers. So the ancient Hebrews and Greeks assigned a numerical value to every letter in their alphabet (like A = 1, B = 2, C = 3). By replacing the letters of a word with its numeric equivalent, you can calculate its gematria.

Adding these numbers have preoccupied some people to the extreme. If calculation makes you miss the plain meaning of the text, rather than enhance it, then gematria becomes a distraction. Yet there is no denying that researchers have found some curious 'coincidences' by calculating the numeric value of Biblical words. For instance, the gematria of the Hebrew word 'pregnancy' is 271. The average length of pregnancy from fertilization to delivery is also 271 days.[1]

How can we stay balanced when it comes to studying numbers? How can we avoid falling into the one ditch of ignoring numbers and the other ditch of being more engrossed with numbers than the Creator of numbers? Here is the balance: the study of numbers is useful so long as it centers on the God of the Bible, the One who made the numbers and assigned to them meaning. But when numerology centers on man and his attempts to make predictions about himself, then it becomes like astrology, a perversion of something good God made. God made the stars to reflect His glory and tell the story of His Son, not which lottery ticket to buy!

> **Studying the stars is astronomy,**
> **but following the stars is astrology.**
> **Studying numbers is Biblical numerology,**
> **but following numbers is idolatry.**

If our understanding of numbers is correct, it should lead us to a better understanding of the words of the Bible and a better appreciation for the beautiful design of life which God gave us. The Biblical study of numbers cannot be separated from the Biblical study of words because God chose to use two languages which did not separate their linguistic symbols from their mathematical symbols. In other words, their letters were their numbers and sometimes their words created interesting sums. The Hebrew gematria of the name "Emperor Nero" (the burner of Christians) is 666. The numeric value of the Greek name "Jesus" is 888. Profound? Read this book and decide for yourself.

INTRODUCTION

THE PURPOSE OF NUMBERS

NUMBERS MAKE US HUMAN. Life would be impersonal without numbers. Numbers tell us our age, height, size, address, phone details, health, pay, portfolio performance, track record, anniversaries, appointments—overall some very personal things. Yet reducing everything to numbers makes it all so.... ah, impersonal. Yes, we seem to have a love-hate relationship with numbers.

We memorize numbers, quote numbers, calculate numbers. But we also want to run away from numbers on our bills, race against numbers on our clocks, fight against numbers of passing years on our calendars, and sometimes ignore numbers on our evaluations or report cards. But I want to tell you why we cannot ignore numbers for too long. Creatures in the animal kingdom can do it. But we can't... for one simple reason.

Numbers also make us divine. No, numbers don't make us god, but numbers elevate us above the animal kingdom and connect us to an intelligent Creator who knows the future! Dr. Peter Plitcha explained it this way in *God's Secret Formula*: "It was a decisive mistake that science began to interpret numbers as a human invention approximately 100 years ago, just so that mysticism could be expelled from science and mathematics. In this way God was also expelled from nature...There is a divine structural plan behind this world."[1]

If you want to know the future, you have to know numbers. If you want to know the projected population of your country, you can by knowing her birth rate, migration rate and mortality rate. If you want to forecast the weather in May, you can by searching the historical temperatures and precipitation in previous Mays. If you want to know how a business will perform long term, you can make a sound projection based on the company's fundamentals, the bank's interest rates, the government's tax rates, the nation's growth rate. If you want to make an educated guess which sports team will most likely win the championship, you need to keep its scores from previous games and seasons. If you want to know the future of God's plan, you will have to know God's numbers — the divine codes.

Our understanding of numbers is necessary to predict the future, which we are inclined to do regularly whether we deal with the weather, the stock market, insurance policies or the state of our own health. We are the unique part of God's creation that is innately preoccupied with the future. My dog does not think about his future. Yes, beavers may build dams for future winters and bears may eat up before they hibernate, but these behaviors are followed out of mechanical necessity.

We, on the other hand, long for the future. Given a moment of solitude, our thoughts soon turn to the prospects of tomorrow. You can put a man in prison by robbing him of his future. You can set a man free from prison by giving him hope of a better tomorrow. When we don't get to ponder or plan our future, we literally feel stuck and shackled - burdened by our past regrets or stressed out about our present situation. When the future cannot be predicted, we feel a sense of uncertainty. We *want* to know the future. We *need* to know our future. And numbers open a divine portal into that future!

NUMBERS TELL US THE FUTURE

There are "prophets" in nearly every field of work and knowledge. Many people are highly sought after and highly paid to make some sort of educated *prediction* about the future. Nearly all of them do it by numbers.

Political analysts use polling numbers to calculate popularity and project an election result. Meteorologists plug numbers into computer models to forecast the weather days, weeks, and months ahead of time. Actuaries are employed to calculate the risk of possible events that could impact insurance claims.

Watch the financial pundits on TV. Little do they report the present. Most of the time they are speculating about the future. Investors analyze the history of price patterns to project potential returns on investments.

Listen to sports commentators. Have you noticed how much of their commentary is *not* about the actual game? How often it's about future games, future outcomes and future champions. Sports analysts use statistics to rank a player's or team's past performance and project who will enter the finals and win.

Numbers have a way of opening a portal into the future for humans. In 1927, W.D. Gann published a book that correctly predicted Japan's attack on America. He also predicted the stock market crash of 1929. He predicted the Great Depression would end in 1932. No one knew exactly how he did it, but two things are certain: 1) he used numbers, and 2) he prospered when many others did not, either because they did not know about numbers or did not believe the numbers.

There is no mysticism about it. No man, including Gann,

knows everything. "For we know in part and we prophesy in part," Paul wrote 2000 years ago (1 Corinthians 13:9). Only when the Perfect comes will our imperfect knowledge be done away. Meanwhile the "prophets" of the world can study probability. We don't "know" what a single coin toss will yield, but we "know" that if you flipped a coin 100 times, 50% of the time it will turn out to be head, 50% tail.

King Solomon tells us the value of studying probability, "That which HAS BEEN is what WILL BE, that which is DONE is what WILL BE DONE, and there is nothing new under the sun" (Ecclesiastes 1:9). I'm sure W.D. Gann as a Christian thought about these Biblical words many times as he sought to forecast the probability of the world's markets turning up or down. In the vernacular, we say it this way, "History repeats itself." If it didn't, there wouldn't be any value to studying history!

This leads me to the uniqueness of the God of the Bible. Our God invented numbers, repeats beautiful patterns, and likes to work in cycles. God is into patterns and prophecy. His Book is the premier book about numbers and the future. Many numbers recorded in the Bible are only beginning to make sense now. Many things recorded in the Bible are repeating themselves. Much of the public doesn't even know about this numeric aspect of God's Word. Patterns are prophetic. History is prophecy. God is far from mythical, He's mathematical. God counts!

NUMBERS KEEP US HONEST

One piece of evidence that tells me the Bible is not intended to be myth is the preponderance of specific numbers and numerical patterns contained in it. There is nothing mythical about a population or military census taken by tribes, clans and families. Anyone who asks, "Isn't the Bible a collection of myths?" can find his answer by studying the numbers in the Bible. Numbers tells us concrete facts about reality in a countable way.

Numbers keep us honest. We may say we are watching our weight, but the number of kilograms on the scale don't lie. We may feel we put a lot of effort in our work and deserve that promotion, but our sales figures show our true performance. We may assume that the Bible has been changed by copyists' errors, but numbers tell a different story.

Every handwritten Torah scroll contains 79,847 words or 304,805 Hebrew letters. Yes, they count the number of words and the letters before sanctioning every copy. Not only were Jewish scribes meticulous in counting the total number of words and letters, they also counted the number of each individual letter of their *alef-bet*. The first letter *alef* appears 27,057 times in the Torah. The second letter *bet* appears 16,344 times. And so on. The last letter *tav* appears 17,949 times.[2]

On a purely mathematical basis, allegations of textual corruption are untenable and were proven so by the "Dead Sea Scrolls." Discovered from 1946 to 1956, this treasure of 972 documents is so called because they were found in clay jars hidden in 11 caves at Qumran near the Dead Sea. Why is it considered one of the greatest archeological findings of modern times? Let me give you three reasons.

First, fragments of every book of the Hebrew canon were found except for the Book of Esther. Second, out of 22 copies of the Book of Isaiah found, one copy was so well preserved you could read it from Isaiah 16 through Isaiah 66. Third, this "Isaiah Scroll" is 1000 years older than any previously known copy of Isaiah, and much to scholars' surprise, it reads virtually the same as our 1611 King James Bible. The minor differences were in spelling and tense errors, but no change to the overall message was found. Counting those 304,805 letters ensured the Bible was transmitted precisely to us.

NUMBERS LEAD US TO TRUTH

By simple math, anyone with a Bible could have calculated or predicted the exact day the Messiah was to come. There are many amazing prophecies in the Bible, but the most startling is the one in Daniel chapter 9. It is the most mathematically precise prophecy ever recorded both in Scripture and in all of world literature. Who knew about this mathematical prophecy?

Those who read the Bible did. Their knowledge of numbers is the reason they came to see the Messiah when He was a baby. How else did Simeon the devout man and Anna the prophetess show up at the right time to worship Jesus, whereas Joseph and Mary still hadn't fully grasped what Child was this who was born to them. These believers came and started worshipping the Savior before He ever preached a sermon. How did they know? Undoubtedly they had read Daniel chapter 9. (You will read about it in Chapter '70 Sevens'.)

Who else in the first century knew the Savior was coming to earth? The magis of Persia. How did they know? Daniel was in captivity in Babylon-Persia for 70 years, during which time this Jewish prophet became the highest advisor to the various kings. His prophecies became well known and studied among the educated, who were called 'magis' (a Persian word from which we get 'magistrates'). By trusting in Daniel's math, these Persians arrived in Bethlehem at the right time to see the Child Jesus. Can you imagine that... math lead educated people to the Savior of the world.

Skeptics who claim the Gospel of Jesus Christ was made up by Paul or a collusion of third-century Christians not only fail to understand the Old Testament prophecies, but they are also unaware of the most basic math contained in it.

Can numbers help you find meaning in life and reveal more about the divine plan of God? Can the knowledge or ignorance of numbers affect your future? You're about to find out! This short guide to divine numbers will open up to you the meaning of the most significant numbers.

1

1 is the number of priority and unity. God is one. "I and the Father are ONE," Jesus said in John 10:30. There are two words for "one" in Hebrew: *echad* meaning a composite unity and *yachid* an absolute singular.

The *shema* or the Jew's daily prayer based on Deuteronomy 6:4-9 starts with, "Hear (*shema*), O Israel, the Lord our God, the Lord is one!" In this prayer, the Hebrew uses the word *echad*, not *yachid*. The Lord is "one" in a similar way a married man and woman become "one flesh"—they become *echad* (Genesis 2:24). This composite unity of God is not made up by the Apostle Paul as anti-Trinitarians accuse, but is taught since the first page of the Bible.

Jewish rabbis have long been puzzled by a grammatical "error" found throughout Scripture. All nouns ending in "-im" or "-in" are plural in Hebrew, like *seraphim* and *cherubim* (angels); *nephillim* and *rephaim* (giants); and *Elohim* (plural of *Eloah* God). *Elohim* is a plural noun that is always used with a singular verb! Genesis 1:1 begins with, "In the beginning, *Elohim* God [plural] created [singular] the heavens and the earth." So is God a singular God or a plural God?

The answer is obvious in the Shema: *Shema Yisrael Adonai Eloheinu Adonai Echad*, which literally says, "Hear Israel Lord God Lord One." Since *Adonai* Lord is a divine title of God, it would be no contradiction to say: "Hear Israel God God God One." The people who deny the Trinity (tri-unity of God) don't understand this concept is not made up by Christians, but revealed by God from the very first words of the Torah.

Another important Scripture to Judaism is the Aaronic or priestly benediction in Numbers 6:24-27:

> **The LORD (1) bless you and keep you;**
>   **the LORD (2) make His face to shine upon you and be gracious to you;**
>   **the LORD (3) lift up His countenance upon you and give you peace.**

The use of LORD 3 times corresponds with God the Father, God the Son and God the Holy Spirit.

The first Lord who "blesses and keeps us" corresponds with God the Father. Ephesians 1:3 says, "The God and Father of our Lord Jesus Christ, who has blessed us with all spiritual blessing in heavenly places in Christ."

The second Lord who "makes His face to shine upon us and is gracious to us" corresponds with Christ, who is "the image of God (2 Corinthians 4:4, Colossians 1:15). "No human has looked into God the Father's face, but Jesus claimed, "He who has seen Me has seen the Father" (John 14:7,9). No one was ever so gracious as Jesus, for "grace and truth came through Jesus Christ" (John 1:17).

The third Lord who "lifts up His countenance upon us and give us peace" corresponds with the Holy Spirit. He was sent to lift up Jesus. Speaking of the Holy Spirit's ministry, Jesus taught,

"He will glorify Me, for He will take of what is Mine and declare it to you (John 16:14)." The fruit of the Holy Spirit is "love, joy, PEACE..." (Galatians 5:22). The Kingdom of God is "righteousness and PEACE and joy in the Holy Spirit" (Romans 14:17). The Holy Spirit lives in us and keeps us in perfect peace.

Is it a coincidence that the 3 most important Scriptures of the Torah—Genesis 1:1, Numbers 6:24-27 and Deuteronomy 6:4-9— all allude to the Trinity? No doubt this is by design.

The Bible is "progressive revelation" which means as we continue to read through the Bible, concepts that begin in seed form grow clearer to the learner. How many Persons do you think King David was referring to in his last words (2 Samuel 23:2-3): "The Spirit of the LORD [1] spoke by me, and His word was on my tongue. The God of Israel [2] said, The Rock of Israel [3] spoke to me: 'He who rules over men must be just, ruling in the fear of God'"? Clearly David had a revelation of 3 Divine Persons in the Godhead.

There are other Scriptures which show God talking to God, and God acting in conjunction with God. In Genesis 19:24, God had come down to earth to judge Sodom and Gomorrah, but another Person in the Godhead was still up in Heaven: "Then the LORD [1] rained brimstone and fire on Sodom and Gomorrah, from the LORD [2] out of the heavens." David recorded this conversation between God Himself in Psalm 110:1, "The LORD [1] said to my Lord [2], Sit at My right hand, till I make Your enemies Your footstool."

IS THE TRINITY NECESSARY?

What philosophers have failed to understand is that a God who is not a Trinity *cannot* be God. One reason is that a lone God would have no understanding of Love, apart from His Creation. He would *need* His creation to experience love, relationship, trust, community, giving, receiving, authority, submission, and countless other virtues which mortal men know and partake of. If God *needs* His creation, He would cease to be Supreme. A God who is alone is no God at all.

Our God is the God of Community. He has known love and relationship since eternity past, without us and without His creation. God the Father, God the Son and God the Holy Spirit existed in a harmonious community from the very beginning and didn't need us. He created us out of His overflowing love.

ONLY THE TRINITY can be God

An attribute of God is that He must be "all-in-all". Humans cannot be "all-in-all" because we live within limitations. To be "all-in-all" means to *understand* human limitations while at the same time *transcend* all human limitations.

There are Scriptures which indicate that no man has seen God at any time; yet there are many Scriptures in which believers claimed they have "seen God face to face and not died!" These Scriptures seem contradictory. How can both be true?

Only the Trinity can remain unseen on the Father's throne and yet seen face-to-face in the Son. Only the Trinity can exist outside of time through the Father and inside of time through the Son. Only the Trinity can be unknowable and intimately knowable at the same time. Only the Trinity can be *above* humans in the Father, *among* humans in the Son, and *within* humans by the Holy Spirit. Only the Trinity can simultaneously be all-in-all. Logic affirms the Trinity is the true God.

WHAT DO Cults Think of the Trinity?

All "Christian" cults[1] deny the Trinity because the central issue to salvation is Christ's Deity. The Bible is clear that man is a sinner and *God* is the Savior. If Jesus is not God, He is also not our Savior.

A Scripture often quoted by cults is Colossians 1:15: "He is the image of the invisible God, the firstborn over all creation." Cults don't know what the term "firstborn" refers to. They think it means Jesus was *firstborn* of creation or first created. The argument goes like this: if Jesus were created then He could not be eternal; if He were not eternal, then He could not be God. This is a cultic attempt to deny the Divinity of Christ. The solution to such misinterpretation is to "let the Bible interpret the Bible." In other words, read the Bible in context.

First we should look at the immediate context. Paul wrote a few verses later, "For in Him dwells all the FULLNESS of the GODHEAD bodily." In other words, Paul believed Jesus is "God in a Body." He would not deny the Divinity of Christ in one sentence then assert the Divinity of Christ a few sentences later.

Next we should look at the broader context; that is, other Scriptures on the same topic. The New Testament explains that Jesus was not called the "firstborn" at the Genesis Creation nor at the Incarnation, but at His mighty Resurrection. Luke recorded this in Acts 13:33 (KJV), "God hath fulfilled the same unto us their children, in that he hath RAISED UP Jesus again; as it is also written in the second Psalm, "Thou art my Son, THIS DAY have I BEGOTTEN thee." "This day" refers not to the day Jesus was born in Bethlehem, but to the day Jesus resurrected from the dead.

Finally we see in Revelation 1:5 that Jesus is called the "firstborn from the dead." Jesus is called the firstborn because He was the *first* to be resurrected. He's not the firstborn of creation, but the firstborn of the resurrection. As God, Christ had no beginning. As man, Jesus had a beginning both at birth and at the Resurrection when He became the *firstborn* from the dead. Nothing is more certain in the Bible than the Divinity of Christ.

IS THE TRINITY LOGICAL?

A skeptic once challenged me on the Trinity by asking, "How can 1 + 1 + 1 = 1? Doesn't 1 + 1 + 1 = 3? You Christians believe in 3 Gods!"

No, in fact, Christians do not believe in 3 separate Gods (called *polytheism*). Nor do Christians believe in 1 God who is merely perceived as 3 different persons (called *oneness*). The Trinity transcends both: God is simultaneously 3 and 1.

I answered this person by saying, "You understand simple math. But this is complex math. It's not 1 + 1 + 1 = 1, which is wrong. It's more like $\infty + \infty + \infty = \infty$ (infinity + infinity + infinity = infinity), which is right." God the Father is infinite, God the Son is infinite, and God the Holy Spirit is infinite. Together they are not 3 Gods, but 1 infinite God.

This kind of unity is hard for our finite minds to grasp, but make no mistake about it: the Tri-unity of God is mathematically sound and perfectly rational. The Hebrew word *echad* or "one" describes this transcendent unity.

MORE ON 1

1 represents the 1st of 10 Commandments: "You shall have no other gods before Me" (Exodus 20:3). Jesus says it positively: "And you shall love the LORD your God with all your heart, with all your soul, with all your mind, and with all your strength. This is the first commandment" (Mark 12:30). The question we can ask ourselves to see if we keep the 1st commandment is, "Who do I put before God?" The Bible says Eli "honored his sons more than Me" (1 Samuel 2:29). That became Eli's downfall. God removed His blessing from Eli's family. "For those who honor Me I will honor, and those who despise Me shall be lightly esteemed" (1 Samuel 2:30b). The number 1 reminds us that we should put God first.

1 represents the 1st of 27 Amendments to the US Constitution: *"Congress shall make no law respecting an*

establishment of religion, or prohibiting the free exercise thereof; or abridging the freedom of speech, or of the press; or the right of the people peaceably to assemble, and to petition the Government for a redress of grievances." The most important freedom upon which all others rely is religious freedom or freedom of conscience. This is why the Founding Fathers made it the First Amendment.

Subsequent legal interpretations have divided this amendment into two parts: the establishment clause and the free exercise of religion clause. Modern legal cases have over-emphasized the establishment clause while ignoring the original intent of the framers and ignoring the free exercise clause. This is partly why a ban on prayer and the Bible in public schools is an injustice and violation of the First Amendment.

Context is key to understanding a text. The biggest debate raging in Europe during the 1500s was between 2 Christian camps: Henry VIII of England who wanted to unite the church and state (much like the Papal State from which he was excommunicated), and Luther and Calvin who saw the church and state as making "Two Kingdoms" and we as citizens of both. None of them ever had the thought of excluding Christianity from government, business or schools.

Henry VII separated the Church of England from the Papal State, but did not separate it from English government. On the contrary, he used political power to impose on the Church in unscriptural ways: declaring himself "Supreme Head of the Church of England," introducing his theory of the "divine right of kings," and dissolving religious bodies. It was in this context of political oppression of religious freedom that the American Founding Fathers thought it wise to curb the power of the State upon the Church, and not the other way around. They did not want the State to establish which Christian denomination was legitimate; they wanted the free exercise of religion. They believed the Church was a positive moral and spiritual influence upon the Republic and without it, government would grow tyrannical and the nation would perish.

1 is the atomic number of Hydrogen, the smallest element in the universe. It simply is made up of 1 proton and 1 electron. The fusion of 2 hydrogen atoms forming 1 helium atom releases the greatest power known to mankind—the solar nuclear energy that makes life possible on earth.

In this age of energy crisis, most people have heard of nuclear power. But there are 2 kinds of nuclear energy: fission and fusion. On earth, nuclear power is achieved by *fission* or *splitting* the atoms of the heaviest naturally occurring element—Uranium (atomic number 92). In Heaven,[2] nuclear power comes by *fusion* or *joining* two Hydrogen atoms together. There are at least 2 moral lessons from God's design of nuclear energy.

First, the greatest power on earth comes from *splitting* big elements; whereas the greatest power in Heaven comes from *uniting* the smallest elements. To become more heavenly, we need to do more uniting than splitting!

Second, unseen power is greater than seen. Coal and petroleum are millions of times larger than a hydrogen or uranium atom, but one such atom can release millions of times greater power. Humans tend to underestimate the power of things they cannot see and to be overly impressed with things they can see. Never underestimate the power of small things or even invisible things! The greatest secrets are locked away in them. God seems invisible to us for now, yet He is the Most Powerful Being. You don't have to see Him or feel Him in order to know Him. But once you know Him, you may see, hear or feel Him everywhere and every day.

1.618

1.618 IS CALLED THE "GOLDEN RATIO" or simply "phi" (pronounced "fi") in Greek. It is the number of wisdom or design. Phi appears throughout nature, classical architecture and Biblical architecture.

Noah's ark, the Ark of the Covenant, and the Golden Altar are all golden rectangles. Noah's ark was 300 cubits long, 50 cubits wide and 50 cubits tall (Genesis 6:15) – *the* ideal proportion for stability. The ratio of 5 to 3 is 1.666, as close to phi as you can get with simple integers. Visually speaking the difference between 1.618 and 1.666 is imperceptible to the human eye.

The Mosaic Ark of the Covenant was 2.5 cubits long, 1.5 cubit wide and 1.5 cubit high (Exodus 25:10). The ratio of 2.5 to 1.5 is 1.666.

The Mosaic altar (Exodus 27:1-2) was 3 cubits high, 5 cubits long and 5 cubits wide. The ratio of 5 to 3 is again 1.666.

Phi is a fitting number to represent God's wisdom as it is a number that can *never be written* or *completely known*, its decimals extending out into *infinity*. We may think we know a lot, but phi teaches us we don't even know phi! Humbling indeed.

2

2 IS the number of union. Jesus has 2 natures—divine and human; Light has 2 natures—wave and particle; the Bible has 2 Testaments—Old and New; humanity needs 2 members—male and female.

2 is also the number of division. Jesus spoke of 2 classes of people—sheep and goats; Paul spoke of 2 kinds of vessels—one for honor and one for dishonor; James spoke of the double-minded man wavering between 2 opinions. When our thoughts are split between 2 options, we become unstable in all our ways.

2 is the atomic number of Helium, the 2nd most common element in the universe, comprising nearly 25% of all matter. Hydrogen is the most abundant element in the universe, compromising 75% of all matter. Hydrogen and Helium together comprise nearly 100% of all elements in the universe.[1] That tells us, despite all the alien watchers out there, that the elements on earth which make life possible are extremely rare. We live on a favored "anthropocentric" planet. We should be in awe at how God made us special and grateful He formed the earth to be inhabited (Isaiah 45:18).

2 bases are needed for a binary number system, the language of computers. Computers reduce all information—whether word, photo, music or movie—to 2 numbers: 0 and 1. Computers use binary numbers to represent everything. Something as simple as capital "A" is rendered 01000001. Small letter "a" is 01100001. The binary number system is the foundation of the technological revolution that has swept the world. It would be impossible to grow a modern economy without computers. 2 is all it takes to change the world.

2 is the number of the Second Person of the Trinity: Jesus Christ. Jesus is both God and man. Jesus has 2 Advents. Jesus multiplied bread twice. Jesus sent His disciples out 2-by-2. Jesus was crucified between 2 thieves. Jesus offers 2 kinds of baptisms: water and fire.

God gave the Hebrews 2 calendars: the Genesis calendar (starting on 1st of Tishri) and the Exodus calendar (starting on the 1st of Nisan—the Passover month when the innocent Lamb was slain and Israel was set free by the blood). The first calendar is considered civil or secular. The second calendar is religious or spiritual. I am not aware of any other major culture or civilization that was given 2 calendars. What could these 2 calendars represent?

No doubt they represent our old life in sin and our new life in Christ! Every Christian has 2 birthdays: the first is natural—none of us chose to be born physically; the second is spiritual—each of us has a choice to be born again spiritually. As the old saying goes, *"Born once, die twice* (die spiritually, then die naturally). *Born twice* (born naturally, then born again), *die once."*

The new birth is what Jesus referred to when He said, "I am the resurrection and the life. He who believes in Me, though he may die [his spirit departs his body], he shall live. And whoever lives and believes in Me shall never die [be alienated from God— the Author of Life]" (John 11:25-26).

When we are born again, it's as if the clock of our life starts again. The calendar turns over to a new year. Truly everything seems new when we repent of our sins and accept Christ for our salvation (2 Corinthians 5:17).

2 represents the 2nd of 10 Commandments: "You shall not make for yourself a carved image—any likeness of anything that is in Heaven above, or that is in the earth beneath, or that is in the water under the earth; you shall not bow down to them nor serve them (Exodus 20:4-5a)."

Idolatry is simply making a god to suit yourself. This can be carved in wood, in stone, in digital format or in our hearts. Idolatry usually begins with this statement, "*To me*, God is like this...." So often I've heard people say, "*To me*, God wouldn't judge anyone" or "*To me*, God wouldn't send anyone to hell." Of course, that God wouldn't, because that God doesn't exist. A god who turns a blind eye to crime, sin and injustice is no God at all.

The true God says He will hold every sinner responsible for his or her sins. In the meantime, He is giving sinners a grace period to repent, believe in His Son and be transformed by His Holy Spirit. To avoid idolatry, we must not make a god in our own imagination; rather we must find out who God really is according to His own words.

2 is the number of twins. How many sets of twins were there in the Bible? Just 2: Jacob and Esau; Pharez and Zerah (Genesis 25:24-26, Genesis 38:27-30). Thomas was called the "Twin" (John 11:16, 20:24, 21:2) but we don't know who his twin brother or sister was. Tryphena and Tryphosa (Romans 16:12), two female ministers in the Church at Rome, may have been twins; this theory is based solely on the similarity of their names.

There are also spiritual twins in the Bible:

- The twins of faith and patience (Hebrews 6:12, 2 Thessalonians 1:4, Revelation 13:10);
- the twins of fear and doubt (Deuteronomy 28:66, Luke 8:50, Acts 9:26); and

- the twins of righteousness and justice (Genesis 18:19, 1 Kings 10:9, Psalm 33:5, 89:14, 97:2).

Hebrews 6:12 says through "faith and patience" the saints inherited the promises! If we ask and instantly receive every time, where would the faith be? We wouldn't need to believe, instead we would *know* by our physical senses that we have received something we wanted. But if we ask and there is a time lag before receiving, then we are trusting God with our hearts and exercising Biblical faith with patience.

Those who truly are in faith will always be calm, in peace, and at rest on the inside (Hebrews 4:1-10, 3:11-19), though storms may rage on the outside. Jesus could sleep during the middle of the storm because He was in faith—He was assured nothing could kill Him before His mission was completed (Mark 4:38).

Once I pray about something, I refuse to think about it anymore. If the thought or burden tries to come on me, I just remind God, "It's not my concern even though it concerns me." You can be strong in faith and patience by saying, "I cast my care upon You, Lord. It's in Your Hands now." Then rejoice and don't worry about it anymore! Just praise God, because faith and patience inherit the promises!

THE JEWISH THEORY of 2 Messiahs

Rabbis have tried to reconcile the apparent "contradiction" that one set of Scriptures claiming the Messiah will be a Mighty King and another set of Scriptures claiming the Messiah will be a Suffering Servant (such as Isaiah 53 vs. Zechariah 12:10). They came up with the theory of "2 Messiahs": one is *Messiah ben Yoseph* (Son of Joseph); the other is *Messiah ben David* (Son of David).

The Talmud (Oral Tradition) unnecessarily adds to Scripture by claiming that *Messiah ben Yoseph* will precede *Messiah ben*

David. They claim *Messiah ben Yoseph* will lead the armies of Israel against the Gentile nations and die at the battle of Gog and Magog. *Messiah ben David* will then come and ask God to resurrect *Messiah ben Yoseph*.[2]

This makes *Messiah ben Yoseph* the forerunner of *Messiah ben David*, which is unscriptural since Elijah is the real forerunner (Malachi 4:5, Matthew 17:10). Error begets more error. Rabbis have to fit Elijah in somewhere, so they add an unfounded speculation that there will be a 45-day period[3] between the death of *Messiah ben Yosef* and the appearance of *Messiah ben David*, during which time Elijah the forerunner of the Messiah will come. This type of human speculation is an illustration of Jesus' words to the Pharisees: "Thus you nullify the word of God by your tradition that you have handed down…" (Mark 7:13 NIV).

The theory of 2 Messiahs can be discarded when one realizes that all Scriptures get fulfilled by one Messiah in two comings; just like Moses came twice to rescue Israel (first time rejected) and the brothers came twice to Joseph (first time they didn't recognize him). The Messiah has come, the first time as a Suffering Servant to pay for the sins of the world, but His brothers rejected Him or didn't recognize Him. Jesus will come a second time as the Glorious King of the Jews, to establish the nation of Israel as the center of His government and to usher 1000 years of peace on earth.

Jesus alone is fully God and fully man. As the only sinless man, He can pay for another person's sin. As the infinite, eternal God, He can pay for all mankind's sins. Jesus qualifies on both counts to be the world's Savior. He will come back as the only Person qualified to be the world's King.

2 DOUBLES

2 IS the number of doubling. The doubling of anything is an interesting numerical milestone.

Elisha asked Elijah for a DOUBLE portion (2 Kings 2:9) of his anointing. On a simple count, Elisha did perform double the miracles that Elijah did. Elijah resurrected one person from the dead. Elisha resurrected two people from the dead. (For a more complete count of miracles in their ministries, read Chapter 16.)

Paul said ministers who teach God's Word should be *"counted worth of DOUBLE honor"* (1 Timothy 5:17) or double pay.

Doubling is an important concept in finance. Any investor knows the *power* of compound interest. Conversely, any debtor feels the *pain* of it. Compound interest is a two-edged sword that can work *against* the borrower, but *for* the lenders and investors.

An interesting question to ask yourself is, "At what rate of interest would I need to invest to double my money every 20 years?" The figure is a surprisingly low 3.49%.

Before you get too excited and deposit your money at a local bank paying 3%, do you know the average rate of inflation in your nation? In America and Australia, it ranges between 2.5% to 4.5%.

Inflation is a result of the government printing more money, thus devaluing money and our purchasing power. The more politically correct way to measure inflation these days is by the CPI (consumer price index) which tracks the change (rise) in prices of goods and services.

Inflation is the reason the first Model T Ford produced in 1913 sold for $575, but a Ford sedan today sells for $15,000. That's over 2000% inflation in a lifetime! At an average rate of 3.4% inflation[1] compounded, we are losing half our wealth every 20 years simply by doing nothing but holding cash!

Understanding the inflation rate and the power of compound interest helps us to appreciate the wisdom of God. This may be one reason why God was so adamant that Israel acquire her own land. When God promised to make Israel wealthy (Deuteronomy 28), He did not give them money. He gave them land.

DEUTERONOMY 15:4 (NAS)
    4 However, there will be NO POOR among you, since the LORD will surely bless you IN THE LAND which the LORD your God is giving you as an inheritance to possess.

Land tends to rise in value while money loses its value. In Australia, land historically doubles its value every 7 years. This certainly is one way to beat inflation.

Many people are counting the rate at which human population DOUBLES. The current global growth rate is 1.17%. (In parts of Africa, Arabia and Latin America it exceeds 3%.) At this rate the world's population doubles every 40 or so years.

Here are the milestones of human population numbers:

YEAR	POPULATION
950AD	250 million
1600	500 million
1804	1 Billion
1927	2 Billion
1959	3 Billion
1974	4 Billion
1987	5 Billion
1999	6 Billion
2012	7 Billion

What this is showing is the speed of compound growth. It took:

- 650 years to double 250 million to 500 million.
- 204 years to double 500 million to 1 billion
- 123 years to double 1 billion to 2 billion, and only
- 47 years to double 2 billion to 4 billion.

What does the speed of compound growth in population tell us? It begs a question for evolutionists, "How many people in total have ever existed if humans have been around for 6 million years (as evolutionists claim)?" Creationists question the very assumption of millions of years. How can we settle this debate?

Mathematician John Heffner proposed a simple way that any person with a calculator can lay aside all evolutionary and creationist bias and calculate for themselves how long humans have most likely been on this planet.

Let's start with the evolutionary timeline that *homo sapiens* appeared 500,000 years ago. Start with only 2 people and multiply that by a conservative growth rate of 0.456% per year.[2] (The current world population growth rate is 1.2%, more than double.) What should the current population be after 500,000 years?

2.45 x 10^{990} people.[3] To put it in perspective, that's 2 with 990 zeros after it. That's more people than ALL the electrons in the universe. There are 10^{130} electrons. That's also more people than ALL atoms on the Earth. 10^{48} is the estimated number of all atoms on the Earth.[4] Clearly something is wrong with the evolutionary timeline.

Let's go with a shorter timeline that humans appeared 100,000 years ago (short in evolutionary terms...what's a hundred thousand years when evolutionists talk in terms of *millions* of years?). Let's also drop the population growth rate to 0.1% (near extinction level, lower than any in recorded history). If the first human pair appeared 100,000 years ago and the growth rate were just 0.1% per year, what should the current population be after 100,000 years?

5.38 x 10^{43} people.[5] That's 5 with 43 zeros after it! To put it in perspective, 10^{21} is the estimated number of stars in the universe. This is obviously wrong. Numbers simply don't lie. We currently have 7.7 x 10^9 or 7.7 billion people.

If *homo sapiens* have been around for as long as a million years, there should be billions upon billions of human remains. *Where are all the people?* Archaeology shows humans have buried their dead from the earliest times (cremation being recent). *Where are all the graves?* All of our cities should be built upon piles of human bones! *Where are all the bones?*

To be fair, everyone with a calculator should test the Biblical scenario. God's account of human history records 4 couples survived a worldwide flood some 4,500 years ago. Start with 8 people and multiply by the average growth rate of 0.456%, what should the current population be after 4500 years?

7.7 x 10^9. In gaming language, we call that a 'Bull's Eye'! The mathematical proof for the Biblical timeline and against the evolutionary timeline is irrefutable. No scientist can challenge this. It doesn't require any twisting and manipulating of data. 2 + 2 = 4 for everybody. The evolution of ape to man never happened and can be disproven by simple crunching of numbers.

As Henry Morris says, *"It begins to be glaringly evident that the human race cannot be very old! The traditional Biblical chronology is infinitely more realistic than the million year history of mankind assumed by evolutionists."*[6]

There is a counter argument that current growth rates cannot be compared to past growth rates, which is true. If anything, past growth rates should be significantly *higher* than now. In all agricultural societies, couples had more children.

The Bible tells us that people lived longer and had more children in the past. Abraham lived to 175, Isaac 180, Jacob 147, Joseph 110, Moses 120, Aaron 123, and Joshua 110. Three of my great-grandparents lived to 104, 99 and 96. How many children could such long-lived people have?

After the Flood, God told Noah's sons to "be fruitful, and multiply, and replenish the earth (Genesis 9:1)." Japheth had 7 sons, Shem had 5, and Ham had 4. If we assume the same number of daughters (usually more females born than males), then they had an average of 10.7 children per couple. In the next generation, Japheth had 23 grandsons, Shem had 14, and Ham had 28. The Biblical average after the Flood was 8 to 8.5 children per couple. My own grandmother had 8 children. So did her grandmother.

This represents a population growth rate of 3.7% per year or a doubling time of about 19 years.[7] At that more realistic rate, it would be mathematically impossible for man to have existed for millions of years!

Another counter argument says modern growth rate should be *higher* with the advent of modern medicine and sanitation. However, evidence tells us the contrary. "First world" nations with modern medicine are experiencing a decline in growth rate, while "developing world" nations like India and China have outstripped the West in population growth. These objections simply do not stand. Facts confirm the Bible.

Humans re-populated the earth after a worldwide Flood about 4500 years ago.

I have studied world history and evolution in well-respected schools with anti-Bible professors. I know how ingrained the mantra of millions of years is. Yet as I was studying, certain questions kept popping up which were unanswerable by the professors.

Why is there no record of human reading or writing beyond 5000 years ago? In evolutionary terms, the human brain did not develop 5000 years ago. That is genetically impossible. Why did man suddenly read and write about 5000 years ago? Linguists are baffled by the *sudden* appearance of languages with complex grammatical rules. Older languages such as Latin and Sanskrit are not "less evolved" than modern languages, they were *more complex!*

No known civilization (Chinese, Mesopotamian, European or Aztec) dates back more than 5000 years. Why the absence of evidence if humans have been around for millions of years?

Both Sumerian and Egyptian civilization began abruptly with *no development*. That means at one moment, no one was there; at the next moment (around 5000 years ago), a society appeared with an advanced form of government, complete written language, legal code, sanitation system, art and music, and complex architecture. It only sounds like a mystery to those who do not believe the Bible.

Within the first few generations after Adam, the Bible names *Jabal* as a cattle rancher and inventor of tents; *Jubal* a teacher of musical instruments; and *Tubal-cain* a teacher of metal workers (Genesis 4:20-22). Noah and his 3 sons were extremely intelligent people who built an ark, kept a record of God's Word, and repopulated the entire earth. Their descendants built cities and towers with precise engineering that would outlast today's constructions.

2 is the number of doubling. Our human population doubled from 3 billion in 1959 to 6 billion in 1999, a period of only 40 years. Doubling reminds us that evolution is impossible and its timeline incredible. Contrary to the mantra on TV documentaries, math disproves mankind has been around for millions of years. The TV producers have never crunched the numbers. The Bible and math agree.

2 DREAMS

2 IS a number associated with dreams. Pharaoh was given 2 dreams. Pharaoh's first dream was of 7 fat cows eaten up by 7 lean cows. Pharaoh's second dream was of 7 plump heads of grain devoured by 7 thin heads of grain. Joseph trusted God for understanding and interpreted the 2 dreams to Pharaoh, *"The dreams of Pharaoh are one; God has shown Pharaoh what He is about to do"* (Genesis 41:16). The 2 dreams were about the same thing: 7 years of prosperity to be followed by 7 years of famine. Then Joseph explained why the same dream was given twice, *"And the dream was repeated to Pharaoh twice because the thing is established by God, and God will shortly bring it to pass"* (Genesis 41:32). Repetition meant confirmation.

The Book of Daniel records 2 dreams about the same future events. In chapter 2, Nebuchadnezzar dreamt of a statue with a head of gold, chest and arms of silver, belly and thighs of bronze, legs of iron, and feet of part iron part clay. Finally a stone cut without hands hit the feet of the statue, destroyed it and filled the whole earth. Daniel trusted God to interpret this dream to Pharaoh. He explained the statue represented successive empires which would deteriorate in glory but increase in strength till the last one:

1. The golden head was Babylon;
2. The silver arms were Medo-Persia (a dual kingdom congruent with the 2 arms) which would defeat Babylon;
3. The bronze belly was Greece which would defeat Medo-Persia;
4. The iron legs was Rome (2 parts again because the Roman Empire would be divided into Eastern Byzantium and Western Rome in 1054 AD);
5. The feet of clay and iron would be the weakest world kingdom, predicting a revived Greco-Roman Empire, which the European Union (EU) partially fulfills.

All of these empires have one thing in common: they all hated and persecuted Israel. They will finally be struck down together by the Messiah, the "stone cut without hands," whose kingdom will grow and surpass all other kingdoms.

There is, of course, no way that Daniel could have known which world kingdoms would rise up to oppress Israel. Most political pundits cannot even predict the outcome of the next election. But a wonderful, omniscient God wants us to know that He knows the end from the beginning. His Word is supernatural and reliable. This dream of future empires was so important, God repeated it to Daniel.

In chapter 7, Daniel saw 4 great beasts coming up out of the sea (the sea typifies Gentile nations): first was a lion with eagle's wings; second a bear; third was a leopard with 4 wings; last was a composite beast with 4 heads, iron teeth, 10 horns and a little horn. Then Daniel saw the last beast and its little horn destroyed by the *"Ancient of Days"* and *"the Son of Man coming with the clouds of Heaven... His kingdom [is] the one which shall not be destroyed "* (Daniel 7:9-14).

The interpretation of Daniel's dream was the same as Nebuchadnezzar's:

1. The lion was Babylon;
2. The bear was Medo-Persia;
3. The leopard was Greece - with 4 wings because after the death of Alexander the Great, his kingdom was divided among his 4 generals into Thrace (east), Macedonia (west), Syria (north) and Egypt (south);
4. The composite beast represented both ancient Rome and the end times Greco-Roman Empire (EU) which shall contain all the elements of the first 4 empires.

The reason I said the EU does not yet completely fulfill the prophetic picture is we are waiting for Iraq (Babylon), Iran (Persia), Syria and Egypt (the northern and southern divisions of ancient Greece) to come into play. Back in 2009 when I first wrote this paragraph, I said, "The 2 Gulf Wars certainly put Iraq back on the prophetic map. Iran's nuclear ambitions put her back on world center stage. We are now waiting for Syria and Egypt to be back in geo-political prominence. Then the picture of the composite anti-Semitic beast would be complete."

No one can claim that we "doctored" the Bible to fit world events or "shoehorned" world news to fit Bible prophecy. This paragraph is one of the foolproof pieces of evidence that it pays to ignore American prophecy fads and stick to the Bible. By 2019 —only 10 years after the first edition—my insistence on letting the Bible lead, rather than following the latest American prophetic theory, has been vindicated.

On 17 December 2010, the Arab Spring revolts began with the self-immolation of 25-year-old Tunisian street vendor Mohamed

Bouazizi. This quickly and shockingly led to the ousting of Egyptian dictator Hosni Mubarak on 11 February 2011, and the assassination of Libya dictator Muammar Gaddafi on 20 October 2011. Note that Libya will be one of four clearly identifiable nations that will invade Israel in the Ezekiel 38 "Gog-Magog" War. Due to the number of nations involved and the use of nuclear weapons in this invasion, this war may be called World War III.

During the lunar tetrad of 2014-2015, more pieces of the prophetic puzzle fell into place. The terrorist organization ISIS declared the establishment of the 5th Caliphate ruling over Iraq and Syria (hence the name the "Islamic State of Iraq and Syria). At its height, ISIS ruled over 7.7 million people living in a territory the size of Portugal. On 19 August 2014, the first public beheading aired on YouTube—its victim 40-year-old James Foley. On 3 Feb 2015, ISIS released a video showing Jordanian pilot Moaz al-Kasasbeh being burned alive inside a cage. The world had not seen such barbaric acts since the 9/11 attacks in 2001.

Russia under the leadership of Vladimir Putin rushed to the aid of Syrian President Bashar al-Assad. The United States rushed to topple him, which was strange as it put President Barack Hussein Obama effectively on the same side as ISIS!

Middle East terror dominated the news from June 2014 until March 2019, when President Donald J. Trump declared victory over the last stronghold of ISIS—a small Syrian town on the Euphrates River called Baghouz. ISIS brought Syria into headline news and I do not believe it is over. The dream of a 5th Islamic caliphate was not realized, but it is not dead.

TURKEY RISING

Turkey's leader Recep Erdogan would like to revive the glory days of the Ottoman Caliphate. But his country's constitution limited his power. Turkey has been a unique Muslim-majority nation in that it has been governed in a secular way. Its founder Mustafa Kemal Atatürk had a vision for reforms which modernized, Westernized and secularized his country after World War I.

Erdogan, on the other hand, sees Turkey as the leading Islamic state, not a secular state. On 21 August 2007, he said, *"The term 'moderate Islam' is ugly and offensive; there is no moderate Islam; Islam is Islam."* On 24 March 2019, Erdogan expressed his desire to reconvert the Hagia Sofia into a mosque. This is highly symbolic because the Hagia Sofia was the architectural wonder of Christendom from 537 AD to 1453, when it was desecrated by Ottoman invaders. The Hagia Sofia was the largest church building in the world for a millennium from 537 AD to 1528, when it was surpassed by the Seville Cathedral, itself surpassed by the Vatican Saint Peter's Basilica in 1626. Erdogan shared his vision on live TV, *"As you know, the mosque was converted to a museum in 1935, as a reflection of the CHP (Republican People's Party) mentality...Hagia Sophia will no longer be called a museum. Its status will change. We will call it a mosque."*[1]

Erdogan has served as Turkey's prime minister from 2003 to 2014, and as president since 2014 till now. After a failed coup on 15 July 2016, Erdogan made sweeping arrests of opponents and called for a referendum in 2017 which changed the constitution and parliamentary system into a presidential system. The office of prime minister was abolished and power was concentrated in the office of the president. Erdogan was reelected on 24 June 2018 and is likely to stay in power till 2023, and if reelected till 2028. This development has tremendous implications on Bible prophecy.

Remember Bible prophecy predicts a loose confederacy, not as united as the previous gold, silver, bronze or iron kingdoms, but mixed of iron and clay – substances that do not stick well together. The little horn of this mixed up beast will be the Anti-Christ.

Turkey is vying to be the leader of Sunni Islam and Iran is already the leader of Shi'ite Islam. According to Daniel 8, they will clash, then according to Ezekiel 38, they will work together with Libya and Sudan to launch a failed nuclear attack on Israel. As unlikely as these events now seem, when they are fulfilled, they will serve as proof again that God protects Israel and the Bible is written by God.

The dreams of Daniel chapters 2 and 7 show that these worldly kingdoms will 1) share a hatred for Israel and 2) pass away when "One like the Son of Man" will rule an eternal kingdom in their stead. This is a prophetic description of Yeshua the Messiah or Jesus the Anointed King!

2 IS **the number of confirmation.**

"In the mouth of two or three witnesses every word shall be established."[2] It a court of law, a minimum of 2 to 3 witnesses are required to establish a truth. In theology, a minimum of 2 to 3 Scriptures are needed to establish a doctrine. Peter saw the vision of God calling unclean animals clean 3 times (Acts 10:16). This was to *confirm* to Peter that God was indeed calling Gentiles to become part of the Body of Christ!

I have found that when a leading is of the Lord, it doesn't tend to go away. Jonah knew he was called to Nineveh no matter how he ran from the call. Paul knew he would suffer by going to Jerusalem, *"The Holy Spirit testifies in every city, saying that chains and tribulations await me"* (Acts 20:23). Because the Lord's voice is persistent, I do not interpret every passing whim and feeling as the leading of the Lord. If it is God's will, it will be confirmed by the Scriptures, in my spirit and often through spiritual people whom I trust (like my wife). I do not demand confirmation from God and I never ask for signs, which are very dangerous for believers to ask. As a new testament believer, I trust that God's leading will be so clear in my born again spirit, I will never be in confusion. When God speaks, I should have only 2 options: obey or disobey. When I'm not sure, it means don't make a move!

I have had several dreams from God. I always checked them against God's Word and the meanings of the dreams were immediately apparent to me. God does not speak to us in dreams to confuse us. He is trying to communicate to us because other methods did not get our attention.

Members of my church have reported unusual dreams and visions. As long as the interpretation lined up with the Word of God, I believed the dreams could be legitimate. More than once, a church member who could not read or write was told by an angel, *"Go back to church!"* That command certainly agrees with Hebrews 10:25, doesn't it? *"Not forsaking the assembling of ourselves together..."*

Some Christians get caught up with dreams and visions and ignore God's Word. This is a mistake that will derail them off course. Even Paul who was caught up to the third Heaven where he heard things unspeakable acknowledged in 2 Timothy 3:16, *"All Scripture is given by inspiration of God, and is profitable for doctrine, for reproof, for correction, for instruction in righteousness."* Paul knew to put God's Word above his own visions. Every true minister of God will elevate the Word of God above his dreams and visions. The clearest leadings and confirmations I have ever received have come from God's Word.

3

3 is God's numerical signature, the number of Divinity, life and language. There are 3 Persons in the Trinity. The very title "Lord Jesus Christ" contains the Trinity—Lord refers to the Father, Jesus refers to the Son, and Christ refers to the anointing of the Holy Spirit.[1] There are 3 parts of man— spirit, soul and body; 3 time periods we know—past, present and future; 3 physical dimensions we live in—width, depth and height; 3 atoms to the molecule of life H2O; 3 states of water which makes life possible on earth. We are the only planet known in the universe where water exists simultaneously as liquid, vapor and solid ice. We live on 30% of the surface area of the 3rd planet in the solar system.

The Trinity made all the elements on the periodic table out of 3 elementary articles: protons, neutrons and electrons. Protons and neutrons form the nucleus of every atom (except hydrogen made of a single proton), and electrons revolve around the nucleus. In chemistry, there are 3 types of bonds: single, double and triple. Only 3 elements can form all 3 types of bonds: carbon, nitrogen and oxygen. Our genetic library—the DNA—is made up of 3 chemical building blocks: phosphates, sugars and nitrogen bases (A, T, C and G). 3 types of alleles (A, B, O) make up the 4 human blood types (A, B, AB and O).

1 John 1:5 says "God is light" and 2 Corinthians 4:4 calls the Gospel "light". The speed of light is 300,000 kilometers per second. When the Human Genome Project (1990-2003) was completed, guess how many DNA base pairs they counted in humans? 3 billion!

The 3rd day of the week (Tuesday) is a favorite day for weddings among Orthodox Jews. Jewish rabbis explain why Tuesday is favored by the fact that the Bible says "God saw that it was good" once every day (except the second day), and twice on the third day. Strangely "God saw that it was good" is missing from the second day (Monday). The Midrash explains this is because the separation of the "lower (earthly) waters" from the "higher (heavenly) waters" brought sadness.[2] I as a Christian would say with due respect that the rabbis miss the point why Tuesday is the Day of Wedding: it points to the original, eternal and most profound love within the Godhead: the Trinity! Love is not 2, it is 3!

The Levites, chosen for divine service in God's House, represented the 3rd tribe of Israel. The Book of Leviticus outlines 3 types of laws: moral, sacrificial and ceremonial (about diet, hygiene, sanitation). Most religious people are aware of the moral rules of do's and don'ts, but if they were sufficient to save us, why is ⅓ of the Law about the need for blood sacrifices to wash away sins? The ceremonial laws were both practical advice and a prophetic picture of our need to be fed and cleansed daily by God's Word.

There were 3 items in the Ark of the Covenant: the 10 Commandments written in stone; Aaron's Rod that budded; and a golden pot of manna or heavenly bread. If the Law were sufficient for us to approach God, why were the other 2 items in the Ark which represents the Presence of God? The Law only leads us to Aaron's Rod that budded - something dead that gives life - a perfect picture of the Cross and Resurrection of Christ. The manna represents the Word which daily renews our mind after getting saved at the Cross.

The Hebrew Bible or *Tanakh* is made of 3 parts: the *Torah* (Law), *Nevi'im* (Prophets) and *Ketuvim* (Writing or Psalms). The first letter of each division spells the acronym T-N-K. Since ancient Hebrews did not write vowels, the 3 consonants T-N-K can be vocalized as TaNaKh.[3]

There are 3 types of mitochondria DNA (mtDNA) which are distributed throughout the world's population. Named M, N and R, these 3 mtDNA provide stunning validation of Noah's Flood and the 4 couples on board. Why? Just as the Y chromosome is inherited only from fathers, mitochondria DNA is inherited only from our mothers. Noah's wife would have passed her mtDNA to her 3 surviving sons. However, their children would have inherited their mtDNA from the 3 wives of Noah's sons. There are other mtDNA which are very closely related to each other but isolated to sub-Saharra Africa. Named L0, L1, L2, L3, Dr. Rob Carter reasons that these may be accounted for by post-Flood genetic mutations in mtDNA N.[4] Advances in human genome studies are disappointing to evolutionary theory because it shows all humans are genetically 99% the same! Where is the genetic diversity after "millions of years"? Where is the mitochondrial diversity? All males have nearly the same Y chromosome and all humans have only 3 lineages of mtDNA. Genetics is adding evidence there had to be 1 "Y-chromosome Adam" and "1 mitochondrial Eve"!

There are 3 types of languages on the earth: **isolating** languages (e.g. Chinese, Tibetan, most Southeast Asian languages except Malay); **fusional** or **inflected** languages (e.g. Latin, Greek, most European languages); and **agglutinative** languages (Korean, Japanese, Turkish, Finnish, Hungarian, Basque).

Interestingly, the 3rd of 10 Commandments is a prohibition on language or the wrong use of our tongue. The 3rd

Commandment reads: "You shall not take the name of the LORD your God in vain, for the LORD will not hold him guiltless who takes His name in vain." This sin is called blasphemy. In an age of increasing disrespect, we tend to make light of blasphemy, but it is the 3rd worst sin in the Bible.

In January 2009, the Australian public was shocked that novelist Harry Nicolaides was sentenced to 3 years of jail by the Thai court for "insulting the King of Thailand." Many people today don't understand the gravity of the crime, but in older times, such a loose mouth would be executed (1 Kings 21:10)! Thais understand the crime and accept the sentence as proportionate to the offense, because they have such love and respect for their king. He was, after all, the world's longest-reigning monarch and ruled the nation benevolently for 70 years. He deserved some respect.

What about God? He has ruled long before anyone else ruled. He is loved by billions of angels and saints. Does He deserve respect? But He says, "My name is blasphemed continually every day" (Isaiah 52:5).

What is blasphemy? It is using God's Name in vain. That includes using the Name of Jesus as an expression of disgust. Could anyone get away with it if in a moment of disgust, they shouted the King of Thailand's name in vain? No! If such honor is paid an earthly king, how much more should be paid to Jesus Heaven's King!

There is a lot more blasphemy going on than we care to admit. God would not have made it His number 3 otherwise. In the New Testament, it is the only unpardonable sin. Jesus said: "Therefore I say to you, every sin and blasphemy will be forgiven men, but the blasphemy against the Spirit will not be forgiven men. Anyone who speaks a word against the Son of Man, it will be forgiven him; but whoever speaks against the Holy Spirit, it will not be forgiven him, either in this age or in the age to come" (Matthew 12:31-32).

What was Jesus' definition of blasphemy? In this context, he healed a blind and mute man, but the religious Pharisees said the devil healed the man. The Pharisees had blasphemed the Holy Spirit. In other words, blasphemy is crediting the work of God to Satan, and the work of Satan to God.

Things that should not be blasphemed are: God, God's Name, God's Word (Titus 2:5), God's servants (Acts 6:11, 13:45, 18:6), God's people and God's tabernacle (Revelation 2:9, 13:6).

The 3rd commandment is one of the most violated commandments in Scripture. The Bible predicts a rise of blasphemers in the end times: "But know this, that IN THE LAST DAYS perilous times will come: For men will be lovers of themselves, lovers of money, boasters, proud, **blasphemers**, disobedient to parents, unthankful, unholy" (2 Timothy 3:1-2).

Have you ever heard a person mocking one of God's servants: "That evangelist is just out to get money"? When the Jews accused Jesus as being a counterfeit and an imposter, He replied, "I do not have a demon; but I honor My Father, and you dishonor Me" (John 8:49). He was saying, "You are blaspheming Me, because I am a true Servant of God." A critical person must have real evidence before he accuses a servant of God, or else he will be liable for blasphemy.

Unfortunately Paul had to instruct some Christians to stop blaspheming: "But now you yourselves are to put off all these: anger, wrath, malice, **blasphemy**, filthy language out of your mouth" (Colossians 3:8). No Christian I know would like to think he or she could possibly be guilty of blasphemy, but if none blaspheme, to whom was Paul talking?

Have you ever heard a Christian say, "That speaking in tongues is of the devil"? According to 1 Corinthians 12:10, it is a gift of the Holy Spirit! How believers can say such things without fear of breaking the 3rd commandment is beyond me. They may not understand it, but the Holy Spirit deserves respect nonetheless. To call God's gift demonic – what is that if not blasphemy?

Have you ever heard a Christian say: "God made me sick to teach me a lesson"? Some Christians do not think there's anything wrong with accusing God of making them sick. Yet Scriptures point to Satan as the source of sickness, and God as the source of healing.

 JOHN 10:10

10 The THIEF [Satan] does not come except to steal, and to kill, and to destroy. I [Jesus] have come that they may have LIFE, and that they may have it more ABUNDANTLY.

Anything that steals, kills and destroys is from Satan. Sickness robs people of their health and destroys their bodies. Jesus never once made anybody sick. He made people well. He came to give us "abundant life".

LUKE 13:16

16 So ought not this woman, being a daughter of Abraham, whom SATAN HAS BOUND—think of it —for eighteen years, be loosed from this bond on the Sabbath?

Jesus called sickness "satanic bondage". Satan bound, Jesus loosed. They never switch roles!

JOB 2:7

7 So WENT SATAN FORTH from the presence of the LORD, and SMOTE Job with sore boils from the sole of his foot unto his crown....

JOB 42:10

10 And the LORD turned the CAPTIVITY of

Job, when he prayed for his friends: also the LORD
gave Job twice as much as he had before.

The Book of Job calls sickness "satanic captivity". One thing is
clear: Satan held Job captive, but God set Job free. Don't let any
religious argument or experience alter the plain teaching of
God's Word: Satan struck Job, God healed Job.

ACTS 10:38
38 How God anointed Jesus of Nazareth with
the Holy Spirit and with power, who went about
DOING GOOD and HEALING all who were
OPPRESSED BY THE DEVIL, for God was
with Him.

Luke the physician called sickness "demonic oppression".
Jesus was anointed to do GOOD and HEAL the sick. Healing is
called good.

ISAIAH 5:20: "Woe to those who call EVIL GOOD,
and GOOD EVIL..."

Despite all these Scriptures calling sickness bad and healing
good, some Christians insist on calling sickness "good" or a
"blessing in disguise." Though some Christians do not think
anything wrong of it, is it not blasphemy? It is crediting the work
of Satan to God!

Everyone who blasphemes feels justified in doing it, even the
novelist who was jailed for insulting the king. But the Bible tells
Christians to not blaspheme. 3 reminds us of blasphemy.

When we humbly obey God's Word, God promises healing
and long life.

EXODUS 23:25-26 (KJV)

> 25 And ye shall serve the LORD your God, and he shall bless thy bread, and thy water; and I will take sickness away from the midst of thee.
> 26 There shall nothing cast their young, nor be barren, in thy land: the NUMBER of thy DAYS I will fulfill.

Healing and longevity are God's promises to the obedient. Here is the same promise in another translation.

> EXODUS 23:25-26 (NLT)
> 25 You must serve only the LORD your God. If you do, I will bless you with food and water, and I will protect you from illness.
> 26 There will be no miscarriages or infertility in your land, and I will give you long, full lives.

It takes 3 witnesses to confirm a truth in the Bible or in a court of law. I have cited 5 witnesses which say Satan makes sick and God makes well. We may praise God through times of sickness or even use a period of hospitalization to witness to other sick folks about God. However, I do not have to be sick to witness in a hospital. I have intentionally gone to many hospitals to witness to and pray for the sick, their visitors, nurses and doctors. God does not use sickness to teach us a lesson. God uses His Word to teach us. We may decide to obey God during times of sickness, but His Word should be enough to cause us to obey.

Our God, being a Trinity, does not need a man, an angel or any other witness to confirm His testimony. He is His own perfect witness.

We should pray 3 times a day. Without the help and infilling of the Holy Spirit, Daniel "knelt down on his knees three times that day, and prayed and gave thanks before his God, as was his custom since early days" (Daniel 6:10). Rabbis teach that the custom of praying 3 times a day was introduced by the Patriarchs: Abraham introduced the morning prayers (*shachant*); Isaac afternoon prayers (*mincha*); and Jacob evening prayers (*maariu*).[5] With the Holy Spirit's power, Christians should be able to pray more, not less, than Jewish believers who have not been baptized with the Spirit.

3.1415

3.1415 IS CALLED "*pi*" not to be confused with "*phi*" (1.618). *Pi* is the ratio of a circle's circumference to its diameter. Like *phi*, it is a constant whose decimal value never repeats and never ends. 3.1415 is only an estimate.

There is a common complaint by Bible skeptics based on the value of *pi*. They say that the Bible gives the wrong value of *pi* in 1 Kings 7:23 and 2 Chronicles 4:2 (NIV):

"He [Hiram the metal worker in Solomon's Temple] made the Sea of cast metal, circular in shape, measuring ten cubits from rim to rim and five cubits high. It took a line of thirty cubits to measure around it."

Ignore the height of 5 cubits; the skeptics are only worried about the 30 cubits circumference divided by 10 cubits diameter. 30 divided by 10 equals 3. Such dimensions, say they, give the wrong ratio for pi; therefore the Bible must not be the Word of God!

Truly this proves nothing but nitpicking. Any math student knows that 3.1 can be rounded off as 3. Any Bible student knows that the Bible doesn't give any decimal for any number. Any history student knows that the decimal point was not in common use at the time of Solomon. Many ancient cultures did not even have a symbol to notate "0", never mind digits to the right of 0.

The Jewish sage Maimonides (1135-1204) commented on 1 Kings 7:23, "The ratio [which Greeks called *pi*] cannot be known. Since it is impossible to arrive at a perfectly accurate ratio, they assumed a round number..." Maimonides is revealing advanced mathematical knowledge based on his knowledge of God. He made this statement in the 12th century, long before Johann Lambert proved *pi* is irrational (cannot end) in 1761 and Ferdinand von Lindemann proved *pi* is transcendental (cannot have repeating patterns) in 1882. God's people should have more wisdom that the world's.

Would Bible skeptics repent of their sins and embrace a life of obedience had the writer of 1 Kings 7:23 written, "Solomon's bowl actually measured 9.64866 cubits in diameter and 30.31213 cubits in circumference"? I seriously doubt it. Perhaps the ancient writer hated fractions, like many students do, and thought any reasonable person would accept 10 and 30 cubits as rounded figures.

But to prove to any sincere skeptic that God always anticipates their questions, I will give a more precise solution.

Whenever someone attacks the Scriptures or misinterprets a Scripture, the answer is often found right there in the context. In other words, most answers to big Bible conundrums have been found by simply reading the verses *before* or *after* the verse in question. In this case the skeptics have omitted to read the following verses:

1 KINGS 7:23-24,26 (NIV)
23 He made the SEA of CAST METAL, circular in shape, measuring TEN CUBITS FROM RIM TO RIM and FIVE CUBITS high. It took a line of

THIRTY CUBITS to measure around IT. [What does "it" refer to? The cast metal of the inner bowl.]

24 BELOW THE RIM, gourds [KJV knops] encircled it—ten to a cubit. The gourds were cast in two rows in one piece with the Sea.

26 IT [the extra outer rim, an addition to the inner bowl] was a HANDBREATH in THICKNESS, and its RIM was like the RIM of a cup, like a lily blossom. It held two thousand baths.

John Boatwright[1] pointed out that the brim in verse 23 was an attribute of the bowl, but *not* that the brim itself was 30 cubits in circumference or 5 cubits tall (making the bowl a cylinder). The measurement of the diameter included this thick brim as a finished bowl, but for the purpose of metal casting, Hiram only needed the circumference of the inner bowl, without the extra thick brim to hang the knops. A handbreadth being approximately 0.225 cubit or 4.5 inches, we would have to subtract 0.45 (0.225 x 2 sides of the brim) from the diameter, which gives us a circumference to diameter ratio of 30 to 9.55. What then is the Bible's value for *pi*? 3.14.

Our estimate of a handbreadth being 4.5 inches could well be slightly off. It would not surprise me that with precise knowledge of a cubit and handbreadth, the Bible's *pi* value would be exact.

If the skeptics were honest, they should admit God is perfectly wise and His Word perfectly accurate. Accusing God of being wrong in math is a smokescreen for a proud heart. We should settle it in our hearts that no accusation will ever stick to God. When we feel like complaining against God, realize that we have incomplete knowledge. When we think His Word is wrong, we can safely assume the Word is not wrong. We should exercise enough humility to admit our understanding may be wrong.

Numbers can teach us about God. Let's see if any skeptic will become a believer after reading this! "Don't let the *pi* hit you in the eye!"

One last note on *pi*. The ratio of the 22 letters of the Hebrew alphabet to its 7 vowels is 22 / 7 or *pi* (3.14). Jewish rabbis claim that Hebrew was the original language of mankind before the Tower of Babel. Perhaps we will be reading and writing Hebrew in Heaven.

3.5

3 ½ IS HALF of 7. It is the number of preparation (half way to completion). Jesus' ministry lasted 3 ½ years; the disciples' training under Jesus lasted 3 ½ years; the Tribulation and Great Tribulation are 2 periods each lasting 3 ½ years or 42 months or 1260 days. The smallest unit of time in the Hebrew calendar is 1 *helek* or 3.33 seconds, which means there are 1080 *halakim*[1] in an hour. It takes 3-4 years to graduate most Bible schools. It takes 3-4 years to obtain a university degree. It takes 3-4 years to complete an apprenticeship in a trade. I suppose 3 ½ years should be the ideal length of time for a season of preparation.

There is a distinction between calling and separation. Paul knew this when he introduced his letter to the Romans, "Paul, a bondservant of Jesus Christ, CALLED to be an apostle, SEPARATED to the gospel of God" (Romans 1:1). Paul was called in Acts 9, but he was not separated until Acts 13, "As they ministered to the Lord and fasted, the Holy Spirit said, 'Now SEPARATE to Me Barnabas and Saul for the work to which I have CALLED them'" (verse 2). Calling comes before separation. Between calling and separation is preparation.

In Paul's case, he sensed his calling since he was young. Paul was schooled under one of the most famous Jewish rabbis named Gamaliel (Acts 22:3), yet he was not ready to serve the Lord. On the contrary he worked *against* the Lord by persecuting Christians! When Paul was miraculously saved on the road to Damascus, he learned the true nature of his calling – to preach Christ among the Gentiles – yet he was not ready to jump into ministry. Paul had to be retrained in the "School of the Spirit."

In Galatians 1:16-18, Paul described God's call on his life and his preparation: "To reveal His Son in me, that I might preach Him among the Gentiles, I did not immediately confer with flesh and blood, nor did I go up to Jerusalem to those who were apostles before me; but I went to Arabia, and returned again to Damascus. Then AFTER THREE YEARS I went up to Jerusalem to see Peter, and remained with him fifteen days." How long did his preparation take? About three years!

It was probably in Arabia and Damascus that Paul received most of his revelations. Then he went to double check his doctrine with Peter and James the Lord's brother. These were the respected Christian leaders in Jerusalem. Even though Paul received visions and revelations directly from Jesus, he did not get into pride and think he was above accountability. Instead, after 3 years of preparing, he submitted all his teachings to Peter and James. This attitude of humble submission is the mark of all true ministers of God.

Paul expected the Corinthian Christians to have grown up spiritually by the time he wrote the book of 1 Corinthians. That letter came 3-4 years after he had established that church.

 1 CORINTHIANS 3:1-3

1 And I, brethren, could not speak to you as to spiritual people but as to CARNAL, as to BABES in Christ.

2 I fed you with milk and not with solid food; for

until now you were not able to receive it, and even now you are still not able;

3 for you are STILL CARNAL. For where there are envy, strife, and divisions among you, are you not CARNAL and behaving like mere [unspiritual] men?"

One can detect a note of disappointment in the Apostle's tone. Paul was disappointed that they were still carnal, as evidenced by their envy, strife, and division, after 3-4 years of learning God's Word. That tells me it is possible to mature spiritually within 3-4 years, if we set our hearts to study God's Word and pray.

I believe it takes at least 3 years to know anyone truly. Judas' heart was not revealed till the end of 3 ½ years. Evidently he had fooled everyone for 3 years as none of the other disciples suspected he was the betrayer, but he could not fool everyone after 3 ½ years.

As a pastor I recommend singles take time to date and really get to know each other for a few years before marrying. Too many young people rush when time is on their side. 3 ½ years is not long compared to being married for a lifetime! Let time prove people's attitudes and motives. Time is your friend.

4

4 IS the number of the Gospel, which is the story of how man can be restored to right relationship with God. By extension, 4 is also the number of relationship. 4 (3 + 1) = Gospel (God + man). That is why there are 4 Gospels (Matthew, Mark, Luke, John); 4 major prophets (Isaiah, Jeremiah, Ezekiel, and Daniel); 4 gates into the Tabernacle (representing the way to God); 4 languages used in the Bible (Hebrew, Chaldean, Greek, Aramaic); 4 women named in Jesus' genealogy[1] (Rahab, Ruth, Tamar, Bathsheba); 4 nucleotides in the DNA (adenine, thymine, guanine, cytosine); 4 personality types (choleric, melancholy, sanguine, phlegmatic); 4 blood types[2] (A, B, AB, O); 4 kinds of soil of the human heart (wayside, rocky, thorny, good); and "4 months till harvest" (John 4:35). Judah, the Messianic tribe from which David and Jesus descended, is the 4th tribe of Israel. The first 4 of 10 Commandments deal with our relationship to God (the last 6 deal with our relationship to fellow man, hardly a coincidence since 6 is the number of man).

Jesus told His disciples to spread the Gospel in 4 places: "But you shall receive power when the Holy Spirit has come upon you;

and you shall be witnesses to Me in Jerusalem, and in all Judea and Samaria, and the end of the earth" (Acts 1:8). Literally, this took place as the Church first grew within Jerusalem and Judea; then was forced out by persecution to Samaria, then to the rest of the world (Acts 8, Acts 11:19).

Personally, this means Jesus wants Christians to preach about Him in 4 places: our home [our Jerusalem]; our neighborhood [Judea]; places we don't like to go to [Samaria]; and distant lands [the uttermost part of the earth].

In the Book of Acts, we find that the Apostle Paul went on 4 missionary journeys to spread the Gospel and establish some of the first churches: (1) Acts 13-14; (2) Acts 15:36-18:22; (3) Acts 18:23-20:38; (4) Acts 23:11-28:31). By reading the Book of Acts, one can see how the local church holds a special place in God's heart and Gospel plan.

A key Gospel verse *"the just shall live by faith"* appears 4 times in the Bible (Habakkuk 2:4, Romans 1:17, Galatians 3:11, Hebrews 10:38). Martin Luther re-discovered this verse while reading the Book of Romans and the world has never been the same since! The Protestant Reformation exploded from this revelation. If the just shall live (be saved eternally) by faith, then we should not depend on our own good works, religious merits or any other form of *self-salvation*. This key verse distinguishes the Christian message from every other religion in the world! God's wisdom says we must be saved by trusting in Someone greater than ourselves; man's pride says I hope to be saved by depending on *no one* greater than myself!

4 is the number of good news, even before Jesus came. The pre-Flood warning was preached to 4 generations: those of Enoch, Methuselah, Lamech, and Noah. Enoch obviously knew about the Flood because he named his son *Methuselah*, meaning "when he is dead it [the Flood] shall come". What a strange name to call your son! I'm sure every believer was concerned about Methuselah's health every time he sneezed! The number of years

each of these 4 men lived all have a unique number. Enoch never saw death nor the Flood because he was translated to Heaven at the age of 365. Methuselah lived the longest life on record and died on the year of the Flood at the age of 969. Lamech died before the Flood at the age of 777. Noah died after the Flood at the age of 950.

After the Exodus, the Jews traveled through the wilderness with God's Tabernacle (holy tent of meeting) at the center. As they journeyed from Egypt to the Promised Land, the 12 tribes were regimented into 4 camps of 3 tribes each, each camp being positioned according to cardinal compass points: the Camp of Dan to the north of the Tabernacle; the Camp of Reuben due south; the Camp of Ephraim due west; and the Camp of Judah due east. Everything God does has significance and thanks to Chuck Missler's calculations, we now have a vivid picture of what these 4 camps represented.

Since God's instruction to the tribes was not to *encircle* the Tabernacle, but to *spread out* due north, south, east, west of the tent, the 4 camps actually formed a Cross marching through the dessert! Based on the number of people in each camp, we can see that the north and south camps had roughly the same number of people, the west camp had the least, and the east camp had the most. By drawing the 4 camps directly north, south, east and west of the Tabernacle, we discover a picture of the Cross on which Jesus would be hung!

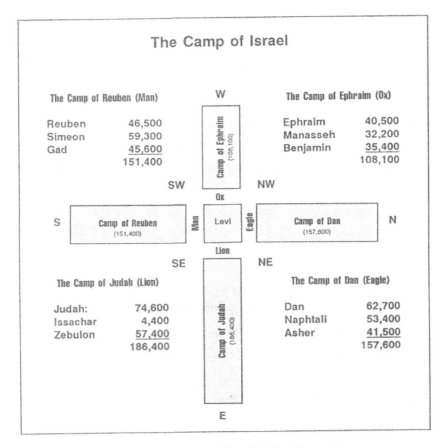

Chuck Missler, The Camp of Israel. Used with permission.

When the prophet Balaam looked down on the approaching Israeli army, he did not see a swarm of soldiers around the Tabernacle, but 4 distinct, tightly-organized camps in symbolic order. Balaam asked, "Who can count the dust of Jacob, and the number of the FOURTH PART of Israel? Let me die the death of the righteous, and let my last end be like his!" (Numbers 23:9). When Balaam looked down on God's marching people, he actually saw the Cross moving through the dessert! 4 is the number of the Gospel, in object lesson form!

4 is the number of restoration. David told Nathan that whoever stole the lamb, "he shall restore FOURFOLD for the

lamb, because he did this thing and because he had no pity" (2 Samuel 12:6). He didn't know that in this case the lamb was Bathsheba and thief was himself! The day Zacchaeus got saved he said, "Look, Lord, I give half of my goods to the poor; and if I have taken anything from anyone by false accusation, I restore FOURFOLD" (Luke 19:8). The Gospel is the news that restores a sinner back to his original position with God.

Jews celebrate the Passover with 4 cups based on the 4 "I will's" of God in Exodus 6:6-7. "I WILL bring you out from under the burdens of the Egyptians, I WILL rescue you from their bondage, and I WILL redeem you with an outstretched arm and with great judgments. I WILL take you as My people..."

1. The 1st cup is the "cup of bringing out."
2. The 2nd cup is the "cup of deliverance."
3. The 3rd cup is the "cup of redemption or blessing."
4. The 4th cup is the "cup of taking out."

Every detail of the Passover feast points to Christ. Each of these 4 cups speak of the 4 phases of Jesus' work in the believer's life.

First, Jesus *brings* our spirits *out* of Satan's kingdom. By faith in Christ, we are saved from sin and given a brand new spirit.

Second, Jesus *delivers* our minds through His Word. Moses may have been the first preacher to make this statement, "You can take Israel out of Egypt, but you can't take Egypt out of Israel!" It means Israel was physically removed out of Egypt, but they were still mentally held captive by their past in Egypt. Like Israel, we too may be saved spiritually but not delivered mentally from our old patterns of thinking. Romans 12:1 tells us to renew our minds by studying and obeying the Bible. The Lord wants to deliver us from our old mental bondage and emotional strongholds. The right way to think is to think in line with His Word.

Third, we begin to experience the fullness of God's *blessings* physically here on earth. Can we really expect blessings here on earth? Jesus told us to pray that God's will be done "on earth as it is in Heaven." Is there any sickness or poverty in Heaven? No! So it's not God's will that there be sickness or lack on earth. Is there any curse in Heaven? No! So it's not God's will that we live under any curse. We can receive physical healing now for "Christ has *redeemed* us from the curse of the law, being made a curse for us..." (Galatians 3:13).

It is the third cup of blessing which Jesus instituted for the New Testament Church at the Last Supper (1 Corinthians 10:16), yet it is probably the most misunderstood one. Too many Christians are still at the first cup, or at best the second cup, but they have not taken the third cup of blessing! Being blessed does not mean we will never suffer persecution from men, but it does mean that we have power over the devil and he should no longer take advantage of us! We have been *brought out* spiritually, *delivered* mentally and emotionally, and *blessed* physically and socially.

Fourth, we await to be "taken out". We long for Jesus, whom we will see either at our death or at the rapture. At the rapture, we who believe and are alive at His Coming will be literally taken up, out and away! The rapture is nothing new. Enoch was raptured or taken up without seeing death 5000 years ago. Isaiah 57:1 records a 2700 year old description of the rapture, "The righteous perish, and no one ponders it in his heart, devout men are TAKEN AWAY, and NO ONE UNDERSTANDS that the righteous are TAKEN AWAY to be spared from evil." The righteous will disappear in an instant but it will not bring understanding to those who reject the truth. They will be confused. They will not realize that a terrible period of time the Bible calls the Tribulation is about to come on earth. Perhaps they will feel so overwhelmed with their own problems or so deceived by the Anti-Christ that they will not care Jesus has taken away the righteous "to be spared from evil."

God loves us and never wants us to suffer as the world suffers, God does not call us to suffer sin, sickness, or poverty, but He does call us to suffer righteously for preaching the Gospel and teaching His Word. If you teach His Word, some people will not like it, because it doesn't agree with their theology. Then you will find out how much you can suffer for Jesus.

Amazingly, the 4 cups of Passover point to Jesus and are symbolic of the entire Gospel plan mapped out in 4 stages.

When Nebuchadnezzar threw Shadrach, Meshach and Abed-Nego into the fiery furnace, intending to kill them, the Bible records that he rose in haste and spoke to his counselors, saying, "Did we not cast three men bound into the midst of the fire?" They answered and said to the king, "True, O king." "Look!" he answered, "I see 4 men loose, walking in the midst of the fire; and they are not hurt, and the form of the fourth is like the Son of God" (Daniel 3:24-25). Who was the 4th man who brought protection from fire to the 3 Hebrew faithfuls? He is the Savior, of course! This is called a theophany or an appearance of Christ before His incarnation. Since 4 refers to salvation, we can be sure of our salvation once we trust in the 4th man.

God wrote 4 Gospel accounts, one for every personality type. Your favorite Gospel may have something to do with your personality.

- The Gospel of **Matthew** is logical, methodical and detailed – perfect for melancholies.
- The Gospel of **Mark** is short, fast-paced, and exciting – fun for sanguines.
- The Gospel of **Luke** is compassionate and contains more healing than any other Gospel – it tugs on the heartstring of phlegmatics.

- The Gospel of **John** is unique (completely different from the other 3 synoptic Gospels) and visionary (John paints panoramic pictures) – it motivates the big thinkers or the cholerics.

There are also 4 major prophets in the Old Testament, one for every personality type.

- **Isaiah** is the choleric pioneer of prophecy, tackling the big topics of judgment and salvation, and showcasing such a grand overview of the future that his book is sometimes called the "5th Gospel", even though it was written 700 years before Christ.
- **Jeremiah** is the melancholy prophet, often seen to be moody and depressed. He wrote two books, one bearing his name, and the other titled "Lamentations" in which he grieved over the destruction of Jerusalem. His writing recorded the most details and depth of any prophet's personal struggles and emotions.
- **Ezekiel** is undoubtedly the sanguine among the prophets, not only speaking prophecies but acting out prophetic dramas! He laid siege on a tile and an iron pan, then lay down on his left side for 390 days, then on his right side for 40 days, and baked a cake with cow dung (chapter 4). He shaved his head and beard, weighed the hair in a balance, then burned a third, cut a third and threw a third into the wind (chapter 5). He pretended to relocate his stuff in the sight of the people, digging a hole through the city wall, then declaring, "I am your sign" (chapter 12). When his wife died, God told Ezekiel not to mourn or cry for her, then said to the people, "Ezekiel is a sign to you" (chapter 24). Ezekiel's ministry was a public performance. Lots of drama!

- **Daniel** is the phlegmatic diplomat, trusted to serve under at least 4 kings of Babylon and Persia: Nebuchadnezzar, Belshazzar, Darius, and Cyrus. He helped his three Hebrew friends get promoted, rarely insisted on his own opinion, and looked for ways to make peace without compromising his faith and core values.

No other religious book in the world has been crafted to suit all 4 major personalities. God knows our make up well because He crafted each personality type to represent a part of Him. Through the 4 Prophets and 4 Gospel accounts, He wants to reach every personality type so that everybody may have a relationship with Him.

4 is the master time factor. Earth times are often divided or multiplied by a factor of 4. There are 4 seasons in a year; 4 financial quarters annually; 4 phases of the moon; a new month about every 4 weeks; a leap year or extra day every 4 years. Is it a surprise that Jesus appeared 4000 years after the fall of Adam? Ancient rabbis believed that the Messiah was due to come during the 4th millennium because the "Great Light" appeared on the 4th day of Creation. They should have known that Christ had come. Jesus the Light of the world appeared at the end of the 4th millennium. He will come again to rule and reign at the start of the 7th millennium.

4 has another special meaning, to which we will dedicate the next chapter.

4 ANGELS

4 is the number of angels. There are 4 living creatures around God's throne; 4 faces on each living creature (lion, calf, man, eagle); 4 wings on the 4 living creatures;[1] 4 angels bound in the river Euphrates; 4 angels named in Scripture (Michael, Gabriel, Lucifer, Abaddon or Apollyon); 4 archangels named by Hebrew sources; and 4 ranks of angels in the Bible.

The Nature of Angels

The word angel simply means "messenger" in both Hebrew (*malak*) and Greek (*angelos*). There are good angels, but there are also fallen angels or demons. Before we explain them, let's clear up some common misconceptions.

People tend to either worship angels or fear demons. The Bible tells us to neither worship them nor fear them. Angels are not to be worshipped because Christ is greater than angels (Hebrews 1:5-14) and one day we will judge and rule over angels (1 Corinthians 6:3). All holy angels in Scripture are male. They are never babies, female, or sexless (as some speculate from Luke

20:36). Demons may appear as a man, woman, child or even animal (remember the serpent in the Garden of Eden). Most angels do not have wings, or else they would be recognized as angels. On the contrary, Hebrews 13:2 tells us that if you met an angel, it is unlikely that you were aware of it; therefore "do not forget to entertain strangers, for by so doing some have unwittingly entertained angels."

All angels are created beings. They are not equal to God. They are not omnipresent, omnipotent, or omniscient. They cannot read our minds, but they do listen to our words. That's why thoughts unspoken die unborn. Our words are vitally important. Jesus said in Matthew 12:37, "For by your words you will be justified, and by your words you will be condemned." Angels and demons cannot act on our thoughts, but they can act on our words.

Gabriel said to Daniel, *"From the first day that you set your heart to understand, and to humble yourself before your God, your words were heard; and I have come because of your words"* (Daniel 10:12). Daniel did not pray silently. His words, not merely his thoughts, were heard. The archangel was sent in response to Daniel's spoken words, not his unspoken thoughts. Jesus spoke to demons to command them to leave. He did not just think the thought, "Please leave." He commanded vocally. Anointed words spoken in Jesus' Name can always defeat the devil.

One third of angels fell in a rebellion against God led by Lucifer, now called the devil or satan (Revelation 12:1-2). Demons, ghosts and evil spirits are not the spirits of deceased humans. When humans die, they are not in a state of limbo or suspension, rather they depart the earth for Heaven or descend the earth to where hell is.

A common ploy of the devil is to impersonate people we once knew. If you have ever seen a dead relative, a common experience among people in the occult, the Bible says you have encountered a "familiar spirit."[2] That is, a spirit that is familiar with the history of your family. Remember angels and demons are not omniscient, they do not know everything, but they have been around before you were born, your parents were born, your grandparents were born, so they do know some intimate details of your life. They know, for instance, what sins work well in your family history. For some families, alcohol destroys male after male. For others, it may be adultery, violence, gambling, or money. Demons are not omnipotent, they are limited in power and numbers, so they follow the path of least effort and resistance. They habitually deploy the same spiritual tactics against you that worked on previous generations in your family.

Do not be afraid of them! They are afraid of you, if you are a Christian and know your rights to use the Name of Jesus. If you suffer recurring nightmares or suicidal thoughts, that is the devil pushing his lies on you. You can end them by believing in Jesus as the Savior of your sins and then commanding, *"Satan, I rebuke you in the Name of the Lord Jesus Christ!"* The visions, apparitions, or nightmares will end. I have seen people set free many times.

I have also seen a few people who unfortunately did not want to be set free, but felt "spiritual" because they saw these familiar spirits. It made them feel special. In reality it is a common method of deception. Read the Bible often to clear your mind. It is better to follow truth as the "truth will set you free."

Now let's explore some details about the good and the bad angels.

Good Angels

Jews believe in 4 classes of good angels. According to a commentary on Genesis dated around 150 BC, the Book of Jubilees, there are: angels of the Presence, angels of sanctification, angels over natural phenomena, and guardian angels over individuals.

Jews believe in 4 archangels, 2 named in Scripture, and 2

named in extra-Biblical Jewish sources: Michael, Gabriel, Uriel and Raphael.[3] Each supposedly corresponds to the 4 divisions of the armies of Israel and 4 directions of the camp: "Michael on my right, Gabriel on my left, Uriel before me, Raphael behind me, and above my head the Shekinah [glory] of God."[4]

- **Michael** means "Who is like God" (*mi* who, *ke* as, *El* God)
- **Gabriel** means "Strength of God."
- **Uriel** means "Light of God" or "Fire of God."
- **Raphael** means "Healing of God."

Gabriel's name appears 4 times in Scripture: Daniel 8:16, Daniel 9:21, Luke 1:19, and Luke 1:26. Gabriel is known as the messenger of God. Michael is the leader of the Lord's hosts and the prince (guardian angel) of Israel.

In Genesis 18:2 "three men" appeared to Abraham after his circumcision. Abraham recognized one of them as the Lord, a pre-incarnate appearance of Jesus Christ. The other two are not identified by name, but Genesis 19:1 calls them "angels." Jews believe Michael and Gabriel accompanied the Lord on His visit. They destroyed Sodom and Gomorrah. The Bible confirms that they work together: when Gabriel was detained by the demonic prince of Persia, Michael came to Gabriel's aid and released him on his mission to help the prophet Daniel understand the end times.

 DANIEL 10:13-14

13 But the prince of the kingdom of Persia withstood me twenty-one days; and behold, Michael, one of the chief princes, came to help me, for I had been left alone there with the kings of Persia.

14 Now I have come to make you understand

what will happen to your people in the latter days, for the vision refers to many days yet to come. [Written 2500 years ago]

The Midrash *Genesis Rabbah 63.24* says that Michael and Gabriel together recorded Esau's selling his birthright to Jacob. Did you know that all your words, attitudes and actions are being recorded? Scriptures confirm that there are books about our lives in Heaven.

 MALACHI 3:16 (NAS)
16 Then those who feared the LORD spoke to one another, and the LORD gave attention and heard it, and a BOOK of remembrance was written before Him for those who fear the LORD and who esteem His name.

If our conversations about God are being recorded "before Him," then God is not the One writing. Who is writing them? Some angels are employed in the task of recording the details of our lives.

 DANIEL 7:10 (NAS)
10 A river of fire was flowing and coming out from before Him; thousands upon thousands were attending Him, and myriads upon myriads were standing before Him; the COURT sat, and the BOOKS were opened.
REVELATION 20:12 (NIV)
12 And I saw the dead, great and small, standing before the throne, and BOOKS were opened. Another BOOK was opened, which is the BOOK of life. The dead were judged according to what they had done as recorded in the BOOKS.

We cannot confirm from Scripture the Midrash's claim that Michael and Gabriel recorded Esau's decision to despise his birthright. Yet it would not be against Scripture. We know according to the New Testament that angels witness men's decisions. Luke 15:10 says they watch our activities, *"Likewise, I say to you, there is joy in the presence of the angels of God over one sinner who repents."* And we know that our decisions are being recorded in books for Heaven's purposes. If the task does not belong to God Himself, then it is safe to say angels are busy recording the evidence that will be used on the Day of Judgment for eternal rewards and punishments.

My rule for study is simple: I consider only stories from the Midrash that are not in conflict with Scripture, and reject all stories that are anti-Scripture. All spiritual information should pass the Bible test. If it doesn't line up with the Bible, I do not accept it.

Here is an instance of conflict. The Midrash says Michael refused to take Moses' soul when he was supposed to die. The New Testament sheds better light this incident, *"Yet Michael the archangel, in contending with the devil, when he disputed about the BODY of Moses, dared not bring against him a reviling accusation, but said, 'The Lord rebuke you!'"* (Jude 1:9). The dispute was over Moses' body, not Moses' soul.

The Book of Enoch claims that Uriel asked God to destroy the *Nephilim* (Giants of Genesis 6:1-4) and that along with other angels, Uriel served as Enoch's guide to Heaven when he was translated. Again, we cannot confirm from Scripture that it was Uriel, but we do know from Scripture that angels accompany righteous saints when they die. Evidently unrighteous souls go alone.

 LUKE 16:22

22 So it was that the beggar died, and was

carried by the angels to Abraham's bosom. The rich man also died and was buried.

The believing beggar was never alone in death but had a triumphant parade to glory. The unbelieving rich man did not receive the same treatment. Jesus simply said his body was buried.

The Midrash *Exodus Rabbah 1.24* claims that Gabriel made baby Moses cry so that Pharaoh's daughter would have compassion on him and adopt him as her son. We know from Scripture that angels surround children.

 MATTHEW 18:3, 10

3 And he said: "I tell you the truth, unless you change and become like little children, you will never enter the kingdom of Heaven.

10 See that you do not look down on one of these little ones. For I tell you that their angels in Heaven always see the face of my Father in Heaven."

By Jewish tradition Raphael is considered to be involved with healing. Although we do not believe in angels to heal us, it is interesting to note that the New Testament mentions an unnamed angel who "went down at a certain season into the pool, and troubled the water: whosoever then first after the troubling of the water stepped in was made whole of whatever disease he had" (John 5:4). An impotent man who met Jesus complained that whenever the angel troubled the water, he was too late to get in and always missed his healing. Jesus ignored the angel and the man's complaint and healed him on the spot! When we have Jesus, we do not need to wait for an angel who was limited in ability and could not heal everybody. By His stripes, we should declare, we were healed!

. . .

Bad Angels

Now concerning the fallen angels. There are 4 ranks of fallen angels according to Ephesians 6:12:

1. *principalities,* being low-level devils; then
2. *powers,* then
3. *rulers of darkness;* and lastly
4. *spiritual wickedness in high places,* being Satan's highest henchmen.

In day-to-day spiritual life and prayer, Christians only have to deal with low-level devils, hence the New Testament's emphasis on *principalities* and *powers* (Romans 8:38, Ephesians 3:10, Colossians 1:16, 2:15). We have authority over these devils in the Name of Jesus (Mark 16:17). When we bind the low level devils on earth, the higher-ranking devils will also be bound in the heavens. Jesus said so:

MATTHEW 18:18
    18 Assuredly, I say to you, whatever you bind on earth will be bound in Heaven and whatever you loose on earth will be loosed in Heaven.

We are supposed to bind some things on the earth and let the Lord and His army deal with some things in the heavens. That means some devils are on earth; while other devils are in the heavens – not the Heaven God lives in, for there are no devils there, but the atmospheric heavens above the earth. Satan is called the "prince of the power of the *air*" in Ephesians 2:2. The fact that believers only need to deal with low-level devils and God's army will automatically deal with higher-ranking devils is clear from Jesus' words:

LUKE 10:19

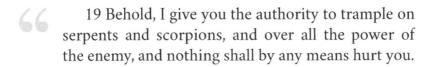

> 19 Behold, I give you the authority to trample on serpents and scorpions, and over all the power of the enemy, and nothing shall by any means hurt you.

Notice two things. Firstly, Jesus compares the devils we face to serpents and scorpions, low-level, belly-crawling enemies.

Secondly, the picture Jesus gives the Church is that we are in a *superior* position *above* those enemies. Our stance is to *stomp on, step on* or *trample down* these low-level devils in the Name of Jesus!

MARK 16:17

> 17 And these signs will follow those who believe: In My Name [the Name of Jesus] they will cast out demons..."

Never does Jesus paint a picture of the Church being underneath the devil and we having to "pull them down" from above us! No, never! The Church is the Body of Christ! We are *above* the fallen demons and they are trodden underneath our feet (Ephesians 1:22-23, Romans 16:20).

A much misunderstood Scripture is the one in which the Holy Spirit admonishes us to "pull down strongholds." What are these strongholds? Read the Scripture in context as Paul defines these "strongholds."

2 CORINTHIANS 10:4-5

> 4 For the weapons of our WARFARE are not carnal but mighty in God for pulling down STRONGHOLDS,
>
> 5 casting down ARGUMENTS and every high thing that exalts itself against the KNOWLEDGE of God, bringing every THOUGHT into captivity to the obedience of Christ.

What is the warfare the Holy Spirit is referring to? A battle of the *mind!* What are the strongholds the Holy Spirit is referring to? The strongholds are synonymous with *arguments* against God's Word, *higher criticism* of God's Word, and *disobedient thoughts* to Christ's Spirit.

We need to understand something basic about our makeup. Humans are made up of 3 parts – spirit, soul and body (1 Thessalonians 5:23). Once our spirits are saved by faith in Jesus, we have a mind or soul that needs to be renewed (Romans 12:2) and a body whose appetites need to be controlled by the Spirit (Romans 8:13-14). The main battle of the believer is the battle of the mind.

Too many Bible preachers have made the strongholds out to be something *outside* the believer or even *above* the believer, misleading Christians into unproductive hours of praying against 'spiritual' or 'demonic' strongholds. I've been in such meetings and other than the benefit of coming together to be with each other and the Lord, I didn't see much good or lasting deliverance come out of those shouting meetings.

Actually the strongholds are *mental* and *emotional*. The battle is not *outside* of us, but *within* the mind of each believer. Strongholds include religious traditions, rationalizations, preconceptions and prejudices that cloud our understanding of God's Word. The religious Pharisees had a lot of mental strongholds that kept them from being saved and healed by Jesus.

The main tool of the enemy is the power of *mental suggestions.* The devil merely introduced a wrong thought to Eve, *"Is God's Word really true? If you disobey God, nothing bad will happen to you. In fact, you'll be better off to reject God's Word!"* That's my paraphrase but it sums up what the devil continues to successfully do to people's minds as soon as they hear God's Word. *"Don't believe it. Don't act on it. It doesn't work. God isn't good. God doesn't help. God didn't answer your prayer. Listen to your feelings instead."* These are variations of thoughts that routinely come into people's heads, which need to be pulled down by a decision to believe and speak the truth. Just opening the Bible and speaking a few verses can defeat the devil.

The devil knows that the worst thing he can do to you is to make you reject God's Word and believe a lie instead. It is not an overstatement to say that every sorrow in the world comes from believing a lie. Every divorce is the result of someone in the marriage believing a lie. Every drug or sexual addiction is the result of someone believing a lie. Every lost soul is lost because someone believed a lie about God or about themselves. That is why Jesus calls Satan "a *liar* and the father of it" (John 8:44) and the Bible summarizes Satan's activity on earth as "*deceiving* the nations" (Revelation 18:23, 20:3, 8).

We must pull down strongholds of wrong thought patterns, lies and deception. We can do this by studying and embracing God's Word for ourselves, no matter what others around us may think. Jesus promised us victory over every stronghold not by praying against devils, but by putting God's Word first: *"If you abide in My word, you are My disciples indeed. And you shall know the truth, and the truth shall make you free"* (John 8:32).

There are spiritual forces to contend with but they are underneath our feet. There are low level devils that bring sickness, lies or mental suggestions; but Jesus and the disciples simply cast them out. There is really nothing for the believer to worry once he or she knows his or her authority in Christ and uses the Name of Jesus in prayer. The devils are afraid of the Name of Jesus!

4TH COMMANDMENT

4 REPRESENTS the 4th of 10 Commandments:

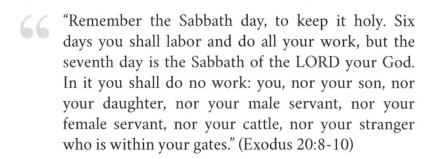 "Remember the Sabbath day, to keep it holy. Six days you shall labor and do all your work, but the seventh day is the Sabbath of the LORD your God. In it you shall do no work: you, nor your son, nor your daughter, nor your male servant, nor your female servant, nor your cattle, nor your stranger who is within your gates." (Exodus 20:8-10)

4 times the Sabbath is called a "sign between God and Israel," never once between God and the Church or Gentiles.[1] The purpose of the Sabbath was for the Jews to remember their deliverance out of Egypt and to look forward to the true rest in the Messiah. The Sabbath was a type of the true rest in Christ.[2] Once the true fulfillment has come, the type is done away. Once Jesus the Lamb of God was crucified, the annual slaughter of lambs ceased to be necessary. Likewise, the abolishing of the Jewish Sabbath was predicted in Isaiah 1 and Hosea 2.

> ISAIAH 1:11, 13
> 11 ...I have had enough of burnt offerings of rams and the fat of fed cattle. I do not delight I the blood of bulls, or of lambs and goats.
> 13 Bring NO MORE futile sacrifices; incense is an abomination to Me. The New Moons, the SABBATHS, and the calling of assemblies— I cannot endure iniquity and the sacred meeting.

> HOSEA 2:11
> 11 I will also cause all her mirth to CEASE, her feast days, her New Moons, her SABBATHS — All her appointed feasts.

Jesus referred to the Sabbath only 4 times in the New Testament[3], and in every instance He 'broke' the Sabbath by working a miracle. Jesus completely ignored the Jewish Sabbath. He taught that no day is lord of man:

> MARK 2:27-28
> 27 The Sabbath was made for man, and not man for the Sabbath.
> 28 Therefore the Son of Man is also Lord of the Sabbath.

Jesus instituted Sunday as a day of Christian worship by resurrecting on Sunday, revealing Himself to His disciples twice on Sunday and giving the Holy Spirit on Sunday. There are 4 Scriptures in the New Testament that specifically say that Christians gathered on Sunday.

> JOHN 20:19
> 19 Then, the same day at evening, being the first day of the week [Sunday], when the doors were shut

where the disciples were assembled, for fear of the Jews, Jesus came and stood in the midst, and said to them, "Peace be with you." [This was the first church service—after Jesus resurrected.]

JOHN 20:26
26 And after eight days [idiom for one week later, counting from the first Sunday to next Sunday][4], His disciples were again inside, and Thomas with them. Jesus came, the doors being shut, and stood in the midst, and said, "Peace to you!" [This was the second church service after the Resurrection.]

ACTS 20:7
7 Now on the first day of the week [Sunday], when the disciples came together to break bread, Paul, ready to depart the next day, spoke to them and continued his message until midnight.

Paul's long service was held on a Sunday. Sabbatarians claim this is the "mark of the beast". That would mean even the Apostle Paul was deceived. On the contrary, he was observing Sunday like all early Christians did, long before Roman Catholicism existed.

1 CORINTHIANS 16:2 On the first day of the week [Sunday] let each one of you lay something aside, storing up as he may prosper, that there be no collections when I come.

Paul assumed an offering would be taken on Sunday. How could it if Christians did not gather on Sundays?

The Holy Spirit fell on the 120 disciples on the Day of

Pentecost (Acts 2). Here is the formula for calculating which day of the week Pentecost, or the Feast of Weeks, is to be celebrated: "Count fifty days to the day after the seventh Sabbath…" (Leviticus 23:15). The day after Sabbath is always Sunday.

Out of the 10 Commandments, all were re-instated in the New Testament except one—the Sabbath law. Out of the 10 Commandments, Sabbath-keeping was the only ceremonial (not moral) law. See Chapter 6 (where Adam was given 6 laws) and Chapter '7 Laws of Noah'. Both sets of moral laws predating Moses did not mention the Sabbath.

Dr. Ken Johnson, a Christian researcher of Dead Sea Scrolls, affirms that this was the historical view of Jews and the Church Fathers, "The Essenes (keepers of the Dead Sea Scrolls) held this same view that the Sabbath was a sign between God and the nation of Israel alone."[5]

"And the Creator of all things blessed it, but **He did not sanctify all peoples and nations to keep Sabbath thereon, but Israel alone**: them alone He permitted to eat and drink and to keep the Sabbath thereon on the earth." (*Ancient Book of Jubilees 2:31*)

There is absolutely no injunction for the Church to keep the Jewish Sabbath. That the early Church met on Sunday—the "first day of the week"—is clear from Scripture.

Despite the New Testament commandments not to make any day holier than another[6], some denominations have fought theological wars to keep the Jewish Sabbath.

COLOSSIANS 2:16-23

16 So let no one judge you in food or in drink, or regarding a festival or a new moon or SABBATHS,

17 which are a SHADOW of things to come, but the SUBSTANCE is of Christ.

> 23 These things indeed have an appearance of wisdom in SELF-IMPOSED religion, false humility, and neglect of the body, but are of NO VALUE against the indulgence of the flesh.

The reason Paul called Sabbath-keeping a pious show of "false humility" that is of "no value" is because even those who sincerely try to keep the Sabbath don't really keep the Sabbath.

According to Mosaic law, every Jew is forbidden to travel far on the Sabbath day (Exodus 16:29). Ancient rabbis fixed the limit to 2000 cubits based on Joshua 3:4-5, which is about walking distance. Driving to church on Saturday breaks the Sabbath! Lighting a fire breaks the Sabbath (Exodus 35:3). To observant Jews, lighting a stove or illuminating an elevator button breaks the Sabbath. Cooking breaks the Sabbath (Exodus 16). Gathering sticks breaks the Sabbath (Numbers 15). Carrying burdens breaks the Sabbath (Jeremiah 17). That would mean *worrying breaks the Sabbath!* Buying and selling breaks the Sabbath (Numbers 13). The truth is, no Sabbath-keeper actually keeps the Sabbath!

We can forget the letter of the law, but we should not forget the heart of the law. The *heart* of the Sabbath is revealed when we:

1. Keep one day entirely dedicated to God;
2. Rest physically once every 7 days;
3. Humbly realize that despite all our best efforts and good intentions, we cannot keep the Sabbath, therefore we need a Savior;
4. Look to the true fulfillment of Sabbath (rest from dead works) in Christ Jesus. It's not the DAY that saves us; it's JESUS alone who saves us when we repent and believe.

GALATIANS 4:9-11

9 But now after you have known God, or rather are known by God, how is it that you turn again to the WEAK and beggarly elements, to which you desire again to be in bondage?

10 You OBSERVE DAYS and months and seasons and years.

11 I am afraid for you, lest I have labored for you in vain.

No one should be against any Christian who wants to worship on Saturday (I worship God on Saturday), but neither should they be against any Christian who chooses to worship on Sunday (I worship God on Sunday, too...I worship God from Monday to Sunday!).

 ROMANS 14:5, 6, 10

5 One person esteems ONE DAY above another; another esteems EVERY DAY alike. Let each be fully convinced in his own mind.

6 He who OBSERVES the day, observes it to the Lord; and he who DOES NOT OBSERVE the day, to the Lord he does not observe it....

10 But why do you judge your brother? Or why do you show contempt for your brother? For we shall all stand before the judgment seat of Christ.

5

5 IS the number of grace. Grace is what distinguishes Christianity from every religion in the world. All religion asks man to try harder; Christianity tells man to give up and ask for help! All religion asks man to save himself by acting good; Christianity alone tells us to depend on the Savior to save him. Grace is a uniquely Christian doctrine. No wonder 5 appears so often in the Bible.

Noah's name first appears in Genesis 5 and on the 5th appearance, the Bible records that "Noah found grace" (Genesis 6:8). There was nothing Noah could do to save himself. Noah could only be saved by believing God and going into the ark for safety. The wooden Ark (like many wooden typologies in the Old Testament) represented the Cross of Jesus Christ. The Ark had only 1 door located on the 2nd floor of the triple-decker boat, representing the Second Person in the Trinity. In the flood of sin, we cannot save ourselves by treading water. We can only be saved by accepting rescue on board the Ark of Jesus.

Noah was 500 years old when he began fathering the only 3 sons who survived the Flood (Genesis 5:32). The Ark of Noah rested on Mount Ararat, which is 5 kilometers above sea level, truly a pinnacle of grace! The Jews who wrote the Bible did not live in Ararat, work in Ararat, and as far as we can tell, never went near Ararat for any reason. Yet they recorded that Ararat was the resting place of the Ark. As it turns out, Ararat is higher than the highest peak of Europe and one of the highest in Asia. The highest mountain in the European Alps is Mont Blanc, at 4810 meters. Ararat stands at 5137 meters (this includes a thick layer of ice cap that would not have been there at Noah's time).

COMPARE THE BIBLE WITH MYTHOLOGY.

Both the Greeks and Romans claimed survivors of a flood landed on Mount Parnassus in central Greece, whose peak is 2457 meters above sea level. The Gilgamesh Epics claimed a flood survivor named Utnapishtim landed in the Zagros mountains in western Iran. The highest peak of the Zagros stands at 4548 meters. Neither of these mountains are ideal for a realistic landing as they would prolong the survivors' wait in the boat, while humans and animals run out of food, water and supplies. But Ararat, towering over 5100 meters, is the most plausible site of a resting Ark.

Mount Ararat is part of historical Armenia (now eastern Turkey). The Armenians believe they are descendants of the great-great grandson of Noah through Japheth, Gomer and Togarmah, a man named Hayk (not found in the Bible). In other words, Armenians claim to descend from a 5th generation patriarch after the Flood. The 5th century historian Moses Khorenatsi recorded in the *History of Armenia*: "Hayk and his people, from the time of their forefathers Noah and Japheth, had migrated south toward the warmer lands near Babylon. In that land there ruled a wicked giant, Bel [or Nimrod by other accounts]. Bel tried to impose his tyranny upon Hayk's people. But proud Hayk refused to submit to

Bel. As soon as his son Aramaneak was born, Hayk rose up, and led his people back to the land of his forefathers, the land of Ararat."[1] Two of the original 12 apostles – Bartholomew and Judas Thaddeus (not Judas Iscariot) – are said to have preached in Armenia and founded the Armenian Apostolic Church, at about 50 AD. Armenia is considered the first Christian country in the world. The number 5 is associated with grace.

God visited Abram 5 times and on the 5th time changed his name *Abram* (a barren man) to *Abraham* (the father of many nations) by inserting the 5th letter of the Hebrew alphabet *"heh"* into his name. The same 5th letter changed *Sarai* (contentious) to *Sarah* (princess).

Benjamin, Joseph's younger brother, was given 5 times as much meal as his elder brothers and 5 changes of garments as opposed to his other brothers' one change (Genesis 43:34, 45:22). Benjamin had done nothing to deserve this. He was the object of his older brother's favor.

5 represents the 5th of 10 Commandments: "Honor your father and your mother, that your days may be long upon the land which the LORD your God is giving you." The New Testament reiterates this commandment as the first commandment with a promise. Paul quotes the 5th commandment in the book of Ephesians:

EPHESIANS 6:1-3
1 Children, obey your parents in the Lord, for this is right.
2 Honor your father and mother," which is the first commandment with PROMISE:
3 that it may be WELL WITH YOU and you may LIVE LONG on the earth.

Children's lives will prosper and be lengthened when parents teach them the 5th commandment. Explain to your children why this Scripture is so important to their future!

God forbade Israel from eating the fruit of a tree until the 5th year after its planting (Leviticus 19:23-25, Deuteronomy 6:11). God wanted to give Israel "vineyards and olive tress which [they] did not plant" as a symbol that God's Promise is by grace. Once Israel entered the land, they were allowed to plant fruit trees, but not forget God's grace.

David had faith he could defeat Goliath with only 5 smooth stones. It was grace, not David's aim, that brought the little shepherd boy victory and saved the nation. Some ask why did David bother to bring 4 other stones? To kill Goliath's 4 other brothers (2 Samuel 21:16-22, 1 Chronicles 20:4-8), but they all ran away.

John is sometimes called the "Apostle of Love" as he understood God's grace and emphasized it more than any other apostle (John 1:16, 1 John 4:19). How many books did God use John to write? Exactly 5.

1. The Gospel of John
2. The Epistles of 1 John
3. 2 John
4. 3 John
5. The Book of Revelation. What a privilege it must have been for John to close the Canon of Scripture!

Moses also wrote 5 Books of the Bible, collectively called the *Torah* in Hebrew or *Pentateuch* in Greek:

1. Genesis
2. Exodus
3. Leviticus
4. Numbers
5. Deuteronomy.

These first 5 books of the Bible are called "The Law". This tells us that law and grace are inseparable. An understanding of the strict requirements of the law leads to a deep appreciation of grace. No one can truly understand the solution Jesus brings without first understanding the problem Moses described.

None of us can perfectly keep all 613 holy laws contained in the 5 Books of Moses, therefore we owe God the penalty of our sins. The law requires the guilty party to pay; but the law will also accept an innocent party to step in and bail the guilty out. The person who does not understand the law will not embrace the grace of Jesus Christ. Jesus bailed us out at a supreme cost to Himself. 5 reminds us that God hid grace as the solution to broken law from the very beginning!

There are 5 "days of grace" between Yom Kippur (the Day of Repentance on the 10th of Tishri) and Feast of Tabernacles (symbolic of the Millennium on the 15th of Tishri).

5 virgins valued grace and were prepared to accept the undeserved invitation to our Lord's wedding; 5 virgins were foolish and squandered grace by being careless.

Mary was the 5th woman mentioned in Jesus' genealogy (Matthew 1:16). The angel Gabriel said Mary had "found grace with God" (Luke 1:30). Mary bore 5 sons: Jesus (while she was still a virgin), James, Joseph, Simon, Judas — Jesus' 4 half-brothers, 2 of which became apostles and writers of New Testament books (Matthew 13:55, Mark 6:3, Luke 8:19-21, John 2:12, Galatians 1:19).

Some people misunderstand the Trinity and think it means God the Father, Mary the Mother of God, and Jesus the Son. Then they profanely assume that God had sexual intercourse with Mary to produce Jesus. This is not a Christian belief!

The Trinity is God the Father, God the Son, and God the Holy Spirit. They conceived a plan to redeem man by coming on earth to take man's punishment as his substitute. To take man's place, God had to come legitimately as a man. How could God do this?

We could not understand the Virgin Birth until our technology caught up with God's. Today, a virgin can give birth through intravenous fertilization (IVF). God borrowed Mary's womb just as a couple today can borrow a surrogate's mother womb. The surrogate mother does not have intimate relation with the couple and does not share any of her DNA with the baby. Mary was blessed to be called of God for this assignment, but she was not divine. She was not omniscient, for she was not privy to the plan of redemption until Gabriel announced she had found grace. Mary was not God, but a human vessel of grace. After she delivered Jesus, she and Joseph had at least four sons and an unknown number of sisters (Matthew 13:56, Mark 6:3).

5 in America

The Name "God" appears 5 times in the US Declaration of Independence. America was founded on the grace of God and many founding fathers openly expressed their faith and reliance on God's gift of grace. Here are what 3 of the signers of the Declaration stated. Samuel Adams, "I...[rely] upon the merits of Jesus Christ for a pardon of all my sins." Charles Carroll, "On the mercy of my Redeemer I rely for salvation and on His merits; not on the works I have done in obedience to His precepts." Benjamin Rush, "Nothing but His blood will wash away my sins. I rely exclusively upon it."[2]

5 in Science

We have 5 physical senses; what a grace it is to be able to see, hear, touch, taste and smell. It's difficult to put to words how we can taste a taste or smell a smell, yet tasting and smelling are part of God's amazing gifts to us. God could have made the universe duller and the earth less colorful, but by His grace life is full of 5 physical sensations.

In an octave, the 5ᵗʰ and 3ʳᵈ notes create the basic foundation of all chords. God's Grace (5) from the Trinity (3) always creates a beautiful sound and perfect harmony.

According to Astronomy.com, nearly all meteors burn up before they reach an altitude of 50 miles over our heads. Considering at least 6 meteors enter the earth's atmosphere per hour (on an ordinary "non-shower" day) and an estimated 100 to 1000 tones of meteoric material fall into our atmosphere per day, it is by grace that our homes, cars and heads are not peppered with meteor showers! Thank God there is an invisible barrier protecting us at 50 miles above!

5 FOR GRACE Overflowing to Gentiles

One of the great expressions of God's grace is the inclusion of Gentile believers in the Family of God. The Jews were originally given the Bible, the covenants and the promises; the Gentiles were by and large excluded. However, hints of God's grace overflowing to the Gentiles were always in the Old Testament (Genesis 17:4, 18:18, 22:18, 26:4; Psalm 72:11, 117:1; Isaiah 2:2-4, 42:1-6; 2 Chronicles 6:32; Micah 4:2-5).

The word *Greece* or *Greek* (*Javan* in Hebrew) is mentioned 5 times in the Old Testament (Daniel 8:21, 10:20, 11:2; Joel 3:6; Zechariah 9:13). *Greek* was synonymous with *Gentile* to the ancient Jews. Since 5 is associated with Greeks, is it a coincidence that more Gentiles have become recipients of God's saving grace than Jews? "Through their fall [unbelief]," Paul wrote, "salvation has come to the Gentiles" (Romans 11:11).

There are 5 books in the Jewish Bible that are NOT specifically about Jews. Why would the ancient Jews who looked down upon Gentiles include 5 "Gentile books" in their Bible? The inclusion was by God's design and is intended to show that His eternal plan of redemption included the Gentiles also. Which are the 5 Old Testament books specifically about Gentiles?

1. **Job** – a Gentile believer. The Book of Job is considered the oldest book of the Bible, evidenced by the fact that there is no mention of Israel, the Mosaic Law, or the Tabernacle. Job was a Gentile who lived before the Nation of Israel was birthed, before the Laws of Moses were written, and before the Tabernacle was built. Though Job didn't have a Bible to read, yet he had a personal relationship with God. We who have easy access to Bibles have no excuse to be far from God!

2. **Ruth** – a Gentile widow from Moab who married a Jewish kinsman redeemer named Boaz. Ruth accepted the God of the Bible and God accepted her. She became an ancestor of both King David and the Lord Jesus;

3. **Jonah** – an unwilling prophet to the Gentile city of Nineveh, Assyria. One of the greatest miracles of the Old Testament is the repentance and salvation of an entire Gentile city through this reluctant man's preaching!

4. **Obadiah** – "an ambassador sent among the heathen" (1:1). Obadiah had a vision about Edom (present-day Jordan). Because Edom gloated over Judah's downfall, Edom would be destroyed. Much of Edom lays waste and deserted today.

5. **Nahum** – a prophet who followed up Jonah's ministry to the city of Nineveh about 100 years later. After the short-lived revival a century earlier, the inhabitants of Nineveh forgot about God and excelled in murder, lies, robbery, wanton wars, whoredoms, witchcraft, and drunkenness (3:1-11). Nahum's message? God spared Nineveh because it repented, but now He will not delay their judgment.

These messages to Gentiles or other nations make the Bible unique. Most nations have their own gods. The Canaanites worshipped Canaanite gods. The Egyptians had Egyptian gods. The Vikings had Viking gods. Till today, many religious people will say they follow a certain religion because they were born in a certain country. I've heard people proud to be "orthodox Christian" because they were born in Armenia, Egypt, Ethiopia, Syria, Greece or Russia. There's nothing wrong with being proud of being Orthodox, as long as one is prouder of being saved by the Blood of Jesus, which is what really makes us Christian.

Biblical faith differs from all traditional faiths in the world because it is not bound to a nation or ethnic group. The God of the Bible does not see Himself as God of the Jews only. Whereas other religions appeal mainly to a specific people group, the God of the Bible sees Himself as the universal Owner of all nations.

Whenever God wanted to highlight people who believed and served Him outside of the Jewish family, He did so. Job from Uz, Melchizedek from Salem, Rahab from Jericho, and Ruth from Moab, these were 4 outstanding examples of Gentile believers. Rahab was a Canaanite prostitute and Ruth was a Moabite widow, yet God accepted both Gentile women into the Davidic or Messianic line. Why? To show that the Messiah is the Savior of the world – both Jews and Gentiles.

Whenever God wanted to send His message to country outside of Israel, He did so. He sent Jonah and Nahum to Nineveh. He sent Obadiah's prophecy to Edom. Other prophets wrote inspired prophecies about Lebanon, Syria, Egypt, Iraq, Iran, etc. The God of the Bible felt He had as much right to call them to repentance and judge them for their sins as He did the Jews. The 5 Gentile books of the Old Testament affirm that God's grace is international and it extends to every person. This is why it's called amazing grace.

5 GIFTS

5 STANDS FOR GIFTS. The anointing oil was made of 5 parts: olive oil, myrrh, cinnamon, calamus, and cassia. God's anointing upon our lives is always a gift . In the secular world, someone who is naturally talented is called a "gifted" child. Did you ever ask, "Gifted by whom?" In 1 Corinthians 15:10, Paul said about his own calling:

"But by the GRACE of God I am what I am, and His GRACE toward me was not in vain; but I labored more abundantly than they all, yet not I, but the GRACE of God which was with me."

When we discover God's call on our lives, we will also discover the supernatural grace, gifting and anointing to help us accomplish that call. We will succeed "not by might, nor by power, but by My Spirit, says the LORD of hosts" (Zechariah 4:6).

5 named individuals in Scripture resurrected others from the dead: Elijah, Elisha, our Lord Jesus, Peter and Paul.[1] On the part of the minister, 3 gifts of the Spirit are required to resurrect someone from the dead: the gifts of special faith, working of miracles and healing. The dead person cannot have faith for his own resurrection or healing, so it can only be done by the

operation of gifts of the Spirit (in 1 Corinthians 12) through a minister. The gift of special faith is required for the minister to call his spirit back into his body, the gift of working of miracles is required to jump start his dead body, and the gift of healing is required to reverse the cause of death in order to keep the person alive after resurrection.

These 3 gifts are in operation today, so resurrections from the dead still occur today. It was never limited to the 5 named ministers. A group of unnamed disciples resurrected Paul from the dead in Acts 14. As long as someone is young and did not wish to die, they are candidates for being resurrected from premature death. Don't go around praying for old people to resurrect - they want to go to Heaven which is far better. God wants the young to live out their full potential and serve Him on earth.

God entrusted the message of grace to 5 ministry gifts. Listed in Ephesians 4:11, they are:

1. Apostles
2. Prophets
3. Evangelists
4. Pastors
5. Teachers

While the Lord Jesus is the Head of the Body of Christ, the Holy Spirit is often called the Hand of the Lord; the 5-fold ministers act like the 5 fingers on the Hand. They are at the forefront of the work of reaching humanity with the gift of salvation.

By contrast there were only 3 main ministry offices in the Old Testament: prophet, priest and king. Today, the Lord has blessed humanity with more ministers of God. Whereas the Law gave the Jews 3, Grace has given the Church 5. One sure way to tell whether a person is deceived by delusions of grandeur is if they believe they're called to be an apostle, prophet, evangelist, pastor AND teacher. The fact is *no one* has been nor ever will be called to stand in all 5-fold ministry offices except Jesus!

Finally, there are 5 instances recorded in the Book of Acts of people being filled with the gift of the Holy Spirit: chapters 2, 8, 9, 10 and 19. The number 5 is there by design. The gift of the Holy Spirit, like the gift of salvation, is not something we can try to earn or receive on our merits.

Too many people delay receiving Christ's new birth or the Holy Spirit's baptism because they are too ashamed to come just as they are. They sincerely want to "clean up their lives first." But if you could clean up your life without Jesus, you wouldn't need Him. You would be the Savior, not Jesus. But the fact is there is only one Savior!

I've seen addicts completely set free by receiving Christ into their hearts and exercising the power of the Holy Spirit by speaking in tongues. What seems hard for you to do is *easy* for God to do. He filled 5 groups of people with the Holy Spirit in the Book of Acts. Why not you?

Ask for the Lord to fill you with the Holy Spirit in Jesus' Name and receive with joy! Begin to pray in your own special prayer language. It's a gift, not something you work for. By grace through faith we can all receive God's best gifts.

5 LOVE LANGUAGES

MANY HAVE HEARD of the 5 love languages popularized by Gary Chapman. Not many have heard that the New Testament story of the "Prodigal Son" links the 5 acts of the father to the 5 love languages. This tells me Jesus understood the 5 love languages long before modern counsellors did. Jesus is the inventor of this teaching on how to love people the way they need to feel love, because God is Love.

In Luke 15, Jesus spoke a parable of a father who loved 2 sons. The younger son asked for his inheritance and ran off to live his own life. The elder son stayed home but never really got to know his father's heart. After a period of suffering, the younger son, known as the "Prodigal Son" or the "Lost Son," found himself in lack and repented for leaving his father. He prepared to go home and ask his father to accept him back, if not as his son, then as his servant. When he returned, the father did 5 things for him to express God's love.

1. **Physical touch** – *he fell on his neck and kissed him* (Luke 15:20). Children need parents who are able to show

physical affection. Too many people go through an entire week without an appropriate touch of acceptance and affirmation. This father, representing our God, knew how to welcome this lost son with a hug.

2. **Gift giving** – *he gave him the best robe, ring and pair of shoes* (Luke 15:22). Children need to see parents who are generous, not stingy or making decisions solely based on money. The heart of God the Father is to give us gifts.

3. **Acts of service** – *he told the servants to cook for him and feed him the fatted calf* (Luke 15:23a). Cooking or feeding is one act of service all parents need to show. Kevin Conner once told me, "Steve, your ability to *lead* comes from your ability to *feed*." Of course, he was speaking to me as a pastor leading the church by feeding the people with God's Word. But it also applies to family. Any parent who refuses to feed her child would naturally lose her ability to lead and her right to speak into that child's life. Any form of help which the child deems helpful is an act of service.

4. **Quality time** – *he sat with him to have a meal, "Let us eat and be merry"* (Luke 15:23b). Many parents do not fail to provide meals for their children, but they fail to invite their children to sit at the table at a set time with them. Too many parents focus on work to provide money for their children, but don't spend enough time with them. Children grow up wanting not only *quality* time, but also *quantity* time. Many children just wish their fathers showed up…to their school play, or sports game, or church service. Having a father who turns up helps a child understand the love of God the Father. God is never too busy for us.

5. **Words of affirmation** – *he affirmed him with restorative words, "For this my son was dead, and is alive again; he was lost, and is found"* (Luke 15:24). Children need to be told they are good in our sight. My wife and I have never called our children "naughty"—not even once! And we never will. That doesn't mean we don't discipline or correct our children. We do! But we don't speak negative, scaring words over them. We speak what God wants them to be and do.

The Bible teaches a principle that we should speak what we want into existence. God said to Abraham, "I have made you a father of many nations" (Romans 4:17-18, Genesis 17:5), before Abraham had even one child. If we were to say our children are spoiled, naughty or dumb, would it be a surprise when they grow up to be spoiled, naughty or dumb?

Solomon wrote in Proverbs 18:21, "Death and life are in the power of the tongue." As our authority increases, the power of our words increases proportionally. You see, if a schoolyard friend says, "You're dumb!" we may not care very much. If a teacher says, "You're dumb!" it may hurt a bit more. But if a parent says, "You're dumb!" it's absolutely devastating! Children need to hear from us words of affirmation and acceptance. Then they will understand God the Father.

Gary Chapman teaches that while most of us enjoy all 5 languages of love, we usually have one that we prefer most and need regularly. We feel emotionally drained when we don't receive love the way we understand it most. Miscommunication and misunderstanding occur when a person tries to communicate love in *his or her own* love language rather than in the language of the *recipient*.

The father in Luke 15 is a type of the ideal father who knew how to give all 5 love languages to his son. God, being the ideal Father, knows how to communicate love to us in all 5 languages, so that each one of us may receive God's perfect love in the way we understand it best. 5 shows us the fullness of the Father's grace.

I think one tragedy of modern discipleship is omitting the Trinity—thereby missing the Fatherhood of God. Some people have met Jesus as their personal Savior; fewer still have met the Holy Spirit as their daily Helper; and almost none have met God as their loving Father. Psalm 68:5 reveals our God as a *Father to the fatherless.*

A minister who understands God as Father will stop focusing on programs, and start looking for potential sons-in-the-faith to father and to mentor. Paul understood the importance of fatherhood when he said, "For though you might have ten thousand instructors in Christ, yet you do not have many FATHERS; for in Christ Jesus I have begotten you through the gospel."

Bible teachers are plenty; but spiritual fathers are scarce. The place to find spiritual fathers is in the local church. That's why God did not think it is enough to give prophets, evangelists and Bible teachers; He also gave us pastors.

Some people may not like to hear it, but a Christian without a pastor is like a son without a father—in other words, he is a spiritual orphan. He has been given a new birth but he receives no love or correction from a father figure or role model. He prefers to be alone. He prefers to take his inheritance and run off to do his own thing. That is not God's best for him.

There is an imbalance in the Body of Christ of more good teachers than good fathers. The responsibility to rectify this falls on both sides. It is incumbent on growing Christians to find spiritual fathers and sit under their love and tutelage. It is also incumbent on spiritually mature Christians to look around the church and ask themselves, "How many people in the church can I truly call my son?" Paul was unashamed to call Timothy "my beloved and faithful son in the Lord" (1 Corinthians 4:17, 1

Timothy 1:2) and Titus "a true son in our common faith" (Titus 1:4).

God is calling us to not only meet Jesus as a personal Savior, but to also know God as Father. God the Father has a Family called the Church, and every Christian is meant to enter a community of relationships where we can truly call other Christians our *spiritual father, mother, brother, sister, son and daughter!* No one is meant to be a spiritual orphan. No one is meant to grow or serve alone. God the Father's heart is revealed inside the Family of God.[1]

6

6 IS the number of man. Adam was created on the 6th day; Adam was given 6 commandments to obey after the Fall;[1] 6 days a week a man is to work; the atomic weight of the building block of life Carbon is 6; 99% of human mass is made up of just 6 elements (oxygen, carbon, hydrogen, nitrogen, calcium, and phosphorus); the first fetal heartbeat is usually detected at 6 weeks (which is why Georgia's 2019 "Heartbeat Bill" prohibiting most abortions after a baby's heart beats is the minimal compassion and protection we should offer infant life); it takes 6 seconds for a man in a strangle hold to pass out; peak performance coaches know that an athlete cannot maintain his maximum speed for longer than 6 seconds; every able man in the ancient Greek *ecclesia*[2] was given 6 minutes to speak; there are 66 books in the Bible containing the only plan for man's salvation.

There are 6 continents man inhabits. 6 feet is the average height of man. As a rule of thumb, the temperature of the earth increases 1° F for every 60 feet in depth. The distance to the earth's core is about 6000 km. The temperature of the earth's core is about 6600°C. The weight of the earth is 6 x 10^{24}

kilograms (6 with 24 zeros after it). The axial tilt of the Earth is 23.4°. 90° minus 23.4° is 66.6°.

The Greek gematria for the word "world" (*cosmos*) is 600. The Hebrew gematria for the word "earthquake" (*ra'ash*) is 600. The world's population hit 6 billion about the same time Israel's population hit 6 million about the same time Jerusalem's population was 600,000. Humans' collective life expectancy is 66 years.[3] There are about 6000 known languages on earth.

World War II, humanity's worst war which introduced 2 atomic bombs, killed about 60 million people.[4] When the Human Genome Project (1990-2003) was completed, guess how many nucleotides (letters of the DNA) they counted in every human cell? 6 billion! What are the chances of such repetitive patterns occurring by chance?

Genesis records that 6 of Adam's descendants lived in excess of 900 years: Seth, Enos, Cainan, Jared, Methuselah, and Noah. Ancient rabbis and early church fathers believed Adam's family was given 6000 years to rule the earth. In other words, Adam's lease on the earth is about to run out, and we are expecting Jesus' Second Coming soon!

The number of soldiers when Israel left Egypt was 600,000 (Exodus 12:37). Nebuchadnezzar's idolatrous image stood 60 cubits high and 6 cubits broad.

6 of the 10 Commandments deal with our relationship with fellow man (the rest deal with our relationship to God). The 6th commandment is so interesting a subject that it warrants its own chapter to come.

6 times in the Sermon on the Mount Jesus contrasted man's misinterpretation of the Law with God's true meaning of the Law. While God gave the Jews the *Torah* (the Laws of Moses) to prepare their hearts to be convicted of sin and search for the Savior; rabbis added their own interpretations and oral laws (called the *Mishna*) to skirt the Law and justify themselves.

In the Sermon on the Mount, Jesus exalted God's holy laws

above the rabbi's oral laws. When Jesus quoted the Bible, He said, "It is written." When Jesus addressed the rabbis' misinterpretations or oral traditions, He said, "It was said." Jesus repeated 6 times variations of "you have heard that it was said" (Matthew 5:21, 27, 31, 33, 38, 43). Here's an example:

> MATTHEW 5:43-48
> 43 You have heard that it was said, 'You shall love your neighbor and hate your enemy.' [The rabbis agreed with this and in their own eyes, they were righteous and worthy of Heaven.]
> 44 BUT I say to you, love your enemies [this they could not keep; the rabbis hated the Romans, the Greeks, the Samaritans, and the Christians], bless those who curse you, do good to those who hate you, and pray for those who spitefully use you and persecute you,
> 45 that you may be sons of your Father in Heaven; for He makes His sun rise on the evil and on the good, and sends rain on the just and on the unjust.
> 46 For if you love those who love you, what reward have you? Do not even the tax collectors do the same?
> 47 And if you greet your brethren only, what do you do more than others? Do not even the tax collectors do so?
> 48 Therefore you shall be perfect, just as your Father in Heaven is perfect.

By God's standard, anyone who does not love in this way is a sinner. No one who refuses to love his or her enemy is worthy of entering Heaven. Jesus set the standard so high, above that of the Pharisees. Why? To show us we are not as good as we think we are. God wants us to repent so He can make us good.

6 is the number of human opinions and man-made theories, in contrast to God's perfect truth (7). Rabbinic commentaries dating from 536 BC to 70 AD were recorded in the Mishna. This was the first written record of "Oral Law". Interestingly, rabbis divide their *Mishna* into 6 orders:

1. *sera'im* (seeds – about agricultural rules and blessings)
2. *mo'ed* (seasons or festivals – about ceremonial rules)
3. *nashim* (women – about marital and sexual rules)
4. *neziqin* (damages – about commercial and criminal laws)
5. *qodashim* (sacred things – about the Temple and its sacrifices)
6. *tohorot* (purifications – about sanitation rules)

Another name for the *Mishna* is the *shas*, an abbreviation of *shisha sedarim*, meaning the "6 orders".

From 300 AD to 500 AD rabbis compiled discussions about the *Mishna* into the *Gemara* (commentaries on the commentaries). Together, the *Mishna* and *Gemara* form the Jewish *Talmud*.

Jesus often attacked religious theories which He said rendered the Word of God "of no effect". To understand what Jesus was saying about Judaism, we must understand that there are really 2 forms of Judaism: **Mosaic** and **Talmudic** (synonymous with Rabbinic); traditional and modern.

As the name suggests, Talmudic Judaism relies on the Talmud (Oral Law); Rabbinic Judaism relies on the rabbis. Mosaic Judaism relies on Moses, who gave us the first five books of the Bible called the Torah (aka Written Law).

The contrast between these two forms of Judaism is nowhere clearer than on the issue of the Messiah. Mosaic Judaism is a religion of blood sacrifice, of substitutionary work, which became impossible after the Temple was gone and unnecessary after Jesus died for sins. Talmudic Judaism is a religion of man's own works, which cannot replace the atoning blood or the Temple.

Jesus attacked the teachings of the Pharisees because they twisted and complicated God's Word with the Talmud. Talmudic Judaism relied on oral teachings not inspired by God. This does not mean the *Talmud* is completely wrong. The early Jewish sages had many wise things to teach us. But it does mean that we must know the Tanak (Christian Old Testament) well enough to be able to discern which parts of the Talmud agree with the Bible and which parts err from its central truths. The fact is, Jews who follow the Scriptures closely end up becoming Jews who believe in Jesus. They form a third group in Jewish religion called **Messianic Judaism**.

THE NEPHILIM & OTHER GIANTS

Goliath was 6 cubits tall and his spearhead weighed 600 shekels of iron. The Bible names 6 kinds of giants who were a cross breed of devils and humans: Nephilim, Anakim, Emim, Zamzummim, Amorites, and Rephaim. Goliath, whom David slew, was a Rephaim who lived among the Philistines. Goliath was not just an abnormally large human, but half-human, half-demon.[5]

Accounts of giants are not only in the Bible, but throughout various cultures. The Greeks named at least 2 races of giants, the *Cyclops* and *Titans*, of which *Atlas* was one. Homer's Odyssey mentioned a race of giants and cannibals called *Laestrygones* who lived in the far north. Scandinavian folklore speaks of many giants among Norse gods, the most famous one called Thor. King Arthur slew one giant named *Rhitta Gawr*. The Knights of the Round Table slew or were slain by other Giants. The Hindu epic of Ramayana credits King Rama with slaying the evil giants of Sri Lanka. Thais and Laotians still have many statues of mythical giants called "Yak", in front of which modern tourists like to take photos.

The traditions of ancient people all over the world are unanimous in asserting that an earlier time, there lived a race of giants on the earth. Who were the giants? Only the Bible explains. Genesis 6:4 makes it clear:

> *"There were giants [nephilim] on the earth in those days [before the Flood], and also afterward [after the Flood], when the sons of God [fallen angels] came in to the daughters of men and they bore children to them. Those were the MIGHTY MEN who were OF OLD, MEN OF RENOWN."*

Don't the mythological figures such as Atlas and Thor qualify as "mighty men of old" and "men of renown"? The ancients called them gods and worshipped them. Although this is a corruption of the facts, there is still a seed of truth in mythology. Because they were partly of supernatural original, giants were easily mistaken for gods. The Ante-Nicene [Early Church] Fathers agreed that poets and mythologists, not knowing demons begot giants, called them "gods". "On the earth," wrote Greek poet Homer in 400 BC, "there once were giants."

6 is the number of the devil. 6 times man dared to accuse the Savior of having a devil.[6] 6 times people asked the Lord for a sign.[7] The greatest apostasy in Jesus' ministry is recorded in John 6:66, "From that time many of His disciples went back and walked with Him no more." God was in the dock and His Son sat through 6 unjust trials whose outcome was rigged from the beginning; the Judge of the Universe was cross examined by 3 Jewish courts and 3 Roman courts, namely: 1) Annas the Jewish High Priest, 2) Caiaphas the Roman appointed Jewish priest, 3)

the Sanhedrin, 4) Pontius Pilate the Roman Governor of Judea, 5) Herod Antipas the Roman appointed tetrarch of Galilee and Perea, and 6) Pilate one final time. All 6 courts knew Jesus was innocent, yet condemned Him to death. Is it a wonder the number of the anti-Christ, a leader who exalts *man* above God, is 666?

6 is the number of manslaughter (unintentional killing). If a man accidentally killed another person, he could flee to one of 6 God-appointed cities of refuge - 3 east of the Jordan River and 3 west (Numbers 35:11-15). The manslayer was to stay inside the "sanctuary city" and never leave until the death of the high priest. If he left, he could be punished by the avenger of blood, which was usually a relative of the victim. This is a typology of how we too are under constant threat from the avenger or Satan until Jesus' death sets us free.

There were 6 instances of unassisted suicide in the Bible: Samson, Saul, Saul's armorbearer, Ahithophel, Zimri, and Judas.[8] Judas was the last case of suicide in the Bible, which suggests to me that the Cross stopped the curse. There was a case of assisted suicide in Judges 9:54, where Abimelech was hit in the head by a millstone and asked his armorbearer to kill him. In my estimate this incident qualifies more as a murder. There was one attempted suicide by the Philippian jailer who thought an earthquake had set all his prisoners free, so he despaired for his career and life. Paul stopped him from taking his life, which tells me the voice of a minister of God can prevent suicide (Acts 16:26-29)! Before I came to Christ, I nearly took my own life, but I turned to the Cross and the Holy Spirit stopped me. Then the voice of a man of God brought me back to life.[9]

6TH COMMANDMENT

6 REPRESENTS the 6th of 10 Commandments: "You shall not murder."

I have heard critics challenge God by saying, "If the Bible says, 'Thou shalt not kill,' how can God command the Jews to kill so many people in the Old Testament? Doesn't that make God a murderer?"

Actually, there is no such command as, "Thou shalt not kill." There is only a command, "Thou shalt not murder." As anyone who has studied law would know, the legal distinction is very important.

The Hebrew word for "murder" is *ratsach;* whereas the word for "kill" is *harag.* It is unfortunate the King James translators translated *ratsach* as "kill" 4 times[1] in the Bible. They translated *ratsach* correctly once in Matthew 19:18, "Thou shalt do no murder." Later translators corrected every instance of *ratsach* to "murder".

Solomon said:

"To everything there is a season, a time for every purpose under Heaven: a time to be born, a time to die; a time to plant;

and a time to pluck up what is planted; a TIME TO KILL, and a time to heal." Ecclesiastes 1:1-3

Harag or killing is sanctioned by God and every government on earth (Romans 13:1-4). There is a time to kill, but there is never a time to murder. What's the difference?

Proverbs 6:16 defines murder for us, "These six things does the Lord hate... a proud look, a lying tongue, hands that SHED INNOCENT BLOOD...." Murder is shedding innocent blood, and the Lord hates it.

There are 3 occasions when it is proper to kill:

1. War – a nation has the right to protect itself when another nation threatens or invades it;
2. Self-defense – a person has the right to protect his own life and/or his family's life;
3. Capital punishment – some nations allow the killing of cruel criminals such as serial murderers, serial rapists and mass terrorists.

Does God believe in capital punishment? God certainly believes in capital punishment or the death penalty. The proof is JESUS. God allowed His Son to be executed for the sins of humanity.

There is hope for the murderer if he repents and turns to Christ. His sins can be paid by Jesus' execution on his behalf. This was the case of Moses who murdered an Egyptian, and also of Paul who was part of a religious gang that murdered Stephen. Their lives were turned around by God's grace and they ended up becoming humble men of God.

However, not all murderers will be spared their just sentence. One criminal who hung on the cross repented before Jesus saying, "And we indeed justly [are condemned], for we receive the DUE REWARD of OUR DEEDS; but this Man has done nothing wrong. [Then he said to Jesus] Lord, remember me when You come into your kingdom." And Jesus said to him, "Assuredly, I say to you, today you will be with me in Paradise" (Luke 23:41-43). The criminal's spirit was saved, but he was not spared the execution of his body.

We cannot conclude a discussion on the 6th commandment without looking at its New Testament application. When we hear of the 6th commandment, many of us justify ourselves by saying, "I'm basically a good person. I haven't killed anybody." However, God judges us by our hearts. Jesus amplified the 6th commandment when He preached His famous Sermon on the Mount:

> MATTHEW 5:21-22
> 21 You have heard that it was said to those of old, 'You shall not MURDER, and whoever MURDERS will be in DANGER of the judgment.'
> 22 But I say to you that whoever is ANGRY with his brother without a cause shall be in DANGER of the judgment. And whoever says to his brother, 'Raca!' shall be in DANGER of the council. But whoever says, 'You fool!' shall be in DANGER of HELL fire.

Jesus said hating or being angry with someone is already murder in our hearts. Road rage, domestic abuse, chewing someone out on the phone would all qualify as murder to God. Just as sure as there will be no murderer in Heaven, there will be no hater in Heaven.

> 1 JOHN 3:15
> 15 Whoever HATES his brother is a MURDERER, and you know that NO MURDERER has eternal life abiding in him."

6 reminds us not to hate anybody, or else we will not have eternal life abiding in us. It is impossible to be truly saved and to hate another human being. If you hate someone, then you are not saved.

> 1 JOHN 4:20
> 20 If someone says, 'I love God,' and HATES his brother, he is a liar; for he who does not love his brother whom he has seen, how can he love God whom he has not seen?

Many Christians unfortunately think they still hate someone, when they are only yielding to their unrenewed mind. If only we would tap into our born again spirit, we will find that "the love of God has been poured out in OUR HEARTS [not in our heads!] by the Holy Spirit who was given to us" (Romans 5:5). We do not need to pray for more love because God's divine love has already been poured into our hearts the moment we got born again! Now we need to renew our minds to believe what our hearts know.

One great way to renew our minds is to daily confess the "Love Chapter" – 1 Corinthians 13. For instance, verses 4-5 say, "Love is patient, love is kind. It does not envy, it does not boast, it is not proud. It is not rude, it is not self-seeking, it is not easily angered, it keeps no record of wrongs." Since God's love is in the Christian heart, we can say, "I am patient, I am kind. I do not envy, I do not boast, I am not proud. I am not rude, I am not self-seeking, I am not easily angered, I keep no record of wrongs." That's the truth about who you are and how God sees you! Don't let the devil bring up some past fault or mistake which Christ's blood has already washed away. You are a brand new creation in Christ Jesus! You are a love child of a love God! When you choose to obey to your spirit, instead of your feelings, you will always walk in God's love.

6 EMPIRES

6 IS the number of Gentile Empires that oppressed Israel in the Bible:

1. Egypt
2. Assyria
3. Babylon
4. Medo-Persia
5. Greece
6. Rome.

Satan has always tried to rule over what God has reserved for Himself.

6 is also the number of regime changes during the Inter-Testament period between Malachi (end of Old Testament) and Matthew (beginning of New Testament). Far too few Christians understand the events leading up to the first coming of our Savior. The reason we should know about these 6 Inter-Testament regimes is that "history repeats itself" and "those who

do not know history are doomed to repeat it." After the Babylonian Captivity ended, the Jews were governed by these 6 successive regimes:

1. **Persian**. Their most notable king was Cyrus the Great, named by Isaiah 150 years before he was born (Isaiah 44:28, 45:1). Cyrus was a friend to the Jews and fulfilled Bible prophecy by issuing a decree to allow Jews to return to their homeland in 537 BC. The rise of the Persian Empire was predicted by Daniel's interpretation of the writing on the wall in 5:28 and the vision of the bear in 7:5. Many Jews have likened Donald Trump to a modern Cyrus. Trump not only recognized Israel's right to call Jerusalem its capital, but also Israel's right to the Golan Heights which it won after being attacked in the Six-Day War. Benjamin Netanyahu has said to President Trump, "Israel has never had a better friend than you."

2. **Greek**. The meteoric rise of Alexander the Great was predicted by Gabriel's interpretation of the *he-goat* in Daniel 8:21 and again by the angel Gabriel in Daniel 10:20. Following Alexander the Great's premature death at the age of 32, his Greek empire was divided up to his 4 generals: Cassander over Macedon (modern Greece or west); Lysimachus over Thrace (modern Turkey or east); Ptolemy over Egypt (south); Seleucid over Syria (north).

3. **Egyptian**. Hellenistic Egypt came under the rule of the Ptolemies, or the Kings of the South, as predicted by Daniel 11. Israel was caught in between the power struggle between the Seleucids to the north and the Ptolemies to the south. From 323 BC to 198 BC, the Ptolemies ruled Israel. Ptolemy I Soter (a Greek)

founded the Ptolemy dynasty. His son Ptolemy II Philadelphus founded the Alexandrian Library. The Ptolemies were benevolent rulers and their promotion of religious freedom and scholarly education resulted in the completion of the *Septuagint*–the Greek translation of the Bible and the Bible of choice for early Christians.

4. **Syrian**. Hellenistic Syria came under the rule of the Seleucids, or the King of the North, as predicted by Daniel 11. Seleucid I Nicator founded the dynasty. His son Antiochus I Soter made Antioch capital of their empire. In 198 BC Antiochus II seized Judah from Egypt. From 198 BC to 167 BC, the Syrians spread heathen altars and heathen festivals all over Israel; and outlawed reading the Torah, observing the Sabbath and circumcision. Ironically, Antioch became the headquarters of Christianity and the missionary base from which Paul conducted his missionary journeys. Christ is able to redeem the vile and turn all things for good. Antiochus IV Epiphanes ordered a pig to be offered in every Jewish village and one in the Temple of God on his birthday – the 25th of Kislev (our December) 167 BC. This prompted the Maccabean revolt.

5. **Maccabean**. When Antiochus' agents arrived in the village of Modein to carry out the pig sacrifice, an aged priest named Mattathias Maccabeus killed both the first Jew who approached the pagan altar and the royal officer. This sparked a spontaneous revolt throughout Israel. After his death, his 5 sons carried on the struggle. Through guerrilla warfare, Judas Maccabeus (the "Hammer") defeated the Seleucid army and restored Temple worship 3 years later, on the 25th of

Kislev 164 BC. This victory is commemorated at *Hanukkah* or the Feast of Dedication, which Jesus attended in John 10:22. Judas died in battle and his brother Jonathan became leader and high priest. Thus the Hasmonean Dynasty of priests / civil leaders began. After Jonathan was killed, his brother Simon became commander and high priest. After Simon was murdered, his son John Hyrcanus ruled for 30 years. John conquered Idumea or Edom (southern Israel or Jordan) around 140 BC and required all Idumeans to obey Jewish laws or leave; most Idumeans converted to Judaism. From here came Herod's family, who although were Edomites or descendants of Esau, claimed they were Jewish. John Hyrcanus' great-great granddaughter married Herod the Great.

6. **Roman**. The 6th regime brought in the reign of the Herodian Dynasty. In 47 BC Julius Caesar appointed Antipater II, an Idumean or Edomite, Procurator over Judea. Antipater appointed his son Herod Governor of Galilee when he was 25. Although not a Jew, Herod tried to court the Jews' favor by marrying a Hasmonean princess; he was circumcised and adopted into the Jewish religion. In 40 BC Rome appointed Herod "King of the Jews". This is "Herod the Great," called *great* mainly for his colossal construction projects such as expanding the Temple for 46 years (John 2:20), building the fortress of Masada, and developing Caesarea as a coastal tourist destination. Herod the Great tried to kill Jesus at the time of His birth. After his own death, his son Herod Antipas became tetrarch of Galilee, beheaded John the Baptist and presided a mock trial of Jesus in which he "arrayed Him in a gorgeous robe" (Luke 23:11). Herod Agrippa

I, nephew of Herod Antipas and grandson of Herod the Great, ordered the execution of James the brother of John (Acts 12:2), and arrested Peter (Acts12:3). His son, Herod Agrippa II, was the king before whom Paul spoke in Acts 25 and 26. He said, "You almost persuade me to become a Christian" (Acts 26:28). Herodians became a term for Jewish agents of Rome. The rise of the Roman Empire was predicted in both Nebuchanedzar's vision of the irons legs (2:40) and Daniel's vision of the fourth beast with iron teeth (7:7).

7. **Jesus**. We add Jesus' rule here because His victory over Satan demarcates the greatest regime change of all! Man's 6 imperfect regimes and empires serve as a contrast to Christ's perfect leadership and kingdom.

Ecclesiastes 1:9 makes this end time prediction, "That which HAS BEEN is what WILL BE, that which IS DONE is what WILL BE DONE, and there is nothing new under the sun." In other words, there is a high probability of a very similar power struggle between these 6 groups leading up to the Second Coming of Jesus Christ.

It is easy to identify the parallels between ancient history and modern history so far. Just as the Ptolemies were friendly to the Jews, so too modern Egypt became the first Arab country to sign a Peace Treaty with Israel in 1979. For that peace agreement, Egyptian President Anwar El Sadat was gunned down in 1981.

Just as the Seleucids instigated a reign of terror over Jews, so too Syria and Iran (territories of the Seleucids) are avowed enemies of the nation of Israel today. How accurate and predictive is the Bible!

Just as Rome did not directly rule over Israel, but appointed an Idumean governor over the province of Judea, so too Western Europe is not likely to meddle directly with Israel, but may appoint an Anti-Christ diplomat to broker its will over the Middle East.

We should be on the lookout for a future *Antiochus* or *Herod*, a Middle Eastern figure popular among the Europeans, because he may well be the forerunner to the Anti-Christ, or even the Anti-Christ himself (see Chapter 666).

7

THE NUMBER 7 is the heartbeat of Scripture. 7 represents perfection or completeness. The conjunctions of 7's in Scripture, nature, history and prophecy are beyond random.

7 IN NATURE and History

There were 7 days of Creation and there are still 7 days to complete a week. Apart from the Genesis account of the 7-day Creation, there is no reason for a week to equal 7 days. The universally accepted 7-day week has no correlation to any movement of the earth, moon, sun or other astronomical body. We have 24 hours in a day because the earth rotates on its axis in 24 hours. We have 365 days in a year because the earth revolves around the sun in 365.25 days. But why do we have 7 days in a week? Why not 10 days? Why not 5? Only the Book of Beginnings – Genesis – explains this! God created the world in 6 days and rested on the 7th.

The fact that every culture and nation recognizes the 7-day week attests to the plain truth that the God of the Bible is the original God all cultures once knew and His Word is the oldest revelation of God.

There are 7 continents (Africa, Antarctica, Asia, Australia, Europe, North America, South America); 7 seas or largest bodies of water (the Arctic, Atlantic, Caribbean, Gulf of Mexico, Indian, Mediterranean, Pacific); 7 full notes on a music scale. There can only be 7 eclipses per year: 5 solar and 2 lunar; 4 solar and 3 lunar; or 3 solar and 4 lunar. There cannot be more than 7! Since the Protestant Reformation (1517), there have been 7 years with 7 non-penumbra eclipses.[1] Twice in the 20th century, a year with 7 eclipses of any kind fell on milestones in Israel's history:

1917—coinciding with the Balfour Declaration (Britain's recognition of the need for the state of Israel) and the Russian Revolution (when communism became the religion of Russia)

1973—coinciding with the Yom Kippur War (the 4th time Arab nations invaded Israel, whose resounding victory led Egypt to concede she could never win a war against Israel and to become the first Arab state to sign a peace treaty with Israel in 1979).

The Jewish people descended from 7 people: 3 patriarchs— Abraham, Isaac and Jacob, and 4 matriarchs—Sarah, Rebekah, Rachel, and Leah. The 5 letters making up the word "Israel" in Hebrew (YiSRaEL) contain the first letter of every ancestor's name: Yod (Ya'akov, Yizhak), Shin (Sarah), Resh (Rahel, Rivkah), Alef (Avraham), Lamed (Leah).

The name Israel itself is prophetic in other ways. It contains two words: YaShaR + EL. The root word means "honesty" or "straightforwardness"; the suffix means "God". Therefore the name God gave Jacob contains the mission of the Jewish people: to be honest and straightforward with God.[2]

The name Israel contains the smallest letter of the Hebrew alef-bet (yod) and the largest letter (lamed). From being the "least of all peoples" (Deuteronomy 7:7), they will grow into the strongest nation on earth during the Messianic Age.

What makes them great comes from the meaning of the largest letter lamed—to teach. This gives a deeper meaning to the Messiah's words, "whoever does and teaches [God's commandments], he shall be called great in the kingdom of heaven" (Matthew 5:19). Lamed, meaning to teach, is literally the greatest letter in the Hebrew alphabet.[3]

7 in Scripture and Prophecy

In his book *God Counts*, W.E. Filmer revealed the unusual patterns of 7 God concealed in His Word. The very first sentence of the Bible –

> *"In the beginning God created the heavens and the earth"*

– contains 7 Hebrew words. Of these 7 words:

- The total number of letters is 28 (4 x 7).
- The first 3 words contain 14 letters (2 x 7).
- The remaining 4 words contain 14 letters.
- The 3 nouns – God, heavens and earth – together have 14 letters.
- The gematria of these 3 nouns is 777 (111 x 7).
- The gematria of the verb "created" is 203 (29 x 7).
- The gematria of the first, middle and last letters of the verse is 133 (19 x 7).
- The gematria of the first and last letters of the first and last words is 497 (71 x 7).
- The gematria of the first and last letters of all 7 words is 1392 (199 x 7).

No wonder Filmer made this challenge, *"I defy anyone to construct another sentence which incorporates such an amazing set of numerics. I should never have believed that such a sentence could exist if it were not for the fact that it is there.*"[4] This is only the first sentence of the Bible! Such supernatural patterns are replete throughout the Scriptures.

Russian born mathematician Ivan Panin (1855-1942) discovered patterns of 7 that are beyond chance in the first pages of the New Testament. The first 17 verses of Matthew outline the genealogy of Jesus. In this section:

- The number of generations (42) is divisible by 7.
- The number of vocabulary words (72) is divisible by 7.
- The number of nouns (56) is divisible by 7.
- The frequency of "the" (56) is divisible by 7.
- The gematria of all 72 vocabulary words (42,364) is divisible by 7.

From verse 1 to 11 is Jesus' genealogy up to the Babylonian Captivity. In this section, the number of vocabulary words (49) is divisible by 7. Of these 49 words:

- The number of letters (266) is divisible by 7.
- The number of vowels (140) is divisible by 7.
- The number of words beginning with a consonant (21) is divisible by 7.
- The number of words beginning with a vowel (28) is divisible by 7.
- The number of words appearing more than once (35) is divisible by 7.
- The number of words appearing only once (14) is divisible by 7.
- The number of nouns (42) is divisible by 7.
- The number of proper names (35) is divisible by 7.
- These 35 names are used 63 times (9 x 7).
- The number of male names (28) is divisible by 7.

- These male names occur 56 times (8 x 7).
- The number of words which are not nouns is 7.
- The only city named - Babylon - contains 7 Greek letters.

The rest of Matthew chapter 1 from verse 18 to 25 tells the history of Christ's birth. In this section:

- The number of words (161) is divisible by 7.
- The number of vocabulary words (77) is divisible by 7.
- The gematria of vocabulary words (52,605) is divisible by 7.
- The number of unique words used in this passage and never again in Matthew is 6 - these 6 words contain 56 letters (8 x 7).
- The number of proper nouns is 7.
- The number of words spoken by the angel to Joseph (28) is divisible by 7.

The second chapter of Matthew tells the history of Jesus' childhood. In this section:

- The number of vocabulary words (161) is divisible by 7.
- The number of letters (896) is divisible by 7.
- The gematria of vocabulary words (123,529) is divisible by 7.

There are more patterns of 7 in Matthew chapter 2 than we can include. These heptadic patterns appear in the next book Mark. The more you get into it, the more mind-boggling it gets!

If these patterns appeared in only 1 book or by 1 writer, it would be astonishing enough. But they also appear in coordinated fashion among different writers who did not know each other and could not know whose writings would be included in the Bible.

The Hebrew word "seven" occurs 287 times in the Old Testament (41 x 7). The word "seventh" occurs 98 times (14 x 7). The word "seven-fold" occurs 7 times. "Seventy" occurs 56 times (8 x 7). "Seventy" in combination with any other number occurs 35 times (5 x 7).

Vocabulary unique to Matthew is used 42 times (6 x 7) and contains 126 letters (18 x 7). How is this possible? One possibility is that Matthew contrived this by getting all other 7 writers of the New Testament to agree not to use those words. That doesn't seem likely. Another possibility is that Matthew was the last writer of the Bible, thereby he knew exactly what words the other 7 New Testament writers did not use. The only one problem with this argument is all 8 writers of the New Testament used unique vocabulary not used by any other writer and the occurrence of unique words are in multiples of 7 for every writer: Mark, Luke, John, Paul, James, Peter and Jude. No wonder Psalm 12:6 tells us, "The words of the LORD are pure words, like silver tried in a furnace of earth, purified SEVEN times."

7 times the God of the Bible says He is the "first and last".[5] There is no one else before or after Him.

7 people are called a "man of God" in the Old Testament: Moses, David, Samuel, Shemaiah, Elijah, Elisha, Igdaliah.

7 Old Testament writers are named in the New Testament: Moses, David, Isaiah, Jeremiah, Daniel, Hosea and Joel. The numeric values of these names is 1554 (222 x 7). David's name is found 1134 times (7 x 162).[6]

There are 7 named prophetesses in the Bible: Miriam; Deborah; Huldah; Noadiah; Elizabeth the mother of John; Mary the mother of Jesus; Anna the prophetess.[7] Add to these 5 unnamed prophetesses[8] and there were 12 female prophets in total!

Psalm 69 is quoted 7 times in the New Testament: twice by Matthew (23:29-38, 27:34,38); twice by John (2:13-17, 15:18-25) and three times by Paul (Romans 11:7-10, 15:3; 1 Thessalonians 2:15,16).

THE MYSTERY of Symmetry

All of these patterns of 7s throughout the Bible are breathtaking. Could they be contrived by humans? The reason the writers could not 'stage-manage' the Word of God was that God used at least 33 different authors living in different places and at different times over a period of 1600 years, writing in different languages (Hebrew, Chaldean, Greek, Aramaic). They did not all know each other. They also did not know whose writing and which of their own writings would be included in the Canon of Scriptures. That decision was made independently of the writers by independent Councils. God used so many people to remove the possibility of human engineering. All this precaution which God took silences every false accusation of human contrivance.

God wants people to know His Word is His Word! He went to great lengths to prove it! Some skeptics cast doubt on the Bible, claiming it's not original, not pure or not true. They insinuate that perhaps the Bible has been doctored or changed since its original form. If that were really the case it would destroy all the symmetry we find in it! Notice that if we changed even a single letter in the first sentence of the Bible, we would not find the heptadic symmetry or patterns of 7's.

APPLYING 7 to Your Life

When Joshua led Israel into the Promised Land, Jericho was the first city they had to conquer. In this first "battle," 7 priests carried 7 trumpets while the Jewish men marched around Jericho once for 7 days and 7 times on the 7ᵗʰ day. At the end of the silent march, the people gave a loud shout and the walls of their enemy came tumbling down!

God wanted to make sure that His people learned that victory came by His grace and not by their own works. God ensured they understood this in a number of ways: He told all the soldiers to be circumcised 4 days before, which would have made them weak and sore; He told them to march silently for 7 days, so they were not allowed to taunt the enemy; He told them to march 7 times on the 7ᵗʰ day. Even if Jericho was a small city of 7 km circumference, circling such a city 7 times would have required a 50 km march and depleted most soldiers of energy before a fight. Sometimes God has to wait until we are depleted of all our own devices and strength before He can show us His grace.

Elisha told Naaman the Syrian leper to go wash in the Jordan 7 times. The funny thing was the Jordan was not a wide or a spectacular river. It didn't have the fertility of the Nile, the religious fame of the Ganges, or the commercial value of the Mississippi. In fact Naaman disdained it, "Are not Abanah and Pharpar, the rivers of Damascus, better than all the waters of Israel? Could I not wash in them and be clean?" (2 Kings 5:12). But he yielded to the prophet's word and dipped 7 times, and his flesh was restored like the flesh of a little child. God may ask us to do things that don't seem to bring us closer to the solution we want, but 7 dips remind us His ways are perfect. Don't give up on only the 5ᵗʰ dip or 6ᵗʰ dip! Do what God says and do it fully the way He says it!

7 THE NUMBER of Jesus

If 3 is the number of God the Father, then 7 is the number of God the Son. As the number of perfection, 7 befits Jesus who alone lived a Perfect Life, finished a Perfect Work and is the Perfect Savior. There are 7 feasts in Israel, each pointing to events in Jesus' first and second coming. Jesus spoke 7 Kingdom parables in Matthew 13. Jesus sent 7 letters to 7 churches in the Book of Revelation. The 7 letters to 7 churches represent both 7 historical churches and 7 prophetic ages or stages of the Church since the first century. The 7 letters contain 7 basic elements: region, role of Christ, recognition, rebuke, recommendation, wrap up, reassurance.[9] In the Book of Revelation, there are 7 seals opened by the Lord, 7 angels blowing 7 trumpets, and angels releasing 7 vials of judgement upon the rebellious earth.[10]

7 people are named before birth: Ishmael, Isaac, Solomon, Josiah (325 years before birth), Cyrus (175 years before birth), John the Baptist, and Jesus (1500 years before birth). While no one knew for certain the Messiah's Name, a big clue was given long ago. Before completing his ministry, Moses prophesied about the Messiah.

> DEUTERONOMY 18:15 (KJV)
> 15 The LORD thy God will raise up unto thee a PROPHET from the midst of thee [born in Israel], of thy brethren [a Jew], LIKE UNTO ME; unto HIM [not unto Moses] ye shall hearken.

When Moses said this, there were two applications to his prophecy: one immediate, and one in the distant future. His listeners were obviously not looking for the Messiah to come thousands of years later. They were looking for Moses' successor to fulfill this prophecy. Who was Moses' successor? What was his name? JESUS in Greek or JOSHUA in Hebrew!

Joshua's name was prophetic of the One who was to be a "prophet like unto Moses," a title of Messiah.[11] Joshua historically was the prophet like unto Moses, succeeding directly after him, whereas Jesus was prophetically the Prophet like unto Moses, arriving about 1500 years later. They both shared the same name!

The Messiah's Name was revealed in type first, then revealed in person by Gabriel to Mary (Matthew 1:21 and Luke 1:31).

How was Jesus a "prophet like unto Moses"? The most glaring similarity is that both came *twice* to their own people: the first time they arrived to help, they were rejected; the second time Moses returned (after 40 years of being away), the Jews accepted him but with much grumbling; the second time Jesus will return (after 2000 years of being away), one-third of the Jews will accept Him with much repentance. Zechariah 12:10, written 500 years before Christ, predicts this event, "Then they will look on Me whom they pierced. Yes, they will mourn for Him as one mourns for his only son, and grieve for Him as one grieves for a firstborn."

The Savior was named before birth, if only we have eyes to see it. Every instance of the Hebrew word *Yeshua*, *Jehoshua* or *Joshua*, meaning *God is Salvation*, was a clue that God would be the Messiah and He would be named JESUS - the Greek form of *Yeshua*. Try inserting *Yeshua* where the word "salvation" appears in these Scriptures and see if you can see the Savior prophetically: Genesis 49:18, Exodus 14:13, 15:2, Deuteronomy 32:15, 1 Samuel 2:1, Psalm 20:5, 21:1, 85:9, 91:16, 96:2, 118:14. For example:

> PSALM 91:16
> 16 With long life I will satisfy him, and show him My Yeshua. [Salvation is a Person. His Name is Yeshua. At the end of a life of faith, we will get to see Him!]

> PSALM 96:2
> 2 Sing to the LORD, bless His name; proclaim the good news of His Yeshua from day to day. [Good news was always about Yeshua from the beginning!]

 PSALM 118:14
14 The LORD is my strength and song, and He has become my Yeshua. [When God was born in the flesh, He became Yeshua! God is my Savior.]

Jesus called Himself Lord of the Sabbath or Lord of the 7th day. Jesus intentionally performed 7 miracles on a Sabbath, irritating the Pharisees, but delivering 7 individuals from oppression:

1. A man with an unclean spirit (Mark 1:21-25)
2. Peter's mother-in-law (Mark 1:21, 29-31)
3. A man with the withered hand (Mark 3:1-5)
4. A woman bent over for 18 years (Luke 13:10-17)
5. A man with dropsy (Luke 14:1-6)
6. A man paralyzed for 38 years (John 5:1-10)
7. A man born blind (John 9:14)

7 times Jesus said for Christians to pray, command and cast out devils "in His Name". That means Jesus has given the believer His own authority to use on earth!

1. In My name [the Name of Jesus]...cast out demons...speak with new tongues...lay hands on the sick (Mark 16:17-18)
2. Whatever you ask in My Name, that I will do...(John 14:13)
3. If you ask anything in My Name, I will do it.
4. Whatever you ask the Father in My Name He may give you (John 15:16)
5. Whatever you ask the Father in My name He will give you (John 16:23)

6. Until now [under the old covenant] you have asked nothing in My name. Ask, and you will receive, that your joy may be full (John 16:24)
7. In that day [when the new covenant has been established] you will ask in My name...(John 16:26)

Most of the time, the sick approached Jesus for healing. In a minority of instances, the Lord approached the sick first. How many individuals did Jesus approach to heal? You guessed it - exactly 7! You can read about them in the chapter on "19 Healings".

Jesus described the torments of hell 7 times.[12] There will be "weeping, wailing and gnashing of teeth." Anyone who disbelieves in hell has to assume they know something Jesus didn't. It's safer to assume Jesus knew what He was talking about and was preparing us to not go there!

Jesus was crucified on a hill called *Golgotha* in Aramaic or *Calvary* in Latin. Calvary is 777 meters above sea level.

7 is **Perfect**

All these patterns of 7's are breath-taking because they transcend the frame of reference of the individual writers. As many Bible critics have been quick to note, the 4 Gospel accounts do not match in timeline and detail. The stories are not presented in the same chronological order and the words are not always quoted the same way. Uncoached eyewitnesses do not tend to give the exact same account of the same events, simply because they have not colluded and naturally come from different perspectives.

Clearly God intended the Gospel accounts to be this way precisely to meet the skepticism of pre-believers. What the minor differences prove is that the 4 Gospel writers did not collaborate. That means Luke wasn't saying to Matthew, "You put 6 references to weeping in hell and I'll put 1—that will make a nice, neat 7." Matthew could not say to Mark, "You write about 2 healings on the Sabbath, I'll write about 1, hopefully Luke and John will have enough sense to put together 4 Sabbath miracles and no more." They didn't know what each other was writing. John could not say to Matthew, "You quote Psalm 69 twice, I'll quote it twice, and we'll leave Paul to quote it 3 times to make a perfect 7." The heptadic structure constantly found in Scripture happened beyond the frame of reference of the writers. In other words, the patterns were not contrived by man, but superimposed by Divine sanction.

This simply is another proof of the inspiration of God's Word. To those who ask, "How do I know which book is truly God's Word?" the answer is: "The Book with His signature of 7 on it!"

When voices come to cast doubt on the authority of God's Word, the 7-day week reminds me that the God who created the world in 7 days also commanded us to believe in His Word which is full of 7s. The 7-day week points to no other Person but Jesus —the Lord of 7. When we meet Him, we will be without excuse because every week of our lives pointed to Him as the Creator God.

7 SURROUNDS Donald Trump

The following pattern of 7s will prove to an impartial reader that Trump is inextricably connected to Israel and God chose him to be the President of the United States, not Hillary Clinton.

- On 14 June 1946, Donald Trump was born. **700 days** after Trump was born, Israel was reborn on 14 May 1948.
- On 8 November 2016, Trump was elected President— **7 years, 7 months and 7 days** after Israeli Prime

Minister Benjamin Netanyahu's first full day in office on 1 April 2009.

- On 20 January 2017, Trump was inaugurated at the age of **70 years, 7 months, 7 days old**.
- How many electoral votes did Trump win? The New York Time election results showed he won 304, compared to Hillary Clinton's 227. Trump beat Hillary Clinton by **77 electoral votes**, because 7 "faithless electors" defected and ignored the will of the American people (two voted against Trump and five voted against Clinton).
- Trump won and was inaugurated in Hebrew year **5777** (which began on 3 Oct 2016 and ended on 20 Sep 2017).
- On 7 July 2017, Trump met Russian President Vladimir Putin for the first time when Putin was **777 months old** to the day.
- On 21 August 2017, exactly **7 months** after his first full day in office on 21 Jan 2017, there was a total solar eclipse over the continental US. It was the first a total solar eclipse was seen in no other country but the United States since the nation's founding in 1776.
- Called the "Great American Eclipse," it marked the beginning of a **7-year period** that will end with another solar eclipse crossing the continental US on 8 April 2024. I preached in Houston, Texas that this was a divine warning in the sky for Americans to repent. A few days later, the sign was confirmed. Hurricane Harvey made landfall 5 times from 23-29 Aug 2017! The damage it caused made it the costliest natural disaster in US history. God doesn't cause disasters, but God gave warning before it happened. We are now within the 7-year period to repent and pursue righteousness and justice.

- On 6 December 2017, Trump announced that the US would recognize Jerusalem as Israel's capital and move the US Embassy to Jerusalem. This came **70 years and 7 days** after the United Nations passed Resolution 181, which called for the creation of the State of Israel on 29 November 1947.
- On 26 April 2018, Mike Pompeo was sworn in as the **70th** Secretary of State.
- On 11 July 2018, 77 **weeks** after Trump's inauguration, Forbes published that Trump was the 777**th richest person** on earth (worth about $3.1 billion at the time, making him the first billionaire President).[13]

Undeniably 7 surrounds Trump. Knowing that 7 is the number of Christ and the number of perfection, we have divine assurance that Trump was chosen by God. Despite the savage attacks by the media and biased news about the President, he is perfectly suited for the job.

70 is also the number of Jerusalem: it was restored after 70 years of Babylonian Captivity and destroyed 70 years after Jesus' First Coming. 70 weeks is the number of God's dealing with the Jews. Daniel 9:24 says, "Seventy weeks are determined for your people and for your holy city…"

It's no wonder Trump is good friends with Prime Minister Benjamin Netanyahu and his face is on the Temple coin alongside an image of Cyrus the Great. It is as though God wanted to assure the Christians: though you disapprove of his past, you've got the right man in the White House! Look with faith to the future!

7 reminds us that God is doing a perfect work on imperfect people.

7 FEASTS

GOD REVEALED to Israel that there are certain *moed's* or "appointed times" in which He will do certain things. These *moed's* divide up time and help us to commemorate as well as anticipate a major event in God's prophetic plan. There are 12 months in a Hebrew non-leap year with 7 Feasts of Israel on the following months:

1. **Nisan**[1]. Nisan 14: Passover (*Pesach*), Nisan 15-21: Feast of Unleavened Bread (*Chol Moed Matza*), Nisan 17: Feast of Firstfruits (*Yom Bikkerim*).
2. Iyyar
3. Sivan. Sivan 6: Pentecost or Feast of Weeks (*Hag Ha Shavout*) or Feast of Harvest (*Hag Ha Kazir*).
4. Tammuz
5. Av
6. Elul
7. Tishri[2]. Tishri 1: Feast of Trumpets (*Yom Teruah*) or the Civil New Year (Rosh *Hashanan*), Tishri 10: Day of

Atonement (*Yom Kippur*), Tishri 15-21: Feast of
Tabernacles or Booths or Ingathering (*Sukkot*).
8. Heshvan
9. Kislev
10. Tebet
11. Shebat
12. Adar
13. A leap year adds a 13th month called Adar II, which has
1 day less than Adar I, i.e. 29 days instead of the
usual 30).

It's readily apparent to us that there are 2 groups of 3 feasts
separated by a long gap of nearly 6 months. The first 3 feasts are
concentrated in the first month of the religious calendar (Nisan),
followed shortly by Pentecost in the third month (Siva), then a
long gap of nearly 4 months till the last 3 feasts in the seventh
month (Tishri). Why such grouping?

Agriculturally speaking, the first 3 feasts coincide with the
Spring harvest of barley, Pentecost with the Summer harvest of
wheat, and the last 3 feasts with the Fall harvest of grapes. But
surely God's "appointed times" refer to more than barley, wheat
and grapes!

Spiritually speaking, the first 3 feasts foreshadow Jesus at His
first coming; the last 3 feasts foreshadow Christ at His second
coming. Many Jewish rabbis have struggled with 2 apparently
contradictory sets of Scriptures about the Messiah. One set
seems to show Him as a suffering servant; another set as a
victorious ruler. Some of the ancients concluded that there must
be 2 Messiahs! They named the first one *Messiah ben Yosef* after
Joseph who suffered much because of his brothers. They named
the second one *Messiah ben David* after Israel's greatest king. The
truth is the contradiction is resolved in Christ. The first 3 feasts
point to Christ's first coming as a Suffering Servant; the last 3
feasts point to Christ's second coming as a Conquering King!

The 4th feast represents the harvest of the nations into the Church, which began on the Day of Pentecost in the 4th Millennium. The early feasts have thus had their fulfillment, the gap corresponds to the present Church Age, and the last feasts await their fulfillment in the latter days.

Let's highlight the meaning of each feast which is God's annual object lesson pointing to the Messiah:

1. PASSOVER (PESACH)

On the first Passover, each Jewish family took an innocent lamb, sacrificed it and applied its blood to the wooden doorposts, so that the Angel of Death would "pass over" the believers inside the house. The blood sacrifice of an innocent lamb represents the crucifixion of the sinless Son of God, which occurred precisely on Passover Day around 32AD.

2. FEAST OF UNLEAVENED BREAD (CHOL MOED MATZA)

On this feast, Jewish families eat unleavened bread. Leaven represents sin, false doctrine and religious self-righteousness (Jesus dubbed it the 'leaven of the Pharisees'). **Unleavened** bread or *matza* was a flat bread that was stripped, perforated, and slightly burned. Without doubt the *matza* points to Jesus Christ. Like bread without leaven, Jesus was sinless. Like bread with stripes, Jesus was whipped 39 times and "by His stripes we were healed" (Isaiah 53:5, 1 Peter 2:24). Like bread pierced with holes, Jesus' hands and feet were pierced by nails and His side by a spear. Finally the burn marks on the *matza* reminds us Jesus went to hell for 3 days and 3 nights, the place of burning (Acts 2:27; Proverbs 23:14).

During a traditional Passover meal, Jewish adults remove the 2nd *matza* out of 3, wrap it in cloth, and hide it for the children to find. This game amazingly speaks about Jesus, who is the 2nd

Person of the Trinity; He came down to earth to die for us; His body was wrapped in graveclothes and hidden in a tomb for 3 days and 3 nights; but He has risen in victory. If we seek Him like little children seek the 2nd *matza*, we will find eternal life! The Messiah is a great discovery and great reward!

3. FEAST OF FIRSTFRUITS (YOM BIKKERIM)

Historically the Red Sea parted on the Feast of Firstfruits. Israel's "baptism" through the Red Sea is a type of New Testament baptism, because they left their Egyptian enemies forever (Exodus 14). Prophetically firstfruits represent resurrection. Christ was the First One to rise from the dead precisely on the Day of Firstfruits. He is called *the* Firstfruits (1 Corinthians 15:20-23).

The Bible states that Noah's Ark rested on Mount Ararat on the 17th of 7th month of the Genesis calendar, which is the 1st month of the Exodus calendar—the Day of Firstfruits! Just as the old world had a new beginning on the Feast of Firstfruits, so too we can experience a new beginning through faith in the Resurrection of Jesus Christ!

4. PENTECOST OR FEAST OF WEEKS (HAG HA SHAVOUT) OR FEAST OF HARVEST (HAG HA KAZIR)

Pentecost celebrates the "wheat harvest," which represents the first wave of mainly Gentile believers swept into the Kingdom of God since the first century.

This is the only feast which *allows* leavened bread, giving it a distinct "Gentile" flavor. Pentecost always falls on a Sunday, being the "morrow after the Sabbath" (Leviticus 23:15). The Law was given on the Day of Pentecost. The Holy Spirit was given on the Day of Pentecost. And the Church was birthed on the Day of Pentecost.

5. FEAST OF TRUMPETS (YOM TERUAH) OR THE CIVIL NEW YEAR (ROSH HASHANAH)

Occurring on the 1st of Tishri, or the Civil New Year, this is a special day for several reasons.

First, ancient rabbis believed the birthday of the world is on *Rosh Hashanah*.

Second, there is scholarly consensus that Jesus was not likely born on the 25th of December. When was the most likely month of Jesus' birth? The month of Tishri (our September). Commentators' estimates vary from the 1st of Tishri (coinciding with the Feast of Trumpets) to the 15th of Tishri (Feast of Tabernacles). Chuck Missler believed a possible date for the birth of Christ is 29 September 2 BC (1st of Tishri 3758 Jewish Year). Roy Reinhold believes a possible date is 11 September 3 BC (1st of Tishri 3759).[3] If the latter were true, it might explain why Satan wanted to defile the date 9/11 with his most audacious act of terrorism so far. Satan perverts what is good.

If Jesus was born on the Feast of Trumpets, then ancient Israel would have been blasting the trumpets while Jesus was being born. God supernaturally arranged for the nation to unknowingly announce the birth of her king!

We may never know the exact date of Jesus' birth till we see Jesus face-to-face and ask Him, so I will not linger on speculations and let the interested reader pursue his or her own further study.

Third, the Feast of Trumpets may symbolize the blast that raptures the Church! We know that a trumpet will sound when the dead in Christ shall be raised and the living saints will be raptured to meet the Lord in the air! Two New Testament Scriptures fit well with this feast:

1 THESSALONIANS 4:16-17 (emphasis added)
16 For the Lord Himself will descend from Heaven with a shout [*teruah*], with the voice of an

archangel, and with the TRUMPET of God [*shofar of Yahweh*]. And the dead in Christ will rise first.

17 Then we who are alive and remain shall be caught up together with them in the clouds to meet the Lord in the air. And thus we shall always be with the Lord.

1 CORINTHIANS 15:51-52

51 Behold, I tell you a mystery: We shall not all sleep, but we shall all be changed—

52 in a moment, in the twinkling of an eye, at the last TRUMPET (*shofar*). For the TRUMPET will sound, and the dead will be raised incorruptible, and we shall be changed.

The Feast of Trumpets is known by many alternative names, all of which support it being prophetic of the Church's Rapture:

- *Yom HaKeseh*—the Hidden Day, when the raptured saints will be hidden from Tribulation.
- *Yomim Noraim*—Days of Affliction, when Israel's main friend, the Christians, will have disappeared, leaving the Jews without ally in the world.
- *Yom HaDin*—the Day of Judgment, when the 7 seals of judgment will be opened and 7 year Tribulation will occur.
- *Ha Kiddushin* or *Nesuin*—the Wedding of the Messiah. While the earth suffers Tribulation, Revelation 19:7 says the Church will be in Heaven celebrating the Messiah's wedding feast. This once again indicates the Church has been raptured.
- *Ha Melech*—the Coronation of the Messiah. While the earth suffers Tribulation, the saints will be before His throne casting our crowns before Him (Revelation

4:10). The Messiah will be adored as King of kings and Lord of lords!

Yom Teruah was known among Jews as the *"Unknown Day"* because it was the only feast with an uncertain start date. The people had to wait for the rabbis to confirm when Yom Teruah would begin. This was done by the sighting of the new moon by two witnesses. If the visibility of the moon was poor, they would have to wait for a second day. To be safe, modern Israel celebrates this feast over two days. Ezra celebrated this feast over two days (Nehemiah 8:2-3, 13). The Rapture may occur on a future Yom Teruah; certainly it qualifies as an *Unknown Day* the general population will not anticipate.

6. DAY OF ATONEMENT (YOM KIPPUR)

Occurring 10 days after *Rosh Hashanah*, this commemorates the day the high priest used to go into the Holy of Holies (when the Temple existed) and apply the blood of an innocent animal on the "mercy seat" (lid of the ark of the covenant) to "atone" (or cover) the sins of Israel. The number 10 points to the Tribulation (Revelation 2:10). *Yom Kippur* symbolizes Israel's National Day of Repentance, predicted in Hosea 5:15 and Isaiah 53. On that day in the near future, Israel as a nation will finally recognize her Messiah!

Then Hosea 5:15 will be fulfilled, *"I will return again to My place [meaning Messiah has already come once] till they acknowledge their offense [of rejecting Messiah]. Then they will seek My face; in their affliction [the Tribulation] they will earnestly seek Me."* This recognition will come when the Jewish survivors of the Tribulation will finally read and understand Isaiah 53, a Messianic passage that is currently forbidden in the synagogues.

The Tribulation will be a time of Jacob's Trouble, yet the end of it will be a time of great salvation for the Jews who choose their Messiah! How many will be in this believing remnant? Zechariah predicted a third will be saved.

> ZECHARIAH 13:8-9
> 8 In the whole land, declares the Lord, two thirds shall be cut off and perish, and **one third** shall be left alive.
> 9 And I will put **this third** into the fire, and refine them as one refines silver, and test them as gold is tested. They will call upon my name, and I will answer them. I will say, 'They are my people'; and they will say, 'The Lord is my God.'"

REVELATION 19:15 says Jesus will come to tread the "winepress of the fierceness and wrath of Almighty God." This is Hebraism indicating the fall season in Israel or the harvest of grapes, when these judgments are likely to begin.

While Jesus' first coming was tied to Passover, Jesus' Second Coming will be tied to Yom Kippur. Prophecy indicates Jesus' feet will touch down on the Mount of Olives on Yom Kippur (Zechariah 14:4).

7. FEAST OF TABERNACLES OR BOOTHS (SUKKOT)

A joyful feast 5 days after Yom Kippur. During this time, Jews build tents and temporarily live in them for 7 days. The Transfiguration of Jesus likely occurred on the Feast of Tabernacles, because of Peter's reference to building tents for Moses and Elijah (Matthew 17:4). Peter was not making a strange offer since Moses' Law required everyone to stay in tents.

This feast is a Sabbath of Sabbaths, for it is the 7th of 7 feasts celebrated on the 7th month for 7 days. After the 7 days, they were to leave the temporary for the permanent. Solomon's

Temple was dedicated on the Feast of Tabernacles, so these two things are connected. Whereas Moses' Tabernacle was a portable tent of worship, Solomon's Temple was built of stone and represented a permanent place of worship. This idea of moving into the permanent leads us to believe that this final feast represents the 7th Millennium (1000 years of Sabbath rest) or the Messianic Kingdom (a permanent Kingdom that will never end).

There is another Scripture that connects the Millennium with the Feast of Tabernacles. Revelation 7:9 says: "After these things I looked, and behold, a great multitude which no one could number, of all nations, tribes, peoples, and tongues, standing before the throne and before the Lamb, clothed with white robes, with palm branches in their hands." Why palm branches? An orthodox Jew should know, but a Gentile might miss the clue. These are the building materials to celebrate Tabernacles!

According to Zechariah 14, Sukkot is the only feast all nations are required to attend during the Millennium. If Jesus will proclaim the start of the Millennium 5 days after His Second Coming on Yom Kippur, then Sukkot shall be remembered as the feast that ushered in the Messianic Kingdom. Just as we look back to the Last Supper and the sacrifice of Jesus Christ through communion, the nations will look back to the start of the Millennium and the Messianic Kingdom through the Feast of Tabernacles.

The 7 Feasts of Israel are God's way of illustrating the Messiah to our sight, sound, touch, taste and smell. The Feasts are audio-visual, multi-sensory object lessons about what Christ did in the past, and what He's about to do in the near future!

How could Jesus have contrived to be born into a society that had 7 feasts about Him? Even the coincidence of one feast like the Passover falling on the same day Jesus died would be an outstanding miracle! Could Jesus have orchestrated His own birth into a society that killed innocent lambs to atone for sins, or His own death on the very day they killed Passover lambs, or the nation's cessation of lamb sacrifice shortly after His resurrection? For nearly 2000 years, the Jews have not killed a Passover Lamb. Why not? Because the true Passover Lamb has already been slain! How could Jesus have accomplished all these things unless He were truly God! He is the very One who instituted the 7 Feasts prior to His own coming.

The more we study the Bible in detail, the more absurd the claim appears that Jesus was no more than a good teacher. Jesus was definitely something far beyond. He was, is and will always be the Eternal One. God the Father has set 7 holidays on His calendar for every believer to celebrate the His Son.

7 LAWS OF NOAH

ACCORDING to ancient and Jewish sources [1], God gave Noah and his descendants 7 laws to obey. Together they are called the '7 Noahide Laws'. The main reason they are named after Noah is that every human being alive currently is a descendant of Noah.

Although most Christians are unaware of this, it is common knowledge among Jews that any Gentile who keeps these 7 laws as an act of devotion to God is considered a Noahide or a "righteous Gentile". Note that heart matters: if a Gentile keeps them merely for the benefit of peace, but has no devotion to God or faith in the Messiah, it does not count towards personal salvation.[2] A true Noahide keeps these laws while he waits for the Messiah, just as Jews are supposed to.

Long before Moses, the entire world was obligated to keep the following moral laws as a sign of fearing God and for the benefit of social order.

1) Do not worship idols.
2) Do not blaspheme God.
3) Do not murder.
4) Do not commit sexual immorality.

5) Do not steal.

6) Do not eat blood or the flesh of an animal while it is still alive.

7) Establish courts of justice (so humanity will not forget God or these laws).

The New Testament is clear that eternal salvation does not depend on our obedience to law—whether Noahide or Mosaic— but is a gift of the Messiah to be personally received "by grace... through faith" (Ephesians 2:8).

Christians do not depend on the law for salvation, yet must understand that there remains important applications of God's laws. Each use of the law must be carefully distinguished in order for God's plan to be fulfilled. One application is personal, the other is national. One application is as a standard of righteousness, the other is as a standard for social justice. The main advantage of the Noahide laws is for social order so people can live in peace with each other.

It may surprise Christians to know that rabbis do not believe that a Gentile must convert to Judaism in order to be saved. They believe that a Noahide who accepts the Messiah will enter the "world to come". Therefore Christians who believe that they must follow all Jewish laws, dietary requirements and customs in order to be an authentic believer are trying to be *more Jewish than the Jews.*

Honoring God's Law without Legalism

To be clear, I believe that there is nothing wrong with Christians learning the original languages of the Bible (Hebrew, Greek and Aramaic), or appreciating the Hebrew cultural context of Scripture, or seeking to please God by celebrating the 7 Biblical Feasts as prophetic acts that point to Jesus. The line is crossed when those emphasizing Hebrew culture believe that they are "holier than thou" and better than other believers. It's not true.

I have heard of so-called "Hebrew Roots" people criticizing people who call on the Name of "Jesus" instead of saying "Yeshua". They criticize those who pray to "God" instead of "Yahweh," "Jehovah" or some other attempt to pronounce the "Yud-Hey-Vav-Hey" Name of God. They will go so far as to call Christians who don't keep the Jewish Sabbath "idolaters" and "devil worshippers".

As often becomes the case, their strength becomes their weakness. Their zealousness in immersing themselves in Hebrew culture makes them blind to other areas of Scripture, and even deceived into thinking they are superior to others due to their strictness.

God put no such requirements on believers of Messiah. God wrote the Bible in 3 languages and if He wanted everyone to speak and pray only in Hebrew, He would have written the Bible in one language. God the Father resurrected Jesus on a Sunday (the first day of the week) and sent the Holy Spirit upon 120 believers on a Sunday. If that's not a church service, I don't know what is! And if God had wanted to be worshipped on only one day, He would have resurrected Jesus on a Saturday. He didn't.

I will tell you the root of the problem. Most of these legalistic extremes arise from the fact that Christians, who are mainly Gentile converts to the Messiah, are not aware of the 7 Noahide Laws.

As non-Jews, they tend to swing to the extremes of either trying to keep all the Laws of Moses or else rejecting all laws altogether. But Jews are well aware that the 7 Laws of Noah are God's requirements for every nation. (Remember as Christians, we are learning this not to apply to personal salvation, but to social justice).

COURTS OF JUSTICE

We can now say that many politically-appointed courts are no longer courts of justice, for they have forgotten the very basics of the Noahide laws.

If Christians wish to take law-keeping seriously as an act of worship, then I would point out that the most neglected of these 7 laws directed at Gentiles is establishing courts of justice.

The courts in the Bible were not like our courts today. The ancient Jews did not have a professional class of lawyers whom they must hire to argue their cases. Two disputing mothers were able to approach King Solomon for a verdict—a verdict that would outrage most Christians today because they tend not to think judicially; rather they tend to swing between the extremes of legalism or hyper grace. King Solomon's verdict called for the murder of the baby! How many Christians would condemn King Solomon's wisdom and demand his resignation? Thank God, modern Christians were not there and the modern lawyers were not there. The women did not have barristers to cover up their reactions for them.

For most of Biblical history there were no police or prisons. Neighbors policed the neighborhood. Your neighbors kept you safe. If your neighbors were taught the Bible, that made for a very good place to live. There were no prisons. If a criminal were found guilty, his debt was not owed to the state, his debt was paid to his victim! Instead of the state paying for him to live for free in prison, while the victim gets nothing from the state or the perpetrator, the criminal had to work to pay off his debt fourfold (2 Samuel 12:6). The victim gains and the criminal may become a blessing rather than a burden on society.

In most legal cases, the people retained the power. The law was easy to understand and every educated citizen was qualified to interpret and apply it. The closest institution we have to Biblical courts is a "swift trial by a jury of impartial peers". The American Founding Fathers considered it the *only way* that citizens can redress the abuse of power by any branch of government—people can veto any law by being a dissenting juror.[2]

Several founding fathers' lives, including William Penn's, were spared because they were tried by a jury of their peers, rather than by a British Crown-appointed judge. Penn was on trial for violating the Conventicle Act (1664), which made the Church of England the only state religion and forbade the religious assembly of more than 5 people outside an Anglican church. Penn was a Quaker leader and, of course, ignored the unjust law as any Christian should. Despite the jurors being abused by the judge who wanted to execute Penn, they stood their ground and exonerated Penn. Had Penn been tried by a judge rather than a jury, there would be no Pennsylvania, no Philadelphia, no Independence Hall, and no Liberty Bell.

As the Founding Fathers feared, modern parliaments and courts attempt to bypass trial by jury whenever possible. They violate the 7th Noahide Law. Throughout the Gentile world they have become halls of injustice. Without justice, there is no peace on earth.

NOAH's LAWS in the New Testament

The laws of Noah were the laws of humanity. (We are calling Christians to learn the Noahide laws not as specified in the Talmud, but as implied for social order by the Old and New Testaments.) Paul said in Romans 13:6 that all the Gentile authorities are ordained by God as "ministers of God". This assumption is *not* found in any Mosaic law, but it is grounded on Noah's 7th law of establishing Gentile courts of justice. The apostles not only knew, but assumed their audiences also knew, the 7 Laws of Noah. That is why the New Testament Council of Jerusalem reminded Christians who were freed from the Mosaic Law to obey 4 things contained in Noah's laws.

> ACTS 15:19-20 [Apostle James speaking]
>
> 19 Therefore I judge that we should not trouble those from among the GENTILES who are turning to God,
>
> 20 but that we write to them to abstain from things polluted by idols, from sexual immorality, from things strangled, and from blood.

These 4 commands do not correspond to the Ten Commandments of Moses, but they do correspond to Noah's 1st, 4th and 6th laws. Abstaining from a strangled animal and abstaining from blood were the same dietary restriction as Noah's 6th command because if an animal were strangled, its blood would not be drained from its body, therefore consuming strangled meat would be the same as consuming blood.

When the apostles and elders wrote the letter to the Gentiles, they slightly reordered their warnings.

> ACTS 15:28-29
>
> 28 For it seemed good to the Holy Spirit, and to us, to lay upon you no greater burden than these necessary things:
>
> 29 that you abstain from things offered to idols, from blood, from things strangled, and from sexual immorality. If you keep yourselves from these, you will DO WELL.

Notice the apostles did not say, "If you keep yourselves from these, you will be saved." No, "you will do well." And that is exactly what the world needs, that Christians do better.

The issue was not salvation, for the recipients of the letter were already saved. The issue was **Grace vs. Law**; put another way, how much of the law are Christians supposed to keep. The apostles' verdict was: circumcision is unnecessary for non-Jews, but *pre-Mosaic laws* are necessary. The implication is the *Noahide Laws* remained in effect on all Gentiles in all nations.

This has far-reaching, eschatological implications. When the Bible predicts that the Anti-Christ will be the "lawless" one, we should ask ourselves, "Which law—Moses' law or Noah's law?" Will he violate Jewish law or Gentile law?

When Jesus said, "And as it was in the days of Noah, so it will be also in the days of the Son of Man," we only hear a negative interpretation (and rightly so as the days preceding the Flood were evil). But could there also be a positive connotation too? Following the Flood, Noah was given the sign of a rainbow and the whole world was under one law— Noah's 7 Laws.

Teaching Noah's laws will make the world a better place, but will not save a person. Only repentance and faith in Jesus Christ will make a person born again. Only the new birth will make a person desire to keep God's laws, without the necessity of being forced by authority, soldiers or police. The Gospel program is to get people's hearts to change, but since not everyone's heart will change in this age, the 7 Laws of Noah are the minimal requirements that should be taught for social order.

There are many questions about the applications and misapplications of Noahide Laws by Jews and Christians. They are beyond the scope of "The Divine Code" which focuses on numbers. I will answer common questions and objections in another book by the same title "*The 7 Laws of Noah*". In it, you will learn where in the Bible are 7 Laws of Noah, the Jewish classification of Gentiles, and my contribution to world leaders on how to apply the 7 Noahide Laws to social justice and government policy.[3]

8

8 IS THE FIRST CUBE, the cube of two (2^3 or 2 x 2 x 2). It is the number of new life, new beginning or the resurrection. A day is divided into 3 periods of 8 hours (8 x 3 = 24). Most people work 8 hours, have 8 hours of free time, and sleep 8 hours, after which they are ready to start a new day.

8 people wrote the New Testament divided into 3 parts: Gospels, Acts, Epistles. Noah was the 8th person from Adam and he had 3 sons (Genesis 5:29, 2 Peter 2:5); there were 8 people who survived the global Flood; the world had a new beginning starting with these 3 couples (Genesis 7:13, 1 Peter 3:20).[1] The words "sun" and earth" appear together 8 times in Scripture; it takes 8.33 minutes for the sun's light to reach the earth.[2] 8 is the atomic number of oxygen, the 3rd most abundant element in the universe. Oxygen gives fuel to fire and life to us as we breathe.

Elijah performed 8 miracles, the 3rd one being the resurrection of a widow's son (2 Kings 17:17-23). Jesus was resurrected on the 8th day (Sunday), after spending 3 days in hell. The Holy Spirit descended on the 8th day (Sunday), after 3 years of Jesus' earthly ministry.

8 is the number of new beginnings. Most people require 8 hours of sleep before they wake up ready to start a new day. God will create a new Heaven and new earth at the end of the Millennial reign of Christ, or at the start of the 8th millennium.

The 888th chapter of the Bible—Amos 9—is about a new start for Israel. "The Lord says, 'A day is coming when I will restore the kingdom of David, which is. Like a house fallen in ruins. I will repair its walls and restore it…grain will grow faster than it can be harvested…I will bring my people back to their land. They will rebuild their ruined cities and live there…I will plant my people on the land I gave them, and they will not be pulled up again.' The Lord your God has spoken (Amos 9:11-15 GNB).

These patterns of 8 are found in Scripture, nature, history and the economy. Economist Martin Armstrong noticed an 8.6 year cycle to the financial markets.[3] Every 3 cycles of 8.6 years or 25.8 years, there also happens to be a major earthquake. Natural phenomenon may affect financial markets in ways people do not expect. For instance, the 1906 San Francisco earthquake led to the 1907 Panic as capital flowed from insurance companies on the East Coast to pay for damages on the West Coast. This sparked a shortage of cash on the East which rationalized the creation of Federal Reserve System in 1913.[4] The 8.6 year cycle in earthquakes and other climate changes may influence new economic policies more than governments and politicians!

The 2010 Haitian earthquake which killed 230,000 people came on time: 4 cycles of 25.8 years after the San Francisco earthquake, or 12 cycles of 8.6 years. I suspect the interval between major earthquakes will shorten as the earth goes into what Jesus called "birth pangs"—the labor contractions before the Messiah arrives.

Male circumcision—a sign of new relationship with God—was commanded on the 8th day.[5] The timing of circumcision varies in other cultures from the 1st day to the 13th year. Is there any reason the God of the Bible specifically commanded it to be on the 8th day? Scientific studies have shown that babies do not produce optimal levels of *prothrombin*, a blood clotting glycoprotein that helps healing, until the 8th day of life.[6] How did the writer of the Bible know that before modern medicine did?

There are 8 glycocarbohydrates or biological sugars which spell out the language of life. These 8 sugars on cell surfaces are responsible for the sperm finding the egg and the immune system identifying friends from foes. They are involved in nearly all cell-to-cell communication and most healing of the human body. These sugars also determine our blood type. While there are 4 letters (nucleotides) in our DNA, there are 8 letters (sugars) on our cells. These 8 letters create a vastly more complex combination of codes than the DNA codes. God chose 8 nutrients to spell out the cellular language of life.

There are 8 cases of infertility in the Bible: Sarah, Rebekah, Rachel, Manoah's wife, Hannah, Michal, a Shunammite who fed Elisha, and Elizabeth. All were healed by prayer except two: 1) the Shunammite was told she would have a son after she honored the man of God—there's no record of her praying, and 2) Saul's daughter Michal who despised David's exuberant worship of God; she appeared dignified to men, but in truth she cared more about outward appearance than inward obedience. There is no record of her praying and she remained infertile for the rest of her life after mocking David's worship.

8 women (7 barren and 1 Virgin) had miraculous conceptions and gave supernatural childbirth: Sarah, Rebekah, Rachel, Manoah's wife, Hannah, a Shunammite, Elizabeth and Mary. All 8 sons became great men of God: Isaac, Israel, Joseph, Samson, Samuel, the Shunammite's son, John the Baptist, and our Lord Jesus. We don't know much about the life of Shunammite's son other than he became a type of Christ by becoming the 2nd person in Scripture to be raised from the dead (2 Kings 4:18-37).

If you have had problems conceiving a child, be encouraged that God has given life where it looked impossible. Instead of focusing on a doctor's report, believe the Great Physician's report. He who made the womb can fill it for you! Bring these 8 cases of infertility and 8 cases of miraculous conceptions to God, and humbly ask God to do the same for you in Jesus' Name. Be willing to give your first child to God, as Hannah, Elizabeth and Mary did.

8 THE NUMBER of the Resurrected One

Both 7 and 8 are numbers associated with Jesus Christ. 7 represents His Perfection; 8 His Resurrection. Jesus called Himself the Lord of the Sabbath – the 7th day; Jesus resurrected on Sunday – the 8th day. David, a type of Christ, is called both the 7th and 8th son of Jesse (1 Samuel 16:10-11, 17:12; 1 Chronicles 2:15). How can both be true? The death of a previous son would explain why both numbers relate to David's birth order. These kinds of preconceived patterns in the Old Testament truly magnify Christ because they only make sense to us after Christ is revealed! There is no reason for the Old Testament writers to contrive such details. Only God knew ahead of time they would find meaning in Christ.

8 IN CULTURE

The ancient Chinese were very interested in the study of numbers. (Perhaps that's what made so many of them the wealthy merchants of the old world and the business owners of today!) The Chinese especially liked the number 8 as it represented "luck" or "prosperity" to them. Where did this belief come from?

It seems likely to me that the origin of some Chinese myths could have been passed down from the original believers of *El Shaddai*. Even the Chinese word for God *Shan-ti* sounds a lot like the Hebrew word for The Almighty – *El Shaddai!*

All Asians can trace their common ancestry to Shem, one of

Noah's 3 sons who migrated East after the global Flood. Shem was a godly man and an ancestor of the Messiah. His name is the origin of the Asiatic term "Semite" and "Semitic".

Asians traditionally worship their ancestors and typically cite ancestral obligation as one major reason not to become Christian. My question to them is, "What would our ancestors want?" They would want us to be good people, live a good life, and go to Heaven. Asians should look to Shem to credit much our godly wisdom, heritage, medicines and traditions. No Asian originally descended from a God-hater. All Asians descended from God-fearing Shem—the first Asian. He in turn was the son of a God-believer—Noah—the 8ᵗʰ from Adam. All humanity ultimately descended from 2 God-believers—Adam and Eve. So when we become Christian, we please all of our ancestors.

A FINAL WORD

Some people have asked me how long Adam and Eve lived in innocence before the Fall. It may not be the most pressing question to our spiritual life, but I have found one ancient Jewish source dating from 150 BC which offers an answer.

The Book of Jubilees 3:17 claims that Adam and Eve lived 7 full years in the Garden of Eden, then on the 8ᵗʰ year of Creation, in the 2ⁿᵈ month, on the 17ᵗʰ day, Satan came as a serpent to tempt Eve. On that day, Adam and Eve turned their backs on God and were expelled from the Garden of Eden to the land of Elda—the land of their creation. The mouths of all animals were closed, so that all animals ceased to communicate with mankind.

Some people speculate whether or not Adam and Eve had children before the Fall. Romans 5 indicates that sin entered the world through one representative man, and that sin passed to all mankind because we were all "in Adam". The Book of Jubilee agrees with the New Testament and says that Adam and Eve had no son till the 8ᵗʰ year of Creation.

Although these dates cannot be verified by Scripture, they are congruent with the numerical patterns we observe. It should come to us as no surprise that Adam and Eve lived in perfection for 7 years or 1 "week" of years. Then at the start the 2nd week of years, or 8th year of Creation, Adam had an unfortunate "new" beginning—one of deception and disobedience. The suffering and death which did not exist before the Fall have been continuing ever since. New life, in the form of a newborn son, also came in the 8th year.

Jesus resurrected to new life on the 8th day. Through Jesus, God the Father wishes to reverse this curse first in our lives, then in the earth, and finally in the entire universe. Christianity is the only religion in the world which says that God can come to live inside of man. 8 times in Scripture, Christians are called the "temple of God".[7] Remember, 8 means you can have a new beginning—just put your trust in Jesus who is the Lord of new life.

9

9 IS the maximum single digit number. It is the number of the Holy Spirit, His power, His gifts and His activity. The Jewish 9th hour (our 3pm) was the time Jesus died on the cross. The 9th hour is a Biblical time of prayer. In Acts 3, Peter and John went to the Temple to pray at the 9th hour. At that time a man crippled from birth got healed. In Acts 10, God sent an angel to meet Cornelius at the 9th hour. He and his family were the first Gentiles to become Christian! The Holy Spirit descended upon the first disciples in the 9th week of the Jewish calendar.[1] There are:

- 9 fruits of the Spirit – love, joy, peace, longsuffering, gentleness, goodness, meekness, faithfulness, and temperance (Galatians 5:22-23).
- 9 gifts of the Spirit – word of wisdom, word of knowledge, gift of special faith, gifts of healings, miracles, prophecy, discerning of spirits, tongues, and interpretation of tongues (1 Corinthians 12:7-11).
- 9 Biblical holidays (see the Chapter 9 Holidays).

- 9 inspired songs sung by Biblical figures in the Old Testament at important times in Jewish history (see Chapter 9 Songs).
- 9 months of pregnancy from conception till childbirth.
- 9 planets in our solar system.[2]
- 9 demon-possessed cases delivered by the power of the Holy Spirit:

DELIVERANCE OF	MATT.	MARK	LUKE
A man with an unclean spirit		1:23-28	4:31-37
Mary Magdalene who had 7 spirits			8:2
2 men with unclean spirits who had a fetish for nudity, death and tattoos or mutilation of the flesh	8:28-43	5:1-21	8:26-39
A mute man	9:32-34		11:14
A blind and mute man	12:22-23		
A girl with an unclean spirit	15:21-28	7:31-37	
An epileptic boy with an unclean spirit	17:14-21	9:17-29	9:37-42
A woman with a spirit of infirmity 18 years			13:16-17
A fortune-telling girl with a spirit of divination			Acts 16: 16-18

A common question is: "Did Jesus ever meet a homosexual?" The answer is very likely, because the term "unclean"[3] is a Biblical euphemism for sexual immorality. Jesus met 4 types of spirits:

- spirits of infirmity (spirits that cause certain sicknesses)
- spirits of divination (occult spirits)
- seducing spirits (religious spirits impersonating Christianity or Christians)

- unclean spirits (spirits of porn and perversion).
  Unclean spirits were the *most prevalent* spirits Jesus
  met! Sexual sins were as common back then as they are
  today.

Notice the men at Gadarenes who were possessed with unclean spirits ran around naked and lost their sense of modesty. In Mark and Luke's accounts, the writers could not bring themselves to mention both men living together. But Matthew tells us there were 2 men co-habitating in a tomb, which strongly suggests they were homosexual outcasts of society.

Notice further that Jesus met 2 children with unclean spirits: one boy and one girl. This tells us that sexual thoughts start from an earlier age than most of the church is willing to accept or care to deal with. It also explains the *only* instance in the Bible when Jesus' own disciples "could not" cast out a spirit. They were confronted with an unclean spirit, which was likely a spirit of homosexuality. Notice the great agony it caused in the parents of both these children. Sins that violate sexual boundaries or confuse sexual identities cause the greatest pain in families. The Church has changed little since the disciples could do nothing about that unclean spirit; most modern Christians still do not know what to do with an unclean spirit. The Bible says through Jesus, deliverance and transformation are possible!

Please note it is wrong to be homophobic, that is, to physically or verbally torment a homosexual. Jesus never did, even though it was likely He encountered several homosexuals. He responded to them the way He did all sinners and helped those who wanted to be helped. People can feel happy to live in sin for a while, but when the consequences of their sin catches up to them, they can bow down to Jesus and He will set them free!

Being linked to the Holy Spirit, 9 is the number of miracles and supernatural power. By the anointing of the Holy Spirit,

Jesus performed 9 recorded miracles or interruptions in the normal course of nature:[4]

1. Turning water into wine, called the "beginning of miracles" in John 2:11. This verse alone dispels all cults' claims that Jesus performed childhood miracles such as turning clay into birds or men into monkeys. Turning water into wine at a wedding was His *first* miracle. All of His miracles shared the same tone and tenor: to bless mankind and to show us how to live above the dominion of Satan by trusting in Christ. None of Jesus' miracles were gratuitous, showy or done merely to prove His Deity. He performed all of them as a "Son of Man" anointed by the Spirit of God (Luke 4:18, Acts 2:22, 10:38).

2. Multiplication of 5 loaves and 2 fishes to feed 5000 men, with leftovers filling 12 baskets (Matthew 14:15-21).

3. Multiplication of 7 loaves and a few fishes to feed 4000 men, with leftovers filling 7 large baskets (Matthew 15:32-38).

4. Causing a net-breaking, boat-sinking catch of fish when in the natural the professional fishermen could catch nothing all night (Luke 5:1-11, Matthew 4).

5. Causing a second miraculous catch of 153 fish when in the natural the fishermen could catch nothing all night (John 21:1-11). Notice 5 miracles were about food! Did not Jesus say in Matthew 6 that you should not worry about what you shall eat, what you shall drink or what you shall wear, because God clothes the lilies of the field and feeds the sparrows, and "you are of more value than many sparrows" (Matthew 6:26; 10:31)? Jesus loved to reveal Himself as the Provider of all our needs. If God fed so many people, why would He not

do it for you! The key is to believe God loves to give and receive it by faith with thanksgiving.

6. Walking on water (Matthew 14:22-32). This was an exceptional miracle—one done apparently for convenience to catch up with the disciples who had gone ahead of Him while He was praying alone. Lest anyone should accuse Jesus of acting showy to prove His Deity, the Holy Spirit noted 2 details for us: a) He "would have passed them by" (Mark 6:48), meaning He intended to go unnoticed; and b) when the disciples saw Him walking on water, He invited any of them to come out and join Him. Only Peter had enough courage to follow Him. Walking on water does not prove someone is God. What makes Him God is His pre-existence before Creation (John 1:1-3, 8:51-58; Colossians 1:16-17). Only God pre-existed everything.

7. Resurrection of Jairus' daughter (Mark 5).
8. Resurrection of a widow's only son (Luke 7).
9. Resurrection of Lazarus (John 11).

Some may wonder why I do not count among the miracles Jesus' stilling the winds and the waves in Mark 4 or Jesus' cursing the fig tree in Mark 11? On both occasions Jesus indicated these were ordinary uses of faith and any believer could have done them.

Jesus could barely contain His disappointment that the disciples did not do them instead of Him! In Mark 4:40 Jesus asked them, "Why are you so fearful? How is it that you have no faith?" If only Jesus could calm the storms, then the disciples had every right to be afraid. I have known several men of God who have stilled storms, tornadoes and hurricanes coming their way. I know of one church in Louisiana where not a single pane of glass was broken during Hurricane Katrina on 29 August 2005.

The pastor of the church spoke to the storm just like Jesus

did. He believed for protection over his property. Why, some may want to know, didn't he ask for all other properties to be protected? It wasn't his right to. In the natural we have authority over our own property, but not over other people's. It is the same in the spiritual. Unless someone gives us their key and asks us to guard their house, we cannot walk in and stay in their place. That's called "breaking and entering"! It's criminal.

Likewise, unless someone asks us to pray protection over their property, we have no right to meddle in their affairs spiritually. It is their right to believe God, or trust in other human beings or rely only on themselves. We have a right to pray for people who are under our care and related to us. But we cannot pray for strangers against their will and volition. God respects everyone's personal right to ask for His assistance or reject His interference.

In Mark 11, Jesus cursed a fig tree and the next day the disciples "saw the fig tree dried up from the roots" (v.20). Rather than saying, "Only God can do this miracle," Jesus used the occasion to teach His listeners about ordinary faith in God.

 MARK 11:22-24

22 So Jesus answered and said to them, Have faith in God.

23 For assuredly, I say to you, whoever SAYS to this mountain, 'Be removed and be cast into the sea,' and does not doubt in his heart, but believes that those things he SAYS will be done, he will have whatever he SAYS.

24 Therefore I say to you, whatever things you ask when you pray, believe that you receive them, and you will have them.

Too many Christians have underestimated the power of their words. We daily experience how words shape destinies and change futures. Have you ever had a teacher, a coach or a role model lift you up with words of affirmation? You can soar on those words for days! Have you ever experienced a Christian praying over you in such a powerful way that all burdens simply seem to evaporate away? That's the power of faith-filled words!

It works not only for adults, it works for children, too. Harsh words can scar a child's life. (Thank God Jesus can wash those past wounds away when we ask Him.) Scriptural words can encourage a child to see himself or herself as a champion! Positive words lift children up to believe that anything is possible! This is what Jesus wants every Christian to believe every day: "I say to you, if you have faith as a mustard seed, you will SAY to this mountain, 'Move from here to there,' and it will move; and nothing will be impossible for you" (Matthew 17:20). The number 9 reminds us of the power of God at work in our lives.

9 AV

THE 9TH of Av (5th month of the Hebrew religious calendar) is considered the "saddest day in Jewish history." It is one of 4 fasts which the Jews observe by tradition, not by commandment of the Torah. The fasts are:

1. Shiva Asar Be Tamuz or 17th of Tamuz (4th month):

the day the city walls protecting Jerusalem were breached by Nebuchadnezzar in 587 BC. The Talmud states that Roman General Titus also breached the walls of Jerusalem on the same day in 70 AD! The Talmud claims that this was the day Moses descended Mount Sinai and found Israel worshipping a golden calf, upon which he broke the two tablets of stones containing the Ten Commandments.

2. Tisha Be Av or the 9th of Av (5th month):

the day the First Temple was destroyed by Nebuchadnezzar, and the day the Second Temple was destroyed by General Titus.

3. Tzom Gedalia or the Fast of Gedaliah on the 3rd of Tishri (7th month):

the day Ishmael assassinated Gedaliah the Jewish governor appointed by Nebuchadnezzar, a final blow which ensured the scattering of the Jews under Babylonian rule. Jeremiah 40-41 recorded this tragedy and the Jews remember it not only as a historic, but a prophetic event that may likely happen again in the end time.

Why would God allow a believer to be assassinated? This is a great lesson in leadership and in hearing the voice of God. Just as God warned Noah before the Flood and Lot before the destruction of Sodom, God sent Johanan (John) and other leaders to warn Gedaliah of a betrayer named Ishmael. Gedaliah failed to see the evil intentions of Ishmael and would not believe God's warning. Ignoring God's voice cost him his life, the lives of those with him, and the lives of 70 Jews who came up to worship God in Jerusalem (see Jeremiah 40:13-41:10).

In the end times, tragedies will occur, but God will always send forewarning. Amos 3:7 promises, "Surely the Lord God does nothing, unless He reveals His secret to His servants the prophets." The lesson from Gedaliah is we all need to get as *close to God* as possible and learn to listen to His voice – whether by the Word, by the Spirit, or through His leaders. We need to *hear God* in the end times and we will be safe!

4. Asara Be Tevet or 10ᵗʰ of Tevet (10ᵗʰ month):

the beginning of Nebuchadnezzar's siege of Jerusalem. Today, this fast is also the occasion to remember the Jewish victims of the Holocaust whose day of death is unknown.

Though not instituted by Moses, God recognizes these 4 fast days in Zechariah, which indicates that they may be prophetic.

 ZECHARIAH 8:19

19 Thus says the LORD of hosts: The FAST of the fourth month, the FAST of the fifth, the FAST of the seventh, and the FAST of the tenth, shall be joy and gladness and cheerful feasts for the house of Judah. Therefore love truth and peace.

The 9th of Av is the most significant fast as both Temples were destroyed on the same day—first by Babylon, then by Rome. Rabbis hold a tradition of calling Esau or Edom the ancestor of the Romans. Geographically, Italians did not descend from Edomites. But there is some basis for this link. During much of the Old Testament, the enemy of Israel was Edom. By the first century, the enemy of Israel was Rome. Herod the Great was from Idumea (a cognate of Edom) and ruled as a Roman-appointed king of Judah. The Jews hated him. Therefore Rome, in the mind of many Jews, is Esau. The first letters of the names of the nations responsible for destroying the House of God spell the month of Av: Alef (Esau or Rome) and Bet (Babylon). In the Hebrew language, days, months, years, and names are all potentially prophetic!

Jewish tradition says the 9th of Av was the day the 10 spies returned from Canaan with an evil report of unbelief. They doubted Israel could inherit the land God promised them, whereas Joshua and Caleb brought the minority report of faith. They believed and 38 years later entered the Promised Land.

The 10 leaders who doubted died in the wilderness, along with 3 million Israelites who believed them instead of Joshua and Caleb. Joshua is the same name as Jesus; the former is Hebrew, the latter is Greek. How prophetic that millions of Jews perished unnecessarily for not believing in "Jesus". They should have believed the minority report.

This story is a lesson for the modern Church too. The majority will doubt; only a minority will believe. It is the believer who receives. It is the believer who enters the Promised Land. It is the believer who obtains the provision, the healing, the baptism of the Holy Spirit, and the full blessing of God! When you choose to have faith while others cast doubt, you are following Joshua instead of the 10 spies.

The 9th of Av has proven to be prophetic several times. Jews and Protestants suffered the Spanish Inquisition and were expelled from Spain on the 9th of Av 1492. World War I started when Germany declared war on Russia on the 9th of Av 1914. Adolf Hitler began the extermination of Jews on the 9th of Av 1942. President Richard Nixon resigned from office after the Watergate scandal on the 9th of Av 1974.

According to Zechariah 8:19, God will turn these 4 fast days of Israel into occasions of joy and gladness. Therefore we need not expect only bad things to happen on these dates. If we have faith in the Messiah, then every day can be a Sabbath rest, a celebration, and a good day!

9 HOLIDAYS

9 IS the number of the Holy Spirit. There are 9 fruits of the Spirit, 9 gifts of the Spirit, and 9 holy days (holidays) ordained in the Bible by the Holy Spirit: Passover, Unleavened Bread, Firstfruits, Shavuot (Pentecost), Yom Teruah (Feast of Trumpets) aka Rosh Hashanah (Civil New Year), Yom Kippur (Day of Atonement), Sukkot (Feast of Tabernacles), Hanukkah (Feast of Dedication), and Purim (Feast of Esther)

God ordained the first 7 by commandment to Moses. Jews added the last 2 by human decision based on historical events of religious importance.

Does God honor man's decisions to worship Him? He does! Jesus made a point of celebrating Hanukkah in John 10:22, even though it was not commanded by Moses or any prophet in the Old Testament.

This fact alone tells us that God works with human decisions of spiritual importance. Why wouldn't He! He accepted human decisions about which books should be included in the Bible. All Bible-believing Christians have no qualm accepting that interweaving of wills. God delights to work with humans. He created us for the purpose of working with our free choice. Human decisions that reject Him are unsanctified. Decisions that worship Him are sacred.

The celebration of the 9 holidays gives me pause when I consider how some claim Christians should not celebrate Christmas because it's not explicitly commanded in the Bible. My question is: why would Jesus honor the Jews' decision to celebrate Hanukkah (which is not in the Old Testament) more than the Christians' decision to celebrate Jesus' birth (which is the first story at the opening of the New Testament)? Why would God object to the most joyous holiday on earth, one which brings universal rest and the best opportunity for the whole world to think about His Son Jesus!

Christmas Tree

Some say it is wrong because the Christmas tree is of pagan origin. This gives too much weight to paganism. God created trees, not pagans. For instance, if pagans are superstitious about the 13th, it doesn't mean they "own" the 13th. As a believer, I have more freedom and more power than they do, and I can redeem it by doing good on the 13th! But if I'm afraid of the 13th and believe "the number 13 is pagan," then I have conceded that the pagans lord it over me. Pagans may pray in mantras, that does not make me stop praying! Their counterfeit praying does not invalidate or make me afraid of the Scriptural gift of praying in tongues! Unless there is a Scriptural injunction, I should not be overly cautious or concerned about what pagans do. There are clear injunctions against worshipping stars and praying to dead people. Is there an injunction about Christmas trees? Some quote Jeremiah 10:2-4 out of context:

 Learn not the way of the nations, nor be dismayed at the signs of the heavens because the nations are dismayed at them, for the customs of the peoples are vanity. A tree from the forest is cut down and worked with an axe by the hands of a craftsman. They decorate it with silver and gold; they fasten it with hammer and nails so that it cannot move. (ESV)

The tree referred to in this passage is not a Christmas tree, but the raw material pagans used to carve their wooden idols. Jeremiah had not seen a Christmas tree in his life and was not condemning it. Christians do not use a Christmas tree to make an idol, nor do they bow down and pray to a Christmas tree. They simply decorate their homes with it. The next verse makes it clear Jeremiah wasn't referring to the tree itself, but to the idols made out of wood:

 JEREMIAH 10:5 (ESV)
>
> 5 Like a scarecrow in a cucumber field are they [the idols], And they [the idols] cannot speak; They must be carried, Because they cannot walk! Do not fear them [the idols, not the tree], For they can do no harm, Nor can they do any good.

Where did the Christmas tree come from? It was a product of the Protestant Reformation during the 1500s. German Christians were likely the first to adopt tree decoration as a part of their Christmas celebration. To equate an idol that pagans worship with a Christmas tree that Christians do not worship is to do injustice to the Scripture!

CHRISTMAS DAY

Others say Christmas must be wrong because it is commemorating Jesus' birth on the wrong date. How would they know the right date? There is no absolute certainty about which day Jesus was born. The Bible did not specify the date and all claims of certainty are spurious.

How do scholars conjecture a date for Jesus' birth? The best guess is derived from the date of John the Baptist's conception. Zechariah, John the Baptist's father, was told he would have a son while he was serving in the Temple. In Luke 1:5, we are told that Zechariah served as a priest in the division of Abijah. We know from the Old Testament that the religious calendar started on Nisan 1, and each priestly division served one week. 1 Chronicles 24:10 says that Abijah served in the 8th division. So the 8th course should have served 8 weeks after Nisan 1, except within those 8 weeks, there were two pilgrimage feasts, during which all priests served to accommodate the large crowds in Jerusalem. The ordinary course was suspended till the pilgrims went home, throwing the priestly rotation off by 2 weeks, which means Zechariah would have been serving 10 weeks after start of Nisan. This would put his service well into June on our calendar. If he went home and his wife Elizabeth became pregnant within two weeks, John the Baptist would have been conceived by the end of June.

In Luke 1:36, we are told in the annunciation by Gabriel that Mary would conceive the Messiah in the sixth month of Elizabeth's pregnancy. Six months after June would put Jesus' conception at the end of December, around the time of Hanukkah, which coincides with Christmas. Nine months later, Jesus would have been born during another Biblical holiday season:

- if He were born on the **Feast of Trumpets**, He would have been born on the birthday of the world;
- if He were born on the **Feast of Tabernacles**, He would have been born during the holiday that means "God

tabernacles with man" or "God makes His home
with us"!

By the above calculation, Jesus was likely conceived on
Christmas Day and born during another Jewish holiday season
from the Feast of Trumpets to Feast of Tabernacles. This does
not disprove Christmas but *confirms* it!

In God's eyes, when does life begin—at delivery or at
conception? Conception! When did God arrive on earth—at
Jesus' birth or conception? Conception! Therefore conception is
the best date to recognize Jesus' coming to earth, which was very
likely on Christmas Day!

Even if we have calculated the right date to celebrate, some
will still argue that December 25th is on the wrong calendar. The
Bible recognizes only the Hebrew calendar. The Gregorian
calendar is not ordained. By that logic, no Christian should
celebrate birthdays, no Chinese should celebrate Chinese New
Year, and no citizen should celebrate any national holiday (like
Thanksgiving or the 4th of July), because we are celebrating
either on the wrong dates or on the right dates but on the wrong
calendar.

Many Asians in the older generation do not know their exact
birth date, because birth registration was not required by the
government and because everyone of Chinese descent turns one
year older on the same day—at winter solstice. Yet most of them
have a birthday their family recognizes. My mother celebrates her
birthday on the wrong date because her mother didn't register
her till many months after birth! All her passports and driver's
license show the wrong date, but we still celebrate that date as her
registered birthday. It is about relationship, not mathematics.

American historians cannot pinpoint the exact date for the
first Thanksgiving, yet Americans still enjoy celebrating
Thanksgiving. Relatives crisscross the country to come home,

spend time with family and be thankful. That's the heart of the American holiday.

The 9 Biblical holidays prove to me God is not as legalistic as some religious people are. Jesus Himself celebrated the Feast of Dedication even though it was never commanded by Moses or the Bible.

LET us close this chapter with a brief explanation of the 2 holidays added by Jewish authority after Moses.

Purim (Lots) commemorates Esther and the Jews' victory over Haman. Coincidentally the last day of the first Gulf War in 1991 was on the Feast of *Purim*. Just as God had delivered Esther's people from Haman, so too God delivered the Jews from Saddam Hussein! He is still delivering those who dare to believe Him!

Hanukkah (Feast of Dedication or Feast of Lights) commemorates the cleansing of the Temple from the "abomination of desolation" or the Greeks' pig-sacrifice in the Temple of God. This feast happens in Israel's winter or around the month of December, often coinciding with our celebration of Christ's arrival!

The 7 Mosaic Feasts speak of Jesus and His work in God's Plan of Salvation. The addition of 2 other feasts takes the number of feasts from 7 to 9, which symbolizes the additional gift of the Holy Spirit after the gift of salvation! The Temple menorah has 7 branches, representing the light of Jesus Christ in the world. The Hanukkah menorah (called Hanukkiah) has 9 branches, representing the supernatural provision of the Holy Spirit.

9 SONGS

THERE WERE 9 inspired songs (shirot) corresponding to the most important events for Old Testament believers. Here are the 9 songs of praise:

1. **A Psalm for the Sabbath** (Mizmor Shir I'Yom ha'Shabbat) sung by Adam at the completion of Creation. Rabbis believe the text is Psalm 92 and Jews recite it at the beginning of every Sabbath at sunset of Friday.
2. **Song of the Sea** (Shirat ha'Yam) sung by the Jews when they crossed the Red Sea and the Egyptian army drowned behind them. The text is Exodus 14:30-15:19.
3. **Song of the Well** (Shirat ha'Be'er) sung by Jews as God gave them water at a well. The text is Numbers 21:16-18.
4. **Song of Moses** (Ha'Azinu—literally, to listen) sung by Moses on the last day of his life. The text is Deuteronomy 32:1-44.

5. **Song of Gibeon** (Shirat ha'Givon) sung by Joshua after God made the sun to stand still and gave Israel victory over Adoni-Zedek a Canaanite king of Jerusalem. The text is Joshua 10:12-15.
6. **Song of Deborah** (Shirat Devorah) sung by Deborah the prophetess when she defeated Jabin king of Canaan and Sisera his army's commander. The text is Judges 5:1-31.
7. **Song of Hannah** (Shirat Chana) was sung by Hannah after God healed her infertility and granted her a son— the prophet Samuel. The text is 1 Samuel 2:1-10.
8. **Song of David** (Shirat David) sung by David towards the end of his life after "the Lord delivered him from the hand of all his enemies, and from the hand of Saul." The text is 2 Samuel 22 and repeated with variation in Psalm 18.
9. **Song of Songs** (Shir ha'Shirim) sung by Solomon to a Shulammite woman he loved. The sexual love is a type of the love between God and Israel, and Christ and His Bride.
10. *Song of Redemption* (Shir ha'Geula) or *Song of the Messiah* (Shir ha'Moshiach). It has not yet been sung! When it is, the lyrics will be from Isaiah 26 and may include an introduction from Isaiah 9:2-7. Isaiah 26:1 predicts it will be sung in the end times, "In that day this song will be sung in the land of Judah." The song has clear descriptions of the Tribulation, Resurrection, Judgment and Salvation of Israel.

Singing to God should be a normal part of a believer's life. Jesus said to the Samaritan woman, "But the hour is coming, and now is, when the true worshipers will worship the Father in spirit and truth; for the Father is seeking such to worship Him.

God is Spirit, and those who worship Him must worship in spirit and truth" (John 4:23-24).

Worship does 5 things: it brings God's tangible Presence into your home and your life; it makes you connect what's in your heart with your mouth; it makes you count your blessings; it helps you control your feelings so you walk by faith not by sight; and when you're tempted to worry, it makes you look up. Turn on some worship songs or play an instrument if you can, and begin to sing to God before you read on. As you do, you might find the Holy Spirit giving you new songs from the heart. Sing by faith—don't hold back!

10

10 IS the number of these related things: law, sin, test, trial, witness, justice, judgment and conscience (the moral seat of responsibility). Moses gave Israel the 10 Commandments; we have 10 fingers to remind ourselves of God's moral laws; if God had found only 10 righteous in Sodom and Gomorrah He would have spared the wicked cities; Daniel asked the eunuch to test him and the other Hebrew servants on a kosher diet for 10 days;[1] Pharaoh suffered 10 plagues for worshipping idols, enslaving the Jews and disbelieving God's prophet Moses. 10 times Israel tempted God, mainly by murmuring about God and complaining to Moses (Numbers 14:22). When God delivered Esther, Mordecai and the Jews from Haman's evil plot, the 10 sons of Haman were killed and hung on gallows (Esther 4).

10 males above barmitzvah age constitute a quorum (Hebrew *minyan*) for conducting a religious service, including weddings. There are a number of reasons why 10 is the minimal amount required. Moses appointed rulers of thousands, rulers of hundreds, rulers of fifties and rulers of tens (Exodus 18:21, Deuteronomy 1:15). Numbers 13:26 calls the ten spies who

brought an evil report of unbelief a "congregation" (Hebrew *edah*). Boaz called for 10 men to be witnesses of his redemption of Naomi's son's estate and his marriage to Ruth the Moabitess widow (Ruth 4:2).

The Talmud (Berachot 47b) says that nine people plus the Torah scrolls in the Ark[2] or held by a boy suffices for a quorum, as the Torah itself counts as a Person! How true, Jesus is the Torah of God in the flesh. Today, born again Christians count the presence of the Holy Spirit among attenders of a religious gathering. The Apostle James agreed with this practice when he gave his final ruling at the First Council of Jerusalem, "For it seemed good to the Holy Spirit, and to us, to lay upon you no greater burden than these necessary things" (Acts 15:28). He treated the Holy Spirit as a real Person involved in and asserting His influence over the meeting.

Rashi, Rambam and the Book of Jubilees[3] all say that Abraham was tested 10 times and found faithful in spirit. If 10 is the number of testing, it would be good to know what makes one pass a test in God's sight. According to the Book of Jubilees, Abraham's last test was Sarah's death and arranging her burial. Jubilees 19 describes for us how he passed the test:

 "And Abraham went to mourn over her and bury her, and we[4] tried him [to see] if his spirit were patient and he were not indignant in the words of his mouth; and he was found patient in this, and was not disturbed. For in patience of spirit he conversed with the children of Heth, to the intent that they should give him a place in which to bury his dead... This is the tenth trial wherewith Abraham was tried, and he was found faithful, patient in spirit. And he said not a single words regarding the rumour in the land [of God's promise] how that God had said that He would give it to him and to his seed after him, and he begged a place there to bury his dead; for he was found faithful, and was recorded in the heavenly tables as the friend of God" (Jubilees 19:3-9).

Both Old and New Testaments call Abraham a "friend of God", but the Book of Jubilee explains that this expression was correlated to Abraham's 10th trial. Why was he a friend of God? How did he pass his test?

Four times Abraham was noted as "patient" when things did not go his way; twice that he was "faithful". In other words, he was "full of faith," fully persuaded that God would give him the Promised Land. It was not up to him to take it for himself. Contrast Abraham's reaction to trials with that of Pharaoh and other evil characters in the Bible. Evil is presented as impatient. Being impatient is not a minor flaw, it makes us an enemy to God's plan.

Was Abraham always patient? I don't believe so. He rushed to get a baby boy through his maid Hagar (Genesis 16). This one act of impatience resulted in four thousand years of conflict between the children of Ishmael and the children of Israel.

Abraham learned to be patient after he had Isaac. He saw patience worked God's purposes better than self-reliance and self-insistence. He did not insist on his own rights with the children of Heth. He could have; after all God promised their land to him! Rather he humbly asked for the value of their land. He bought a plot of ground owned by the children of Heth in order to bury Sarah and eventually himself (Genesis 23). When I go through trials, when I am waiting on God's promises, I cannot forget how Abraham reacted — with *patience*.

10 times fire fell from Heaven upon:

1. **Sodom & Gomorrah** (Genesis 19:24)
2. **The first offering** (Leviticus 9:24)

3. **The disobedient priests** Nadab and Abihu (Leviticus 10:2)
4. **The complainers** at Taberah (Numbers 11:1)
5. **The rebels** Korah and his company (Numbers 16:35)
6. **Elijah's offering** at Mount Carmel (1 Kings 18:38)
7. **Jezebel's first set of soldiers** coming to arrest Elijah (2 Kings 1:10)
8. **Jezebel's second set of soldiers** (2 Kings 1:12)
9. **David's offering** (1 Chronicles 21:26)
10. **Solomon's offering** (2 Chronicles 7:1)

Joseph gave his 10 brothers 10 "Tests of Justice" before giving them mercy and grace. These tests are recorded in Genesis chapters 42 to 44 and enumerated in my video *"10 Tests of Justice: How to Handle People Who Mistreat You"*.[5]

Joseph is an Old Testament type of Christ in that he was rejected by his brothers, but ended up saving them. They did not recognize their own brother the first time they saw him; only when he appeared to them a second time did they recognize him. He did not punish them as they deserved, but forgave them and blessed them. Preachers thus lift up Joseph as an example of mercy and grace towards his offending brothers. However, Joseph did not give mercy and grace the way most Christians do. He pretended not to even know them and emphasized justice instead.

There are 10 instances of leprosy in the Bible:

1. **Moses** twice - first time privately (Exodus 4:6-7)
2. **Moses** - second time publicly (Exodus 4:29-31)
3. **Miriam** (Num 12)
4. **Naaman** (2 Kings 5)
5. **Gehazi** (2 Kings 5)
6. **The 4 lepers** in the days of Elisha (2 Kings 7)
7. **King Azariah** (2 Kings 15)

8. **A leper** who asked if Jesus was willing to heal him.
   (Matthew 8) Jesus said He was! He still is willing to heal
   you, since He never changes.
9. **Simon the leper** in Bethany (Matthew 26)
10. **Another 10 lepers** Jesus healed (Luke 17)

Leprosy was incurable and infectious. It was the most
dreaded disease in the ancient world. Lepers were ostracized
from society. Contracting leprosy was as good as a death
sentence. Consequently the Bible uses leprosy as a type of sin and
lepers a type of sinners. Sin is incurable, infectious, bars us from
Heaven, and is a death sentence! Since sin is associated with the
number 10, it is no surprise that God put 10 instances of leprosy
in the Bible.

Just as Jesus cured leprosy, so too He cured sin. There has
been only one sinless Person in the World – Jesus Christ – and
He came to die for our sins! His sacrifice becomes effective in our
lives when we put our faith in His Name for our salvation. To
cure sin, we must repent of rebelling against God and verbally
say,

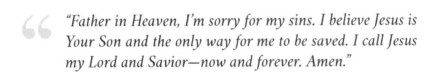

*"Father in Heaven, I'm sorry for my sins. I believe Jesus is
Your Son and the only way for me to be saved. I call Jesus
my Lord and Savior—now and forever. Amen."*

10 people experienced temporary[6] resurrection from the
dead in the Bible:

1. **Widow's son** in Zarephath, raised by Elijah (1 Kings
   17:17-24)
2. **Shunammites's son**, raised by Elisha (2 Kings 4:18-37)
3. **Moabite man**, raised by Elisha's bones (2 Kings
   13:20-21)
4. **Jonah**, raised by God (Jonah 2:1-10, Matthew 12:40)

5. **Jairus' daughter**, raised by Jesus (Matthew 10:18-26)
6. **Widow's only son** in Nain, raised by Jesus (Luke 7:11-16)
7. **Lazarus**, raised by Jesus (John 11)
8. **Dorcas**, raised by Peter (Acts 9)
9. **Paul**, raised by disciples (Acts 14)
10. **Eutychus**, raised by Paul (Acts 20)

Sin and its consequence death are represented by 10. Because God's heart is not for death, but life, it is fitting that in the Bible He raised 10 dead people back to life!

10 DAYS

> *"Do not fear any of those things which you are about to suffer. Indeed, the devil is about to throw some of you into prison, that you may be tested, and you will have tribulation TEN DAYS. Be faithful until death, and I will give you the crown of life."* (Revelation 2:10)

10 IS A PERIOD OF TESTING. Human pregnancy lasts on average for 10 sidereal months (a sidereal month is 27.3 days long; an average female is pregnant for 273 days). Daniel the prophet asked the royal eunuch to test him for 10 days on a kosher (Biblical) diet. Jesus told His first disciples to wait 10 days in the Upper Room for the baptism of the Holy Spirit.

Since the Holy Spirit has come, we no longer have to wait for the Holy Spirit. He has never left. We just believe and instantly receive!

We patiently wait for other things...such as seeing justice served in an unjust world, or seeing skeptics turn to Christ. Such things are difficult to wait for, but God promised, "Rest in the LORD, and WAIT patiently for Him; do not fret because of him who prospers in his way, because of the man who brings wicked schemes to pass...For evildoers shall be cut off; but those who WAIT on the LORD, they shall inherit the earth" (Psalm 37:7-9).

The Seleucid king Antiochus Epiphanes IV erected a statue of Zeus in the Temple of God and 10 days later sacrificed a pig on the altar of God. This infamous event in Jewish history occurred on the 25th of December[1] 167 BC and was predicted by the prophet Daniel 400 years in advance. It is called the "transgression of desolation" in Daniel 8:13 and the "abomination that makes desolate" in Daniel 9:27, 11:31 and 12:11. The "abomination of desolation" will be mimicked (or re-enacted) by the Anti-Christ according to Jesus (Matthew 24:15), Paul (2 Thessalonians 2:4) and John (Revelation 13:15).

Jesus told the church of Smyrna she would be tested for 10 days. This could literally mean she would be tested for a very short period of time, 10 literal days. Or it could mean she would be tested for a period of 10 years of persecution under Emperor Diocletian. Or it could figuratively mean she was going to be tested during 10 periods of persecution by 10 Roman emperors. All of the above could be true as Biblical prophecy is often fulfilled multiple times. The last view was held by Eusebius the Bishop of Caesarea (260-340 AD), who identified 10 wicked emperors who persecuted Christians; he was an eyewitness of the persecution by the 10th emperor.

1. **Nero** (54-68 AD) – killed his own mother, burned Christians alive to light his garden [origin of the disc burning software called *Nero*], accused Christians of burning Rome in 64 AD, beheaded Paul and crucified Peter upside down, finally committed suicide in 68 AD.
2. **Domitian** (81-96), brother of Titus who sacked Jerusalem in 70 AD – exiled John on the Greek island of Patmos where he saw the vision of Revelation.

3. **Trajan** (98-117) – persecuted Christians including Ignatius the Bishop of Antioch.
4. **Marcus Aurelius** (161-180) – killed Polycarp the Bishop of Smyrna and the Christian martyrs of Lyon and Vienne, France.
5. **Septimus Severus** (193-211) – killed Origen's father Leonides [Origen wanted to follow his father into martyrdom, but was prevented by his mother]; Septimus extended persecution of Christians to North Africa.
6. **Maximus** (235-238)
7. **Decius** (249-251) – imprisoned and tortured Origen.
8. **Valerian** (253-260)
9. **Aurelian** (170-275)
10. **Diocletian** (*Gaius Aurelius Valeris Dicletianus* 284-305) and his co-regent Maximian (285-305) – the Diocletian Persecution from 303-311 (10 years) was the largest and bloodiest official persecution of Christianity; he burned Christian books and churches; outlawed Christian gatherings; denied Christians the right to fair trial; imprisoned, tortured and killed multitudes of Christians.

However, Diocletian failed to destroy the Christian Church. Just as Jesus had promised the Church of Smyrna, early Christians did go through only 10 periods of testing. Then in 311 Diocletian committed suicide.

By 313, his successor Constantine the Great (306-337) issued the Edict of Toleration (Milan), ending the persecution of Christianity and proclaiming religious tolerance throughout the empire. At this time half of the population of the Roman Empire professed Christ![2] Constantine became the first Christian Roman Emperor, exempted Christian ministers from taxes and military service, and favored Christians in positions of leadership. He appointed Eusebius as his chief religious advisor. Slavery, gladiator fights, infanticides and crucifixions were abolished.

Disturbed by the aristocratic and pagan influences in Rome, Constantine relocated his capital to the Greek city of Byzantiumm and renamed it Constantinople in 330 AD. This became the "New Rome" and capital of his new Christian empire.

Contrary to many teaching, Constantine did not make Christianity the official religion of the Roman Empire. It was his second successor, Theodosius II (379-395) who declared "Catholic Christianity" the official state religion on 27 February 380, thus marrying religious and political power. This was a tragic mistake because the Bible would be neglected, the Gospel would be forgotten, and so-called Christian leaders would be pre-occupied with political struggles instead of saving souls. Western Christianity fell into idolatry, syncretism and religious dead works; out of which many Christians today still have not escaped! Penance replaced true repentance. Earning merits replaced God's grace. Medieval Christianity became a false religion of self-salvation like every other religion in the world.

With a strong arm Theodosius II tried to stamp out paganism, destroying pagan temples and prohibiting pagan festivals. His persecution of pagans is reminiscent of his predecessors' persecution of Christians; his severe actions did not uphold freedom of religion nor exemplify Christ's love for sinners. Christianity cannot be legislated; it has to be chosen! When the true Gospel is preached, sinners are presented with a choice to continue in sin and suffering, or to repent and receive Christ. Theodosius II did not present this choice to pagans. To avoid persecution, masses of pagans called themselves Roman Christians. With good intentions, Theodosius II did much harm to the mission of Christ.

By exalting Catholic Christianity, Theodosius II prepared the way for 3 great schisms between East and West.

Politically, the Roman Empire was divided in 395 AD into

Eastern and Western legs, just as Daniel's vision of the 2 iron legs had predicted.

Religiously, Christianity divided in 1054 into the Eastern Orthodox Church and the Roman Catholic Church, a religious landmark known as the Great Schism.

Spiritually, the last great schism occurred during the Protestant Reformation which saw numerous churches breaking away from Papal authority to return to Biblical authority. In 1517 Martin Luther posted his 95 Theses on the door of Castle Church in Wittenburg, Germany, causing the break away Lutheran Church. In 1845, Henry VII rejected the Pope's authority to not grant him a divorce, causing the break away Anglican Church (Church of England and Episcopal Church in the USA).

Emperor Constantine built an Eastern "Byzantine Empire" that would outlast the Western "Holy Roman Empire" by 1000 years. He also left a lasting legacy for Christianity – the Nicene Creed. Refuting the heresies that had crept up in the past 3 centuries, Constantine convened the first ecumenical council in the city of Nicea (modern Turkey) in 325 AD to write a Christian "statement of faith". The Council of Nicea reaffirmed what the Bible, the apostles and the early church fathers taught: the Trinity and the Deity of Christ. This may well represent the last universal decision of the Church agreed upon by the Eastern Orthodox Church, the Roman Catholic Church and even the Protestant Churches such as the Lutheran, Anglican, Presbyterian and Methodist!

By the Edict of Toleration, Constantine fulfilled Jesus' words that the early Church would go through no more than 10 days of testing.

10 represents tests and trials. The persecution of early Christians by 10 evil emperors reminds us of Jesus' words in Mark 13:13, "And you will be hated by all for My name's sake. But he who ENDURES TO THE END shall be saved." It is a great

day of victory when we can say, "No matter what comes, I will never abandon my faith in Jesus Christ!" and to say with all Christians the following declaration...

THE NICENE CREED[3]

"I believe in one God, the Father Almighty, Maker of Heaven and earth, and of all things visible and invisible;

And in one Lord Jesus Christ, the only-begotten Son of God, begotten of the Father before all worlds; God of God, Light of Light, very God of very God; begotten, not made, being of one substance with the Father, by whom all things were made;

Who, for us men and for our salvation, came down from Heaven, and was incarnate by the Holy Spirit of the virgin Mary, and was made man; and was crucified also for us under Pontius Pilate; He suffered and was buried; and the third day He rose again, according to the Scriptures; and ascended into Heaven, and sits on the right hand of the Father; and He shall come again, with glory, to judge the quick and the dead; whose kingdom shall have no end;

And I believe in the Holy Ghost, the Lord and Giver of Life; who proceeds from the Father and the Son; who with the Father and the Son together is worshipped and glorified; who spoke by the prophets.

And I believe one holy catholic and apostolic Church. I acknowledge one baptism for the remission of sins. And I look for the resurrection of the dead and the life of the world to come. Amen."

10 COMMANDMENTS

GOD GAVE the 10 Commandments to Moses from the very early part of the Bible. Yet very few people can name the 10 Commandments and fewer still know *why* they were given.

Most people make the assumption that the 10 Commandments were given to us so that by them we might enter Heaven. Some even boast that they live by the 10 Commandments, although I have yet to meet one claimant who can so much as *name* all 10 Commandments!

Can you name the 10 Commandments? We have touched on the first 6 Commandments in this book. Please take a look at the full list below[1] and see how many of them you can keep every day of your life:

1. **Love the Lord your God with all your heart, with all your soul, with all your mind and with all your strength;** or simply, **Always put God first!**
2. **Do not make or bow down to idols.**
3. **Do not blaspheme God's Name.**

4. **Keep the Sabbath holy** or **dedicate one entire day a week to worship God.**
5. **Honor your father and your mother.**
6. **Do not murder.**
7. **Do not commit adultery.**
8. **Do not steal.**
9. **Do not lie.**
10. **Do not covet.**

We are not meant to use God's Laws to judge others. I'm not your judge. You're not my judge. But we *are* to judge ourselves.

So how did you go judging yourself? Can you keep the 10 Commandments perfectly? These laws have been written into our hearts (Romans 2:15) and our conscience will convict us whenever we break them. Everyone in the world, even people who have never read the Bible, know that these laws are good and breaking them is bad!

The big trap of religion is to misuse rules and laws. The Pharisees read the same Bible and studied the same laws as we, yet somehow they did not see themselves as sinners who needed a Savior. One weakness religious people tend to have is applying good laws on others but not on themselves. This habit comes from Adam and Eve eating the fruit of the "tree of the knowledge of good and evil". If we were to update the story in modern language, then we would say that the first humans became sinners when they ate the fruit of the "tree of religion". They immediately found fault with each other and the serpent, but no fault with themselves. This is what religion does to people. Those who think they can keep the 10 Commandments have probably never read Jesus' words: "Did not Moses give you the law, yet NONE OF YOU keeps the law?" (John 7:19a).

The Logic of Law

The purpose of God's Laws is to convict our own conscience of sin and bring us to our knees before the Savior! Paul understood this when he wrote, "Therefore by the deeds of the law no flesh will be justified in His sight, for BY THE LAW is the KNOWLEDGE of SIN" (Romans 3:20).

In other words, the Law is not the solution; the Law is a diagnosis of the problem! Paul wrote further, "I would not have known sin except through the law. For I would not have known covetousness unless the law had said, You shall not covet" (Romans 7:7).

Once we realize the true function of the Law and come to terms with our own immoralities, what should we do? Contrary to common assumption, God does *not* want us to try harder to be a sinless person!

A sinner trying to clean himself of his sin is like an insomniac trying to fall asleep. The more you think of falling asleep, the more awake you'll be! The more you try to cleanse yourself of sin without Christ's cleansing power, the more sin-conscious and sinful you will end up becoming! Just as we fall asleep by *surrendering*, so too we are saved by *surrendering* to Christ. God wants us to humble ourselves and depend on His Son's help.

Paul put it this way, "Wherefore the law was our schoolmaster to BRING US UNTO CHRIST, that we might be justified BY FAITH" (Galatians 3:24 KJV). The reason Christ alone can save us is Christ alone is without sin. By trusting in Jesus Christ, we are hanging our entire future on the Only Perfect Person who ever lived! He came without sin, lived without sin, died for our sins, and resurrected to new life.

Our trying harder or resolving to become more religious does not lead to salvation. It only leads to self-centeredness and self-righteousness, all of which is really pride. To become honest about who we really are (expressing humility) and who Jesus really is (expressing faith)... that's the open door to salvation! Job 22:9 says, "He will save the humble person."

10 is the number of law and sin. Is it any surprise the Bible records 10 people who said, "I have sinned"?

1. **Job** (7:20)
2. **Pharaoh** (Exodus 9:27, 10:16)
3. **Balaam** (Numbers 22:34)
4. **Achan** (Joshua 7:20)
5. **Saul** (1 Samuel 15:24,30, 26:21)
6. **David** (2 Samuel 12:13, 24:10,17; 1 Chronicles 21:8,17; Psalm 41:4, 51:4)
7. **Shimei** (2 Samuel 19:20)
8. **Hezekiah,** (2 Kings 18:14, rendered *I have done wrong* in KJV and NKJ. Young's Literal Translation correctly renders Hezekiah's words as *I have sinned.*)
9. **Nehemiah** (1:6)
10. **Micah** (7:9)

Judges **10:10** records Israel half-heartedly admitting their guilt: "And the children of Israel cried out to the LORD, saying, We have SINNED against You, because we have both forsaken our God and SERVED the Baals!" True repentance would not go back to sinning and forgetting God.

God does not expect us to save ourselves from sin. He wants us to ask Him to change our hearts and impart a new nature in us so that we can live and be clean like Him.

10 PERCENT

10 PERCENT OF OUR INCREASE, income and inheritance belongs to God. Giving this 10% is called tithing.

Why would God expect people to tithe?

Because it establishes property rights and brings blessings to subjects of the Kingdom of God. God's right to claim the tithe stems from the fact that He created the earth, and all wealth is derived from His creation. He is the Source, we are the stewards. He is the Landowner, we are the tenants.

God has the right to claim 90% and allow us to keep only 10%, which is what most secular jobs do. If we make the company a million dollars, we may get paid $100,000 a year. But God reverses the order: if we make a million dollars, He says we get to keep $900,000 and give Him the Owner only $100,000. God made it easy so people would have no excuse to disobey. We should be happy!

But as Jesus taught about the tenant farmers in Luke 20, when the Owner sends His representatives to collect rent, the tenants often act as though they were the owner, or they wish to the owner were dead. This is a serious offense in God's economy.

LUKE 20:13-14

13 Then the owner of the vineyard said, 'What shall I do? I will send my beloved son. Probably they will respect him when they see him.'

14 But when the vinedressers saw him, they reasoned among themselves, saying, 'This is the heir. Come, let us kill him, that the inheritance may be ours.'

The Owner came to eject the tenants off His property and to avenge His Son, the true heir. No one who continually skips rent, cheats in taxes, or desires to overthrow the Owner deserves to use His land or benefit from His investment.

To whom should we tithe? Again, we refer back Jesus' words in Luke 20. The Owner does not come Himself to collect rent; He sends representatives, ministers of God.

The Government does the same. The President or Prime Minister does not knock on your door to collect taxes. Our tax to a minor government officer is sufficient to show allegiance to the President or Prime Minister. God expects all of us to tithe to full-time ministers of God, not social charities, orphanages or our own family. As a pastor I tithe to my church and other ministers of the Gospel; my church tithes to missionaries. Everyone is morally obligated to tithe—no exception.

What is the purpose of the tithe? A tithe is a 10th of our income set apart for God's ordained workers to carry out His work on earth, which can be summarized in two words: righteousness and justice.[1] In the Old Testament, one tribe was separated to work full-time for the Lord, the Levites. The other twelve tribes shared their income to support this one tribe. In the New Testament, God increased the number of gifts by calling people from any tribe to become apostles, prophets, evangelists, pastors and teachers. After giving us more gifts in the New

Testament, would God expect us to give less support to His ministers? That is illogical.

All covenant institutions, whether government, church or family, require regular payments as signs of covenant. 1 Samuel 8:15 establishes a principle that civil government may tax at the same rate as God—10%. Today, because 80% of Christians do not accept God's tithe as obligatory, but view taxes as obligatory, they end up paying as much as 4 times the amount of tax permissible by the Bible, while supposedly "saving" 10% of their tithe. It is a net loss for the believer, a net loss for the Kingdom and a net gain for secular state power.

Samuel the prophet warned about state power when he described how much tax a king would charge:

 1 SAMUEL 8:15 (NET)
15 He [the king chosen by the people] will demand a tenth of your seed and of the produce of your vineyards and give it to his administrators and his servants.

This verse gave a *warning* that if "democracy" or the voice of the people prevailed over God's recommended system, one of the worst effects would be a legal tax of 10%. Most modern democratic governments far exceed the Biblical limits of taxation.

Why do Christians accept taxation imposed by politicians but generally refuse the tithe imposed by God? God's way of flat tithe and flat tax is much better than cheating on the tithe and getting a "progressive" tax rate plus sales tax on top. In Australia, the top personal income tax rate is 45% plus 10% GST, for a total of 55% tax. That means a high income earner works from January to July to pay the government, then from July to December to pay himself and his family. The Bible considers this an economic injustice. High income earners, of course, have ways to bypass these oppressive tax burdens and transfer their wealth to tax havens.

Both Christians and secular citizens would do much better following the Biblical model of 10% tithe to the church and 10% tax to the government. Nations that do not burden their citizens with too much tax while encouraging donations to non-profit and religious entities fare much better than oppressive regimes. Singapore has a near flat tax rate: people earning $10,000 a month pay about 5% in real overall personal income tax; those earning $13,000,000 a month begin to reach the top tax bracket of 20%.[2] (For the sake of simplicity I have not included personal contributions into the compulsory saving program called The Central Provident Fund or CPF.) Every Singaporean pays zero capital gains tax. Personal investments are encouraged rather than welfare dependence. Following Biblical guidelines of taxation is one major factor why Singapore has attracted investments and become a prosperous nation that is the envy of Asia.

There is no question giving 10% to support ministers is in the New Testament. Hebrews 7:8 tells us, "Here [on earth] mortal men [ministers] receive tithes, but there [in Heaven] he [Jesus] receives them, of whom it is witnessed that he lives." It is clear tithing remains a New Testament practice to the writer of Hebrews. The writer takes pains to explain that the Christian tithe was not founded on Moses' command, but on Abraham's covenantal tithe to the Priest-King Melchizedek, who was a type of the Messiah.

If Abraham had not tithed to Melchizedek, and if Melchizedek not served him the bread and wine (symbols of the body and blood of Christ), then we would not have any basis for the New Covenant today! Over and over writers of the New Testament pointed to Abraham's faith as the basis for our receiving the promises of God, such as salvation and the Holy Spirit.

Too many pastors beg their congregants to give "whatever is on your heart" as though it were an act of volunteerism. They have not studied the subject of tithing enough to be bold in proclaiming its blessing to their people.

> MALACHI 3:10-11
> 10 Bring all the tithes into the storehouse, That there may be food in My house, And try Me now in this," Says the Lord of hosts, "If I will not open for you the windows of heaven And pour out for you such blessing That there will not be room enough to receive it.
> 11 "And I will rebuke the devourer for your sakes, So that he will not destroy the fruit of your ground, Nor shall the vine fail to bear fruit for you in the field," Says the Lord of hosts;

My family and I have proven to ourselves and our church that tithing works. It is not enough to intellectualize the tithe, you won't comprehend it that way. Only when your heart decides to obey, then the blessings and protections begin to flow and you will see the good results.

God showed me through His Word that tithing is an eternal principle. Have you ever wondered why Joshua was not allowed to take any of the spoils—the silver, gold and clothing—from Jericho after they conquered it? If you count the number of battles in Israel's first military campaign, you will find they fought 10 battles for 10 territories:

1. **Jericho** (Joshua 6)
2. **Ai** (Joshua 8)
3. **Makkedah** (10:28)
4. **Libnah** (9:29-30)
5. **Lachish** (9:31-32)

6. **Gezer** (10:33)
7. **Eglon** (10:34-35)
8. **Hebron** (10:36-37)
9. **Debir** (10:40-41)
10. 'From **Kadesh-barnea** even unto **Gaza**' (10:40-43)

Jericho was one of 10 cities; in other words, the tithe! Therefore Jericho belonged to the Lord!

Israel was not supposed to touch its wealth because the tithe always belongs to the Lord. One man named Achan refused to honour the Lord with his tithe, and consequently the entire nation of Israel lost the next battle at Ai.

It was the only battle Israel lost in the entire Book of Joshua! When Joshua found Achan withholding some of the clothes, silver and gold from Jericho, he ordered Achan and his family to be executed. Achan's theft of the tithe had brought a curse on his family and the nation!

I would never make a business partnership with a tithe-thief. It's too dangerous. I would never marry a tithe-thief. I would never want my children to marry a tithe-thief. The first question I would like to know of anyone who wants to marry one of my children is, "Do you pay your tithes to your home church?"

God is not after your money; He is after your heart. The thing to do is to believe Jesus first. Then tithing will be part of putting Him first.

11

11 IS the number of disorder, disintegration and things falling apart for the ungodly. 12 represents order, therefore taking away from perfect order, 12 minus 1, you get disorder. 11 is the number of judgment. Judgment follows after a broken law and ten signifies the law.

The judgment of the Flood came upon the world in the 10th generation (Noah) and 11th generation (Noah's 3 sons) from Adam. Egypt was judged 11 times in under Moses' ministry: 10 plagues + the Red Sea collapsing upon the Egyptian army (Exodus 14).

The grandson of Noah "Canaan" received the misnamed "curse of Ham" when Noah cursed him: "Cursed be Canaan; A servant of servants He shall be to his brethren" (Genesis 9:25b). Canaan had 11 children who became the 11 Canaanite tribes: Sidonians, Hittites (descendants of Heth), Jebusites, Amorites, Girgashites, Hivites, Arkites, Sinites, Arvadites, Zemarites and Hamathites. The Canaanites occupied Canaanland until the Israelites left Egypt and displaced them in the days of Joshua. For nearly four thousand years the land has been known as Israel.

In 1 Samuel 11, David's life was thrown into chaos after his adultery with Bathsheba and murder of her husband Uriah. To correct this disorder, David pronounced his own judgment that the man who stole a poor man's ewe lamb (Uriah's wife) must "restore fourfold for the lamb" (2 Samuel 12:6). Subsequently, 4 of David's sons died—Bathsheba's firstborn, Amnon murdered by Absalom, Absalom murdered by Joab, and Adonijah executed by Solomon.

Revelation 11 represents the chapter of chaos during the Tribulation. The Anti-Christ, presumably with the approval of Jews who operate the Third Temple, will kill the 2 Jewish witnesses sent by God. People will not only rejoice at their deaths, but also "shall send gifts to one another" (11:10). Many scholars believe the 2 witnesses will be Moses and Elijah. Imagine the Jews, having killed the greatest Jewish man who ever existed Jesus, will also kill their 2nd and 3rd greatest prophets Moses and Elijah! Yet make no mistake about it, the Lord still loves the Jewish people for the sake of His covenant with Abraham. If God can love the Jew who rejects his own Messiah, how much more He loves you who accept His Son!

The 11th hour is the last hour of a clock. World War I ended at the 11th hour (French time) of the 11th day of the 11th month of 1918.

"The Great Crash" occurred on Oct 29, 1929 (2 + 9 = 11). It ended a decade of prosperity called the "Roaring Twenties" and started "The Great Depression".

Wall Street crashed again on Sep 29 (2 + 9 = 11), 2008. The Dow Jones Industrial Average fell 777 points, the largest point drop in history up to that time. This was the market's signal of the Global Financial Crisis (GFC), the worst financial crisis since the Great Depression.

On 20 April 2010, British Petroleum (BP)'s Deepwater Horizon oil rig exploded in the Gulf of Mexico, killing 11 people.

The greatest earthquake to ever strike Japan (magnitude 9-

9.1) occurred on March 11, 2011. It shook the earth's surface for 6 minutes, caused a tsunami, triggered nuclear reactor meltdowns at Fukushima Daiichi Nuclear Power Plant, and killed 15,896 people. 1 + 5 + 8 + 9 + 6 = 29. You guessed it. 2 + 9 = 11.

THE AGE OF GLOBAL TERROR

Al Qaeda was formed on August 11, 1988. Al Qaeda struck the United States with four simultaneous airplane attacks on September 11, 2001. I began preaching my end time messages from this day onwards. It changed and defined every adult who lived through it. It was a day of unfathomable evil rearing its head to the public.

September 11 marked a milestone in terror. It was the worst terrorist attack on American soil. The symbols of this tragedy were the Twin Towers, which look like number "11". Other patterns of 11 are associated with this terrorist attack.

Date of the terrorist attack was 9/11	**9 + 1 + 1 = 11**
September 11 is the 254th day of the year	**2 + 5 + 4 = 11**
Number of floors in the Twin Towers	**110 or 11 x 10**
The first plane to hit the Twin Tower	**Flight 11**
Number of passengers on Flight 11 was 92	**9 + 2 = 11**
Number of passengers on Flight 77 was 65	**6 + 5 = 11**
Number of passengers on Flight 93 was 38	**3 + 8 = 11**
Number of letters in the official name of the President during the attack: George W. Bush	**11 letters**
Number of letters in the code name Secret Service assigned to the President: Trailblazer	**11 letters**
Number of letters in the official name of the most devastated target: New York City	**11 letters**

I think most adults will remember where we were when President Obama announced Osama bin Laden was shot dead. I was sitting in the car of a Bible school director in Brisbane. It was Monday morning Australia time, but it was the 11th hour of Sunday, May 1, 2011 in Washington D.C. time! I do not recall any other president delivering a televised statement at the 11th hour before midnight! Prophetically we have been living in the 11th hour of human history since September 11, 2001.

Al Qaeda bombed trains in Madrid, Spain on March 11, 2004. One of the worst terrorist bombings to hit India happened on July 11, 2006. Islamic terrorists detonated 7 bombs on rush hour trains for a period lasting 11 minutes. 209 people were killed. 2 + 9 = 11.

The Arab Spring successfully deposed Hosni Mubarak as President of Egypt after 30 years of dictatorial rule on February 11, 2011.

The Islamic State of Iraq and Syria (ISIS) announced the

creation of a caliphate (Islamic state) on June 29, 2014. 2 + 9 = 11. Despite ISIS being defeated in Syria on 20th March 2019, the global war on Islamic terror continues.

~

THERE IS an annual 11-day discrepancy between the Hebrew and Gregorian calendars. The former has an average of 354 days a year, the latter 365.25 days a year. This mismatch would cause the two calendars to eventually go completely out of sync. Left uncorrected, it would cause Biblical feasts to be celebrated in the wrong season.

In the 4th century AD, Hillel II instituted a correction to the modern Hebrew calendar by adding an extra month (Adar II) every two or three years for a total of seven times every nineteen years. This 11-day disorder forced the end of the Biblical "observed" calendar, whereby new moons and the Feast of Trumpets (the only major feast falling on the new moon) were announced by the observation of moon by the priest or other eye witnesses. This is why the Feast of Trumpets was also known as the "unknown day," an idiom to which Jesus alluded in Matthew 24:36.

11 SOLAR CYCLE

11 IS the number of the sun. Every 11 years, solar activity[1] reaches a peak and the solar poles actually reverse. While it may seem strange to us, the sun's magnetic poles switch places – i.e. north becomes south and south becomes north - every 11 years. The complete magnetic cycle (time for poles to flip once and flip back to its original position) spans 2 solar cycles or 22 years.

The solar magnetic activity cycle (aka *Schwabe Cycle*) is linked to changes in space weather, earth's weather, and possibly earth's current "climate change". While pollution is certainly a terrible thing to dump into our environment, it is not the most influential factor in our climate change. Two other factors are more important:

1. Solar activity. It is clear that the cyclical nature of solar activity influences our planet more than human activities. It's impossible to speak about climate and ignore the sun! The sun rules earth's temperature. When it goes down, the earth is cooler. When it comes up, the earth is warmer. When there's an eclipse, there's

an immediate drop in temperature. Solar activity overrides all other factors as the chief instigator of earth's cyclical climate.

2. Man's sin. Sin is the worst environmental pollution to our planet, for without sin, moral decay and spiritual pollution, there would be no toxic waste, chemical sludge or industrial pollution. There would be no Chernobyl, Exxon Valdez oil spill or BP Gulf oil spill.

An anti-Scriptural idea that has been promoted through the secular media is that our planet is fragile. Since God made the earth to last forever, we must believe that the earth cannot be fragile. Did you know that one volcanic eruption (recall the 2010 eruption in Iceland) dumps more toxic chemicals into the earth's atmosphere than all the car exhausts in the world combined? The earth absorbs the volcanic plume and recycles it away naturally. It is not the earth that is fragile, but humans living under sinful conditions who are fragile.

The earth can also tolerate changes in temperature – it has been through an ice age before and it has experienced global warming before. That Greenland is called "green" is testament to the fact that global temperatures were once higher than they are now. Should we be worried about global warming? What would be the effect of the earth's temperature rising by a few degrees? While we have all heard of doom and gloom predictions, one report projects that if the earth warmed up a bit, northern European countries would benefit from an agricultural boom![2]

When God made the sun, the sun was intended to play a central role to our planet. It is not we who control the seasons or cycles. The sun has more sway on earth's weather than all of man's activities. While some are convinced that man's CO2 emission is causing global warming, other scientists such as Piers Corbyn are calling it "green religion" with no scientific evidence. His organization Weatheraction predicted more accurately than anybody else a harsh winter of 2010-2011 in the UK and Europe, and has been proven correct.

Astrophysicist Piers Corbyn attributes his predictions to studying the sun's full 22-year cycle, not man's CO2 emission. He believes that oil companies and governments love the CO2 theory because it justifies their raising energy prices, taxing our "carbon footprint", and trading "green". Part of a one world government is a global tax, but the world will not accept the addition of a global tax...unless it was called a "green tax".

Other scientists are asking what is causing the apparent global warming of other planets? They observe at least 4 other planetary bodies – Mars, Jupiter, Triton (Neptune's largest moon), and Pluto – are experiencing global warming. Granted solar activity may not be the only explanation for why these planetary bodies are warming, one can safely say they are not warming because there are too many cars on Mars or too many capitalists opening new factories on Triton! We take ourselves too seriously if we think we are the saviors of the planet. The planet doesn't need saving as much as *we* do!

Salvation through Christ is the greatest clean-up action for this planet. Once Jesus cleanses our inward nature from sin and fills us with the presence of the Holy Spirit, we will automatically become better citizens of this planet and better stewards of God's resources. Solomon wrote in Proverbs 12:10, "A righteous man regards the life of his animal, but the tender mercies of the wicked are cruel." Nothing could be better for the welfare of plants, animals and the ecosystem than for sinners to stop sinning, turn their lives over to Jesus and live clean Christian lives on a planet we share.

11 is the number God assigned to solar activity. The last peak in the solar cycle was 2012.

12

12 IS the number of authority, order or government. There are 12 tribes of Israel; 12 Apostles of the Lamb; 12 months in a year; 12 hours in a day; 12 hours in a night; 12 constellations of stars; 12 musical notes in an octave; 12 foundations of Heavenly Jerusalem, with 12 gates made of 12 pearls and 12 angels guarding those gates. Jesus said He could pray to the Father and He would send Him 12 legions of angels. The measurements of New Jerusalem are 12,000 stadia.

There are 12 minor prophets in the Old Testament: Hosea, Amos, Micah, Joel, Obadiah, Jonah, Nahum, Habakkuk, Zephaniah, Haggai, Zachariah, and Malachi.

Anyone who wants to understand the chronology of the Old Testament needs to read only 12 books in this order: Genesis, Exodus, Numbers, Joshua, Judges, 1 Samuel, 2 Samuel, 1 Kings, 2 Kings, Daniel, Ezra, Nehemiah.

The rest of the Bible books are important and tell the stories within the main plot. For instance, Ruth lived during the time of the Judges and is a Gentile woman who would become an ancestor of Jesus. Most Psalms were written during the period of

2 Samuel. Nearly all major and minor prophets lived during the time of 2 Kings, with the notable exception of Haggai, Zechariah and Malachi who lived during the time of Ezra.

There were 12 prophetesses in the Bible: 7 named (Miriam, Deborah, Huldah, Noadiah, Elizabeth, Mary, Anna) and 5 unnamed (Isaiah's wife in 8:3 and Philip's 4 daughters in Acts 21:9).

There are 12 persons anointed with oil in the Bible: Aaron, Nadab, Abihu, Eleazar, Ithamar, Saul, David [anointed 3 times!], Absalom, Solomon, Jehu, Joash, and Jehoahaz. The first 5 were anointed priests and the next 7 kings. 12 = 7 (perfect) + 5 (grace).

The title "Christ" means the "Anointed One". Jesus was not anointed with oil by man, but was anointed with the Holy Spirit as King, Priest and Prophet at His water baptism. Jesus' first sermon was about His anointing by the Holy Spirit (Luke 4). After His anointing Jesus chose 12 disciples to be His future Church leaders.

13 NEGATIVE

13 HAS OFTEN BEEN ASSOCIATED with evil in the Bible.

Jesus taught 13 evils proceed from man's heart: evil thoughts, adulteries, fornications, murders, thefts, covetousness, wickedness, deceit, lewdness, an evil eye (Hebrew idiom for stinginess), blasphemy, pride, foolishness (Mark 7:21-23); Nimrod the 13th man from Adam was the world's first dictator and founder of the rebellious city of Babel; there were 13 famines (financial recessions) in the Bible;[1] 13 civil wars in Israel;[2] the noun "leaven" representing false doctrine (Matthew 16:11-12) occurs 13 times in the New Testament; the "dragon" representing the devil is mentioned 13 times in the Book of Revelation.

Revelation 13 is *the* premier chapter revealing the Anti-Christ. Actually, the term "antichrist" is never once used in the Book of Revelation, because the word "antichrist" is primarily a Gentile term referring to anyone who opposes Christ as the only way to be saved, whereas the Book of Revelation deals primarily with Israel and the Jews post-Rapture.

Revelation instead uses the term "beast". There is not one but *two* beasts the Jews are to look for during the time of "Jacob's

Trouble". Revelation 13:1-10 describes the first beast "out of the sea". Revelation 13:11-18 describes the second beast "out of the earth". One interpretation is that the first beast is a Gentile (sea is a symbol for nations) whereas the second beast is Jewish (the geo-political center of the earth is Israel).

The first beast is a political leader (perhaps a world leader) whereas the second beast is a false religious leader, belonging to an ecumenical religion of some sort, for the masses will not accept any other kind of religion. The truth it calls 'dogma' and rejects, a lie it calls 'compromise' and accepts.

The second beast imitates John the Baptist while the first beast imitates Christ. The false messiah, his false prophet and Satan make an unholy trinity that will persuade the world to hate Israel and hate God. Considering opinion polls now, Satan doesn't have much more convincing to do. The world's media-driven, Bible-illiterate population is *ready* to embrace anti-Israel leaders. So far America, Australia and England have not given them one. If a charismatic Middle Eastern leader rises with enough power to rival the pro-Israel Western leaders, the world will fall on its knees to follow him and his spokesperson. These two charismatic beasts of Revelation 13 will deceive many. That time doesn't seem far away!

13 is a prime or indivisible number. The series of prime numbers starts with 1, 3, 5, 7, 11, 13, 17, 19, etc. What is interesting is 13 is the 6th of such numbers, 6 being significant of the Anti-Christ.

There were 13 judges in the Book of Judges, the 6th one being the worst one. One of the worst periods in Israel's history was the time of the judges. Israel was under anarchy (Judges 21:25), worshipped false gods (Judges 5:8, 10:10); public streets were not safe (Judges 5:6-7); homosexuality was common (Judges 19:22); one of the worst crimes in the Bible occurred when bisexuals from Gibeah[3] tried to rape a Levite, then succeeded in raping his concubine. Israel asked for the sodomites to be handed over and punished according to the Law of Moses, but the tribe of Benjamin refused and protected them, contrary to the Law of Moses! In retaliation Israel nearly wiped out the tribe of Benjamin, killing 25,100 young men and leaving only 600 left.[4]

Without spiritual and national leadership, Israel was trapped in a cycle[5] of sin, suffering, brief repentance, and being rescued by a deliverer (called judge at the time). Here were the 13 judges in the Book of Judges:

1. **Othniel** of Judah saved Israel from the Mesopotamians and ruled 40 years (3:9-11).
2. **Ehud** of Benjamin saved Israel from the Moabites and ruled 80 years (3:15-30).
3. **Shamgar** (3:31).
4. **Deborah** of Ephraim, with **Barak** of Naphtali, saved Israel from the Canaanites and ruled 40 years (4:4-5:31).
5. **Gideon** of Manasseh, with a band of only 300 men, saved Israel from the Moabites and ruled 40 years (6:7-8:35).
6. **Abimelech**, the son of Gideon, ruled 3 years. He oppressed his own people, killing 70 sons of Gideon,[6] except Jotham. Abimelech created civil strife because he wanted to be king and turned Shechem into his capital. He was killed by a woman of Thebez who threw a millstone on his head (Judges 9). If the 6th judge is a type of the devil or Anti-Christ, then the woman who threw a milestone was a type of the Church who speaks Christ's Word which acts like a Rock (1 Corinthians 10:4) and a Hammer on the devil's head (Jeremiah 23:29)!
7. **Tola** of Issachar ruled 23 years (10:1-2).
8. **Jair** of Gilead ruled 22 years (10:3-6).

9. **Jephthah** of Gilead saved Israel from the Ammonites and from civil attack by the tribe of Ephraim. When Jephthah defeated the Ephraimites, the survivors tried to cross the River Jordan back to their home territory. Jephthah's men were waiting at the River and identified disguised soldiers by asking them to say the word "Shibboleth." If they said "Sibboleth" instead, their mispronunciation gave them away and they were killed. This is the origin of the term "Shibboleth" in English, meaning a linguistic, social or cultural identifier, such as an accent from a particular region, or jargon used by a subculture, or a physical sign such as male circumcision. In WWII, American soldiers used knowledge of baseball as a shibboleth to identify German infiltrators from real American troops. Till today, Thai police uses several shibboleths to identify refugees who cross the Thai border illegally and stay to work. The police may listen for a Burmese refugee to say a word with a Thai "b" in it; the Burmese confuse the Thai "b" with a "w". Sometimes policemen will make the Burmese pretending to be a Thai sing the Thai national anthem. If they can't sing it with the right words or accent, they are sent back to Myanmar! Jephthah was the first to use the shibboleth and ruled Israel 6 years (10:10-12:7). He, Barak, Gideon and Samson are among the great men of faith mentioned in Hebrews 11. Gideon, Barak, Jephthah and Samuel also get honorable mention by the Lord in 1 Samuel 12:11.

10. **Ibzan** of Judah ruled 8 years (12:1-10).

11. **Elon** of Zebulun ruled 10 years (12:11-12).

12. **Abdon** of Ephraim ruled 7 years (12:13-15).

13. **Samson** of Dan saved Israel from the Philistines by his death; he ruled 20 years (13:2-16:31).

After recording the 13 judges, the writer of Judges ends with one of the worst indictments against the spiritual condition of Israel, "In those days there was no king in Israel; everyone did what was right in his own eyes."

13 is the total number of the tribes in Israel, because Joseph's two sons Ephraim and Manasseh were adopted by Jacob and count as 2 tribes. These are the sons in birth order: Reuben, Simeon, Levi, Judah, Dan, Napthtali, Gad, Asher, Isaachar, Zebulun, Manasseh, Ephraim, and Benjamin. All Biblical lists show 12 tribes, which makes for interesting discussion as to why 1 tribe gets omitted and why the tribes are in the order they are.

Most lists give Reuben first place, being the firstborn of Jacob. However, Judah heads other lists because he was chosen to be an ancestor of the Messiah. Long ago Jacob prophesied about his son Judah,

> GENESIS 49:10
> 10 The sceptre [symbol of kingship] shall not depart from Judah, nor a lawgiver from between his feet, until Shiloh [a term for the Messiah] comes; And to Him shall be the obedience of the people.

All of Israel's godly kings came from Judah, including David, Solomon, Hezekiah and Josiah. All of these kings were ancestors to Jesus. Most genealogy in the Bible ultimately exists to link Jesus Christ to David, Abraham, and Adam. No other book in the world presents a continuous account of history from Creation to the first century AD (omitting the 400 year Inter-Testament period).

What about the omitted tribes? In several lists Levi is not mentioned because they are ministers not soldiers. In the Book of Revelation, the tribe of Dan is missing. Why? The omission may serve as a clue to Dan's future: the tribe may become so apostate that it will be rejected during this time, or it may be in cooperation with the Anti-Christ. In Deborah's time, Dan was guilty of cowardice.[7] Deborah asked after victory over the Canaanites, "Why did Dan remain in ships?" After Samson, Dan couldn't handle the Philistines and decided to move to the far north of Israel. (Dan is the only tribe with 2 disconnected pieces of land.) Those of us who study End Times interpret Dan's absence from the 144,000 end-time ministers of God as a clue that the false messiah or else his false prophet may be a Jew from the tribe of Dan. The sign of the tribe of Dan is a serpent.[8] The word Dan means "judgment".

13 POSITIVE

13 IS NOT a number we should be afraid of, because God is able to turn negatives into positives. Oppression is an opportunity for believers to overcome evil with good. The anti-Christs of this world will not prevail. Many have come and gone, but the Gospel continues to advance and the Church continues to grow.

Haman the Agagite (Amalekite) planned to kill the Jews on the 13th day of the 12th month (Esther 3:12-13; 9:1-18), but God turned it for the Jews' good. Israel was delivered from her enemies on the 13th day of Adar and still celebrates the 13th-14th days in an extra-Biblical feast called *Purim* (meaning lots).

13 is the number of times Joshua's army marched around Jericho before it fell: 6 times on the first 6 days and 7 times on the 7th day. They won despite crossing the Jordan River at the most vulnerable point militarily speaking, right in front of Jericho! They won despite having been circumcised just days before. Joshua 5:5 explains why, "For all the people who came out [of Egypt] had been circumcised, but all the people born in the wilderness, on the way as they came out of Egypt, had not been circumcised." While the freshly circumcised men waited to be

healed, they camped in Gilgal where "the Lord said to Joshua, This day I have rolled away the reproach of Egypt from you" (Joshua 5:9). They had not won the physical battle yet and, in God's mind, they were already in victory!

Abraham's circumcision is mentioned 13 times in the Torah.[1] Ishmael was circumcised at the age of 13, whereas the Bible commands sons to be circumcised on the 8th day (Leviticus 12:3).

13 is the age boys become men in Jewish culture. A Jewish boy who comes of age undergoes a confirmation ceremony in which he gets to publicly read the weekly portion of the Torah for the first time. His father typically gives thanks to God that he is released from being punished for his son's sins, and the son becomes a *bar mitzvah* or "son of the commandment." This is the age when he becomes accountable for his own sins and makes a choice to follow God and not turn back.

The bar mitzvah becomes a full-fledged member of the Jewish community: he is able to be called upon to lead prayer or religious services, his presence is counted towards a prayer quorum, his testimony is accepted in the Beth Din (Jewish Court), he is eligible to own property and be legally married. The preparations for this rite of passage include meeting with his rabbi, studying the Torah, and getting involved in charity by giving and serving. The age of 13 corresponds roughly to puberty and males from this age up are expected to fast on the Day of Atonement.

Jesus would not have had a bar mitzvah, for 3 reasons: 1) the custom dates back to the fourteenth century; 2) He wouldn't have needed one. He was, is and will always be the ultimate Bar Mitzvah (Son of the Law). He is the only human born who never violated any of His Father's mitzvahs, qualifying Him to be the Messiah and Savior of sinners. 3) Jesus, like most sons pre-industrialization, would have spent most of His time under the tutelage and apprenticeship of His father. We know the Nazareth community identified Him as a carpenter just like his father (Matthew 13:55, Mark 6:3).

Most ancient cultures had a rite of passage so boys clearly knew when they were identified and accepted by their community as men. Catholics, Anglicans, Lutherans and Methodists are among Christian churches that practice confirmation, an analogous process. My church has helped several boys transition into manhood through what we call a "Christian bar mitzvah". The results have been a lasting boost in male confidence, responsibility and maturity.

I believe a proper rite of passage becomes increasingly important in grooming men into husbands and leaders as industrialization has taken the father out of their homes to work and modern schooling takes children away from their parents. Jesus would have spent most of His time learning both intellectual and professional skills from His father Joseph. As modern children become disconnected from their fathers in particular and from men in general (Western public schools are statistically dominated by females), boys are overly mothered and under fathered. Who pays the price? All of society, especially young women looking for marriageable men.

Compare this to only 200 years ago. Samuel Adams, one of the signers of the Declaration of Independence, entered Harvard University at the age of 14 and graduated with a degree in history and politics 4 years later.

John Quincy Adams, the eldest son of John Adams (America's first Vice President and second President), was responsible for protecting his mother and siblings from the British army at the age of 10 while his father attended to Revolutionary business. From the age of 12 to 17, Quincy accompanied his father on diplomatic missions to France and the Netherlands, studied at Leiden University, and learned French, Latin and Greek. At the age of 15 he served as translator and secretary to the American diplomat to Russia, Francis Dana. At the age of 17, he was admitted into Harvard University, from which he graduated in two years. He went on to become the 6th American President.

By contrast 43% of Millennial men between the ages of 18-34 still live with their parents, without wife, children or a house to their name.[2] What is causing prolonged immaturity and delayed manhood? While there are many factors, I would point out that the rite of passage is gone from non-church-goers. At the same time the culture of public schools has become more feminized; public officials would be "concerned" for boys like Samuel Adams and John Quincy Adams[3] who didn't conform to government standards, skipped grades and grew up "too fast". Today, many of our teachers would either hold such boys back from advancing academically for the sake of "socializing" (a more feminine goal) or else label them as ADHD and refer them to a psychiatrist. Our low expectations and lack of confirmation of manhood have produced a lack of marriageable men. Men are capable of nearly every responsibility from the age of 13.

13 is one of the numbers associated with God. Twice a day observant Jews recite the *Shema* from Deuteronomy 6:4, "Hear, O Israel: the Lord our God, the Lord is one." There are two words for "one" in Hebrew: *yachid* (singular one, one only, one alone - never used of God) and *echad* (one in number or one in unity). The *Shema* uses *echad* (אחד), spelled *alef (1)* + *het (8)*+ *dalet (4)* , with a gematria value of 13.

1 John 4:8 says, "God is love." Love in Hebrew is *AHaVaH* (אהבה), spelled *alef (1)* + *hey (5)* + *bet (2)* + *hey (5)*, with a gematria value of 13. The Love Chapter of the Bible is First Corinthians 13, which has 13 verses about love. God is "the One" (13) and God is "Love" (13); together 13+ 13 makes the number of God (26). God loves the 13 tribes of Israel, making them one.

There are two nations on earth founded on the Bible from its inception. One can say that America is to the New Testament what Israel is to the Old Testament. (No, that does not mean America replaced Israel. It means there are similarities between them.) Biblical Israel was made up of 13 tribes. America had 13 original colonies on the east coast, now the 13 states of New England. Israel influenced the world spiritually by propagating the Law of Moses; America influenced the world spiritually by propagating the Gospel of Jesus. America ended slavery and involuntary servitude with the 13th Amendment.

Moses Maimonides (1135-1204) wrote 13 Articles of Faith summarizing the basic beliefs of Judaism:

1. The existence of God
2. The unity of God
3. God is Spirit
4. God is Eternal
5. Worship God alone and not those that are below Him
6. Prophecy or revelation through prophets
7. The preeminence of Moses among the prophets
8. The Torah was given by God on Mount Sinai
9. The completeness of the Torah, i.e. it is not lacking
10. God knows man's actions and does not ignore them
11. God will punish those who break His commandments
12. The Messiah will come though He delays His coming
13. The Resurrection of the dead, conditional on the Messiah's coming.

Remember 13 is just a number. Let's stay positive and have faith in God, not numbers!

14

14 IS the number of salvation. The first holiday God commanded Israel to celebrate is a commemoration of the 14ᵗʰ of Nisan, called the Passover Feast. On that day, at the start of the Exodus out of Egypt, Jews were spared from the visitation of the angel of death when he "passed over" each home whose the entrance was covered by the blood of an innocent lamb—this was an object lesson of what the Blood of Jesus does to protect our lives from eternal judgment. According to the *Midrash*, the blessing Isaac gave Jacob in Genesis 27 occurred on the 14ᵗʰ of Nisan. According to the *Targum*, Naomi and Ruth arrived in Bethlehem on the 14ᵗʰ of Nisan. Because Ruth arrived in Bethlehem and married Boaz, two great kings were born in Bethlehem: David and Jesus. The first sinner to accept Jesus, the thief on the cross, was saved on the 14ᵗʰ of Nisan.

The number 14 is most prominent in Jesus' life and genealogy. Jesus was crucified for the sins of the world on the 14ᵗʰ of Nisan. Matthew 1:1-17 records:

- 14 generations from Abraham to David
- 14 generations from David to the Babylonian Captivity
- 14 generations from the Babylonian Captivity to Christ

14 may be a reference to Jesus as the Son of David, thus the legitimate heir to the Throne of David. The Hebrew gematria of David's name is 14 (D + V + D = 4 + 6 + 4 = 14).

Luke's record shows:

- 10 generations from Adam to Noah
- 10 generations from Noah to Abraham
- 14 generations from Abraham to David
- 40 generations from David to Joseph

Much theological debate has raged over the differences between Matthew's genealogical account and Luke's. But all confusion is solved when one understands that Matthew records Jesus' paternal lineage whereas Luke records His maternal lineage.

Luke 3:23 contains *italicized words* which are additions by the translators of the King James version. Usually the additions are meant to help us understand the passage better in English, but in case they didn't the translators knew enough to let us know by *italicizing* the additional words:

"And Jesus himself began to be about thirty years of age, being (as was supposed) the son of Joseph, which was the son of Heli."

The words "the son" of Heli is *italicized* because they are not there in the original Greek. It would make much more sense to read the verse as "Joseph, which was *the son-in-law* of Heli [Mary's father]." Luke then traces Jesus' maternal lineage.

Typically ancient records only showed the paternal genealogy of a king or an important person. (Commoners kept no genealogy at all, as most of us can attest. I don't know too many commoners who can trace their family trees beyond 4 generations.) Why would the Gospel writers want to trace Jesus' family tree back through 42 paternal generations and 62 maternal generations?

Writing to the Jews, Matthew was concerned with proving that Jesus was the Jewish Messiah. The Messiah must be of royal descent, heir to the throne of David, descendant of the tribe of Judah, and the seed of Abraham. Nobody today can prove those qualifications, which precludes all other claims to the Messianic title. Jesus is the last Person to completely trace His lineage to David and Abraham.

Luke was addressing the Gentiles. Both the Gospel of Luke and the Book of Acts are addressed to a Roman named "Theophilus," which may have been a real person or a code name for anyone of us who is a "Lover of God". Therefore Luke was more concerned with proving Jesus is the "Seed of the Woman" (Genesis 3:15) or the Savior of the World promised to every generation since Adam. Accordingly Luke 3:23-38 traces Jesus' genealogy back to Adam.

Luke's record is the only complete genealogy of any man which can be traced back to Adam and Eve, clearly disproving evolution. Although some people may not realize it, redemption depends on humans descending from humans. The Incarnation of Jesus as God in human form is proof that only a human descended from a human has the legal right to save mankind. God could not unilaterally intervene to save mankind and defeat Satan. God has given certain rights to humans, the first humans abdicated those rights to Satan, so it would only be just and legal for a human to redeem those rights and give them back to humans. This completely human lineage is necessary for redemption.

Luke's genealogy proves Jesus did not descend from apes, but from the fully human Adam and Eve. Over and over Jesus called Himself the "Son of Man". (Make no mistake about it: Jesus also called Himself the "Son of God".) Whether the Bible refers to Jesus' humanity or to His divinity, there is no reference to any ape in Jesus' genealogy. Jesus did not believe in evolution.

15

15 IS a mysterious number pointing to something "hidden". 10 (law) + 5 (grace) = 15 (hidden in law is grace).

There are 15 places where mysterious "extra points" (*puncta extraordinaria*) appear on one or more letters, or even whole phrases, in the Masoretic text[1] of the Hebrew Bible. Hebrew is normally not written with vowels, but when it is, such as in children's books or in the Masoretic text, the vowels are represented by dots called *nikkud* (singular) or *nekuddot* (plural). There are 15 passages where extra dots appear beyond the ordinary nekuddot. For instance, there is a series of dots over the phrase "he kissed him" in Genesis 33:4.

> "Esau ran to greet him. He embraced him and, falling on his neck, he kissed him; and they wept." (The New Jewish Publication Society of America Tanakh, 1985)

Why would the entire phrase "he kissed him" feature a series of superscript dots over every letter? Rabbis disagree over the meaning, but one thing is for sure, the special dots serve to draw our attention to the word or phrase.

In the case of Esau, most scholars say that the special dots suggest doubt, that Esau's kiss was not genuine, for Esau really hated Jacob. Rabbi Yannai and Church Father Origen, who were third-century contemporaries, agreed on this. Ellicott's Commentary for English Readers echoes the same, "the Masorites are supposed to signify thereby that Esau's kiss was not a sign of genuine love."[2]

However, in the Jewish commentary *Sifre Numbers 65*, Rabbi Shimon bar Yohai suggested the opposite, that the special dots are meant to convey that the kiss was authentic, despite the suspicion the reader might have to the contrary.[3] The special dots in 15 passages convey a hidden message.[4]

There are two Biblical feasts celebrated on the 15th: Unleavened Bread on the 15th of Nissan and Tabernacles (*Sukkot* in Hebrew) starting on the 15th of Tishri. During unleavened bread, the middle bread (matzah) is broken and hidden, then Jewish children enjoy some fun trying to find it. Once found, everyone eats the hidden bread (*afikoman*). The ritual of eating it is called *tzafun*—meaning "hidden". Jesus fulfilled the meaning of the *afikoman* when His sinless body was buried on the 15th of Nisan, one day after Passover.

Jesus will also fulfill the hidden meaning of Tabernacles when He comes to save the Jews from the Anti-Semite Anti-Christ and establish the Messianic Kingdom on earth. The beginning of this 1000-year reign of the Messiah is going to start on the 15th of Tishri. We are given the date, but not the year. It is hidden from us. Faith helps us wait for the time of fulfillment.

15 in Hebrew spells the shortest Name of God Yah (יה), which is half of Yahweh (יהוה). For this reason, Jews customarily avoid writing 15 in a straightforward way: *yod* (10) + *hey* (5) = 15. To keep the Name of God holy, Jews circumvent writing 15 with God's Name 'YaH' and conventionally write it

with *tet* (9) + *vav* (6) = 15 (טו). In this way, the name of God is "hidden" in 15.

15 is associated with marriage or man and woman joining together. In Hebrew, "man" is spelled with the letters *alef-yod-shin* (pronounced "Ish") and "woman" is spelled with *alef-shin-hey* (pronounced "Ishah"). You can see that man and woman share two letters in common, *alef-shin*, which spells the word "fire"; but they also have one letter different from each other, *Yod-hey*, which spells the name of God "YaH" (15). Rabbis interpret this linguistic code to mean that a successful marriage depends on God being in the center of a marriage. If you remove God (*Yod-hey*) out of man and woman, you will be left with only fire (*alef-shin*), an unholy flame that burns both parties.

There are 15 stairs separating or joining (depending on your perspective) the Women's Court and the Men's Court in the Temple of God. This 15-step staircase is where Levitical musicians stood and played their musical instruments during the Feast of Tabernacles (or *Sukkot*). So we can see 15 is associated with love, male and female, and home - tabernacles being a picture of God's home on earth.

Jacob was 15 years old when his grandfather Abraham died and 120 years old when his father Isaac died. Here is a mathematical mystery: if you add all the numbers in a series from 1 to 15, you will get the sum of 120. Jacob's ages at both his father's and grandfather's deaths were hidden in code.

I do not believe God is controlling everyone's time on earth, because His Word tells us that how long we live is often up to us. We can do some things to "prolong our days" and "lengthen our years" (see Deuteronomy 25:15; Proverbs 3:2, 3:16, 9:11; Ephesians 6:3), or we can do foolish things to "shorten our years" (Proverbs 10:27; 28:18, Ecclesiastes 7:17). Psalm 91:16 says that we who dwell in the secret place of the Most High can live till we are satisfied: "With long life will I satisfy him, and show him my salvation."

This is a truth few have learned: God is not ruling over everybody, only those who choose to call Him their Leader. He is not determining whether some die young or some live long. No! There are multiple factors affecting a person's mortality. Some babies are born deformed and die young not because of God's fault, but because the mother abused drugs, drank alcohol, or lived or worked in a place that exposed her to toxic chemicals; that cannot be blamed on God.

Some adults die young because they violate the 5th Commandment, "Honor your father and mother, which is the first commandment with promise: that it may be well with you and you may live long on the earth" (Ephesians 6:2-3). The converse of this command must be that people who dishonor or mistreat their parents will die prematurely. Much of longevity depends on our responsibility.

Some people who don't know God treat their parents very well; in their case I have noticed that they are blessed with a long life. Obeying the *principles* of God works for everybody, even when they do not necessarily know the *Person* of God.

But I do believe that God has a perfect will for the lives and deaths of His own believers, those who welcome God's intervention and ask God to actively guide their lives. Abraham, Isaac and Jacob are illustrations of such Providential care.

Romans 12:2 says, "And do not be conformed to this world, but be transformed by the renewing of your mind, that you may prove what is that good and acceptable and perfect will of God." You see here 3 levels of God's will: the good, acceptable and perfect. Not every Christian is in the acceptable and perfect will of God. The only way to be is to fulfill 2 conditions: 1) to "not be conformed to this world" and 2) to "be transformed" by studying God's Word till His Word changes our pattern of thinking, speaking and behaving.

When we first come to understand that God wants us to be saved from our sins through the sacrifice of His Son Jesus, and we believe it, we are immediately put in the "good will" of God. But it does not mean we move straight into the perfect will of God. There is training and preparation involved to move us into our ultimate destiny. Even though we are saved, we may chose to obey or disobey God's plan.

Here are two examples. When Israel asked the prophet Samuel for a king (so they could be like other nations), Samuel told them this was not God's perfect will. But they insisted and persisted in asking. Therefore God told Samuel to give them what they wanted, not what He wanted. From this point onwards, Israel slid back into God's "acceptable will". They were no longer in His perfect will.

As Samuel warned, the results of being in the "acceptable will" of God were that they paid higher taxes and fought more wars for their human king than they would have under the Lord's theocratic system. Eventually the kingdom of Israel was divided by civil strife and destroyed by multiple foreign invasions.

Every believer is given a choice to discover God's will and follow it. Isaiah 38:1 and 2 Kings 20:1 record another illustration of the contrast between God's acceptable and perfect will: "In those days Hezekiah was sick and near death. And Isaiah the prophet, the son of Amoz, went to him and said to him, 'Thus says the Lord: 'Set your house in order, for you shall die and not live.'"

King Hezekiah wept and prayed to God that He would remember how he had "done what is good in Your sight." God heard his prayer, agreed Hezekiah had been good, and told Isaiah, "Go and tell Hezekiah, 'Thus says the Lord, the God of David your father: 'I have heard your prayer, I have seen your tears; surely I will add to your days fifteen years'" (Isaiah 38:5).

Now, I believe healing is the will of God, but was Hezekiah in the perfect will of God? Clearly not. Isaiah had already told him what the perfect will of God was in this case. Hezekiah had lived a good life and done good. Like Abraham, Isaac and Jacob, God had a perfect timing for Hezekiah's life and death.

Hezekiah refused God's perfect will and asked for God's acceptable will. God agreed and gave him 15 more years to live. 15 is the number of something hidden. Why might God have not wanted Hezekiah to live 15 more years? Did you think about it? What did God know that Hezekiah didn't know?

2 Kings 21:1 tells us what Hezekiah couldn't have known. We find out what happened immediately after Hezekiah's death: "Manasseh was twelve years old when he became king, and he reigned fifty-five years in Jerusalem." What kind of king was he?

> "...Manasseh seduced them to do more evil than the nations whom the Lord had destroyed before the children of Israel...Because Manasseh king of Judah has done these abominations (he has acted more wickedly than all the Amorites who were before him, and has also made Judah sin with his idols), therefore thus says the Lord God of Israel: 'Behold, I am bringing such calamity upon Jerusalem and Judah, that whoever hears of it, both his ears will tingle...Moreover Manasseh shed very much innocent blood, till he had filled Jerusalem from one end to another, besides his sin by which he made Judah sin, in doing evil in the sight of the Lord." (2 Kings 21:9,11-12,16)

Manasseh became one of the longest-reigning and the most wicked kings in David's dynasty. He was 12 years old when he ascended the throne, which means that he was born within the 15 year extension period given to Hezekiah!

Had Hezekiah accepted God's perfect timing, Manasseh would have never been born, Israel would have not suffered for 55 years, and calamity would not have come upon the nation.

God's way are better than our ways, but He offers us free choice. He defines for us 3 levels of His will: good, acceptable and perfect.

The idea that "God is sovereign" and therefore God controls us and forces His will on us is contradicted by many stories in the Bible, including Israel making Saul their king and Hezekiah asking for extra years.

Often people suffer not because it's God's fault, but because they don't wait on God long enough to surrender to His perfect will. They pursue selfish ambition, quick opportunities or good ideas which are not God's plan. God allows freedom while He invites us to pursue His plan.

For some, like Peter and Paul, His perfect plan included suffering, persecution and the death of a martyr. For others, like John, that included persecution, a long life, and a peaceful death.

We must not refuse loss when God calls us to it, because God calls us to the way of the Cross. 15 reminds us of Jesus' burial, of Jacob's age when his grandfather died, of the steps ascending from the Women's Court to the Men's Court, and of Hezekiah's extra years which should have been avoided. 15 is a number of "hidden things".

16

16 IS double new beginning—8 x 2 = 16. 16 is completeness in 'reduced gematria'—1 + 6 = 7. 16 is an important rite of passage for young people. Girls celebrate their "sweet 16." Boys look forward to getting their drivers' permit or license, depending on the country they live in.

In Acts 2, the first disciples to be baptized with the Holy Spirit spoke in the tongues of 16 nationalities. The onlookers from 16 regions of the world thought they were drunk and asked, "And how is it that we hear, each in our own language in which we were born?" (v. 8)

In 1 Corinthians 13, Love has 16 characteristics: "Love

1. suffers long and
2. is kind;
3. love does not envy;
4. love does not parade itself,
5. is not puffed up;
6. does not behave rudely,
7. does not seek its own,

8. is not provoked,
9. thinks no evil;
10. does not rejoice in iniquity,
11. but rejoices in the truth;
12. bears all things,
13. believes all things,
14. hopes all things,
15. endures all things.
16. Love never fails."

16 is most prominent in the ministry of Elisha. Elisha performed 16 miracles exactly double of Elijah's 8. This is a divine response to Elisha's request for a "double portion" of his mentor's anointing. Not only were Elisha's miracles greater numerically, they were sometimes greater qualitatively.

Below is a table of miracles performed by Elijah and Elisha. (We are not counting prophetic utterances as miracles, for then the number would be untold.) By the end of Elisha's ministry, he had only performed 15 miracles. So God granted his dead bones, no doubt saturated with the double anointing, to resurrect a dead man (2 Kings 13:20-21). This posthumous miracle made 16 miracles in total!

We should find comfort in this fact: the anointing can last beyond us. We can all dwell in God's Presence to the point that His anointing saturates our being and bones, and spills over into our shadows or clothes, like it did for Peter and Paul (Acts 5:15, Acts 19:11-12). No doubt we can pass our anointing on to our disciples and children who wish to follow us, as Moses did for Joshua, Elijah did for Elisha, and Paul did for Timothy.

16 is the number of the double portion of anointing.

MIRACLES OF ELIJAH	OT REFERENCE	MIRACLES OF ELISHA	OT REFERENCE
1. Causing rain to stop for 3 ½ years	1 Kings 17:1	1. Parting the Jordan River	2 Kings 2:13-15
2. Multiplying the barrel of meal and cruse of oil	1 Kings 17:4	2. Healing the water	2 Kings 2:19-22
3. Resurrecting the widow's son	1 Kings 17:22	3. Cursing 42 mockers who died by bear mauling	2 Kings 2:23-25
4. Calling fire from Heaven	1 Kings 18:20-40	4. Filling the valley with water without rain	2 Kings 3:16-20
5. Causing it to rain	1 Kings 18:45	5. Defeating the Moabites	2 Kings 3:21-23
6. Outrunning the king's chariot for about 50 kilometers	1 Kings 18:46	6. Multiplying the widow's oil	2 Kings 4:1-7
7. Calling fire from Heaven on soldiers	2 Kings 1:9-12	7. Healing the Shunammite's infertility	2 Kings 4:16
8. Parting the Jordan River	2 Kings 2:7-8	8. Resurrecting the Shunammite's son	2 Kings 4:32-37
		9. Healing food poisoning	2 Kings 4:38-41
		10. Multiplying bread for 100 men	2 Kings 4:42-44
		11. Healing Naaman the leper	2 Kings 5:1-14
		12. Cursing Gehazi with leprosy	2 Kings 5:27
		13. Making an axe head float	2 Kings 6:1-7
		14. Blinding the Syrian Army	2 Kings 6:18-19
		15. Healing the Syrians' blindness	2 Kings 6:20-23
		16. Resurrecting the Moabite man	2 Kings 13:20-21

17

17 IS the number of victory.

5 (grace) + 12 (authority) = 17 (victory).
7 (perfect) + 10 (justice) = 17 (victory).

Victory is defined by the victor. One person's victory is another person's defeat. Noah had victory over mockers when God began to flood the earth on the 17th day of the second Hebrew month (Genesis 7:11). Noah's ark rested on the mount of Ararat on the 17th day of the seventh Hebrew month (in Genesis this was 'Nisan'). The Red Sea parted on the 17th of Nisan. Jesus resurrected on the the 17th of Nisan.

Joseph was sold as a slave by his brothers at the age of 17. It seemed his brothers had gained victory over him, but in reality, God set Joseph on a new path of development which was necessary for him to become a world leader. Neither his father nor mother nor brothers would have chosen this path for him, so really Joseph's victory began from the age of 17. (The Life of Joseph course is one of our best series. If you're going through a process you cannot understand, or you think this is the end, you should watch this series.)[1]

Jacob, the father of Joseph, lived in Egypt for 17 years. They must have been the 17 happiest years of his life, as he was finally reunited with the son whom he thought he had lost. Peace was restored to Jacob for 17 beautiful years.

On the 17th of September 1787, America won a great victory over tyranny. On that day, the US Constitution was signed by 39 delegates to the Federal Convention, including George Washington. Many nations have defeated tyrants only to become tyrannical themselves. Besides the Bible, the most successful legal document ever crafted to limit government power and secure people's freedom is the US Constitution.

EVERY 17 YEARS, with few exceptions, the US is involved in a war.[2]

- 1746—**The middle of King George's War** (1744-1748). Britain and France were enemies in the Old World and when their empires expanded across the Atlantic Ocean, they brought their wars to the New World. This was the Third French and Indian War, known by the French as the Third Intercolonial War. British colonies made a failed attempt to conquer Canada. Remember that land north of the 13 colonies and west of the Mississippi River was part of 'New France'. Under President Thomas Jefferson, America purchased the 'Louisiana Territory' of New France—530 million acres of land in which 15 present states fit. Napoleon parted with the real estate because he needed the money to fund his wars. The 'Louisiana Purchase' cost 68 million francs or $15 million ($600 billion in today's value). Canada was 'New France' from 1534 to 1763.

- 1763—**The end of the Fourth French and Indian War** (1754-1763). In the terms of the Treaty of Paris 1763, France ceded all of Canada to Britain. The lingering frontier disputes and war costs from this war led to the American Revolution.
- 1780—**The middle of the American Revolution War** (1775-1783). America declared independence in 1776 but truly became independent in 1781 at the defeat of the British and surrender of General Charles Cornwallis at Yorktown on **17** October 1781. Yes, another 17! The Peace of Paris ending the war and dealing with Britain's relations with nations that supported the Americans—France, Spain and the Dutch Republic—was not signed until 1783. Only Article 1 of this treaty, which acknowledges the United States' existence as free, sovereign, and independent states, remains in force.[3]
- 1797—**The beginning of the Quasi-War** (1798-1800). Called "quasi" because it was undeclared and fought by naval and privateer forces in the West Indies. The French monarchy was abolished in 1792, and in response the United States stopped paying its large debts to France which had supported it during the Revolutionary War, claiming the debts were owed to the previous regime. France was outraged over this and the fact that Americans were trading with their previous enemy Britain. French and American ships attacked each other for a short time. Despite many anti-French politicians' objections, President John Adams ended the war by offering peace to France.
- 1814—**the burning of Washington, D.C.** The middle of the **War of 1812** (1812-1815). Britain invaded America. America tried to invade Canada but failed. On 24 August 1814, Britain burned down the White

House and damaged the U.S. Capitol building. Although neither side lost territory after the war, there were long-term consequences. Canada's drift to be more pro-British and anti-American may be traced to this war. Canada discouraged immigration from the U.S. and showed favor towards the Anglican Church over the more Americanized Methodist Church.[4] The national tariff policy developed after this war to protect American manufacturers from European competition led to the economic downturn of the 1820s, which in turn led to the next crisis.

- 1831—**the start of the Nullification Crisis** (1832-1833). Though not an actual war, America was on the brink of war. South Carolina was hit badly by the Tariff of 1828 (known as the 'Tariff of Abominations' for setting a 38% tax on imported goods). The South had hoped that the election of President Andrew Jackson would lead to a reduction in tariffs, but Jackson did not compromise. A split between the President and his vice President John Calhoun ensued. A native of South Carolina, Calhoun was an effective proponent of the constitutional theory of state nullification: if a state didn't like a federal law, it could nullify it. In 1832, South Carolina nullified the Tariff of Abominations. Jackson accused South Carolina of treason. With only a few months remaining in his second term, Calhoun resigned as vice president and was elected Senator. Congress backed President Jackson. Under military threat, South Carolina conceded by repealing its Ordinance of Nullification in 1833. Yet the seeds of secession had been planted, and when the American Civil War broke, it started in South Carolina.

- 1848—**the end of the Mexican-American War** (1847-
1848). Tension between the two countries rose after
the American annexation of Texas in 1845. Mexico lost
this war. American victory forced Mexico to accept the
Rio Grande as its northern border with the United
States. In the terms of the Treaty of of Guadalupe
Hidalgo (1848), Mexico ceded 'Alta California' (Upper
California)—land that is now present-day California,
Arizona, New Mexico, Nevada, Utah, Colorado, and
Wyoming. Two years later, California became the 31st
state.
- 1865—**the end of the American Civil War** (1861-
1865). In the 1860 election, Republicans called for the
abolition of slavery in all U.S. territories. Leaders in
Southern slave states felt threatened that the abolition
movement would spread next to the states. In general,
the conflict can be summarized as follows: the North
upheld the Constitution, whereas the South upheld
states' rights. Unfortunately, those rights meant, for the
South, their right to slavery. When Republican
candidate Abraham Lincoln won, 7 Southern slave
states declared secession from the Union (comprising
of 34 states at the time). The 7 then formed a
'Confederate States of America' in rebellion to the U.S.
Constitution. War broke out between the Union North
and Confederate South. (If you think Donald Trump
has it bad with Democrat hostility, Abraham Lincoln
experienced worse!) On 1st January 1863, Lincoln set
all the slaves in the South legally free by an executive
order called the 'Emancipation Proclamation'. The
bloodiest battle of the Civil War was the Battle of
Gettysburg, Pennsylvania—fought from July 1-3, and
considered the military turning point in favor of the
Union. On 19 November 1863, President Lincoln

dedicated a cemetery for Union soldiers who died at
Gettysburg with a short speech which he thought, "The
world will little note, nor long remember what we say
here." On the contrary, it was one of the most effective
and best remembered speeches in the history of public
speeches. It was only 272 words or 10 sentences long.
The Civil War cost 1 million American lives or 3% of
the population, including President Lincoln's. On 14
April 1865, he was assassinated in a theater by William
Booth, an angry actor and Confederate sympathizer.
Slavery officially ended when Congress ratified the
13th Amendment in December 1865.

The Gettysburg Address is one of the must-reads for every
orator. Lincoln began with these now famous words:

"Fourscore and seven years ago (87 years ago) our
fathers brought forth, on this continent, a new
nation, conceived in liberty, and dedicated to the
proposition that all men are created equal. Now we
are engaged in a great civil war, testing whether that
nation, or any nation so conceived, and so
dedicated, can long endure. We are met on a great
battle-field of that war."

- 1882—**no war.** Thank God for grace!
- 1899—**aftermath of the Spanish-American War**
  (April-August 1898). The cause of this war was
  America's support for Cuban independence from
  Spain. War ensued in the Caribbean Sea and Pacific
  Sea. American victory led to the Treaty of Paris 1898,
  by which Spain ceded ownership of Puerto Rico, Guam
  and the Philippines to the United States, and gave the
  U.S. temporary control of Cuba. The course of Filipino

history was altered as America imposed English as the language of schools. In 1935, the constitution recognized English as a co-official language with Spanish. In 1937, the National Language Institute was given the task of developing a national language based on one of the existing native languages. Tagalog was chosen as the base language as it was spoken by one-third of the population. In 1973, the constitution renamed Tagalog as Filipino and made it a co-official language with English. Coming back to the Americanization of the Philippines, after Japan invaded and occupied the Philippines during World War II, America recaptured the Philippines in 1945. America signed the Treaty of Manilla in 1946, by which it relinquished sovereignty over the islands. The Philippines shares the same independence day as America—July 4th.

- 1916—**the middle of World War I** (1914-1918). This war ended the "old world order"—the legal system which European states developed in the 17th century and spent hundreds of years imposing on other nations. Four imperial dynasties collapsed: the Habsburgs of Austria-Hungary, the Hohenzollerns of Germany, the Sultanate of the Ottoman Empire, and the Romanovs (czars) of Russia. This led to the October Revolution (24-25 October 1917), by which Vladimir Lenin the founder and leader of the Bolshevik Party seized control of Russia and became the first head of the Soviet Union. World War I was unprecedented in carnage, killing 37 million humans.
- 1933—**no war.** But...

...something did happen which would lead to the worst war of human history. In 1928, spurred on by the idealism of the "**outlawry of war**" movement, the United States, Japan and 43 other nations signed the Pact of Paris, aka Kellogg–Briand Pact, officially the 'General Treaty for Renunciation of War as an Instrument of National Policy.' Signatories agreed to:

> "Condemn and abandon forever the use of war as an instrument for the settlement of international disputes and for the enforcement of decisions and awards of international tribunals, and hereby outlaw the immemorial institution of war by making its use a public crime as the fundamental law of nations."

Looking back at it now, we can see it was a laughable ideal. It should have never been signed by any nation that understood the Bible. God made nations to be a check and balance on each other; when one nation goes bad—as often does—other nations have a divine mandate to not only protect its people against invasion, but to be an instrument of judgment against evil. Idealistic humanists do not understand why God sanctioned wars in the Bible. They deem it as cruel and barbaric. They think they can do better than God. This same spirit led to the Pact of Paris, which then led to the worst war in human history.

Godless nations will not abide by a code of conduct, keep promises or act morally. Japan was first to violate the Pact of Paris by invading Manchuria (Northeast China), raping and pillaging her people till 1945. According to Dr. Gordon Lindsay, "The League of Nations met, condemned Japan, but did nothing further, thus encouraging Mussolini and Hitler in their later military adventures."[5]

The nations were under *moral* obligation to punish Japan for violating her promise, but under *legal* obligation not to use force to enforce the Treaty. It was utterly stupid. If America had not signed the pact, she would have stopped Japan dead in her tracks. Instead, leaders dallied and war was delayed.

Instead of winning an easy victory against Japan in 1931, America was bombed at Pearl Harbor, then fought Japan on one front and Germany on another front from 1941-1945. At the end of World War II, 55 million souls died violent deaths and another 28 million died from war-related disease and famine.

By outlawing war, idealists who ignored Bible truths increased misery and suffering to worldwide proportions. This is why it does not matter whether we *like* what the Bible says or not, it is true. The Bible indicates: 1) wars will not cease until every sinner is gone, 2) it is better for believers to plan for war than be caught off-guard or destroyed. In God's plan for Israel, He developed a strong, peace-loving people by taking them through battles. We cannot be smarter than God.

 JUDGES 3:1-2 (NLT)
1 These are the nations that the LORD left in the land to test those Israelites who had not experienced the wars of Canaan.
2 He did this to teach warfare to generations of Israelites who had no experience in battle.

The Bible says that one day, another idealist like these 'outlawry buffoons' will rise to dupe another generation by promises of 'peace without God'. This Anti-Christ *"shall magnify himself in his heart, and by PEACE shall destroy many"* (Daniel 8:25). The last days will be filled with promises of peace, but *"the end thereof shall be with a flood, and unto the end of the war desolations are determined"* (Daniel 9:26). I guarantee wars will not cease till every sinner surrenders, one-by-one, to the Prince of Peace.

- 1950—**The start of the Korean War** (1950-1953). After World War II (1939-1945), Korea was split into communist North Korea and republic South Korea. The North invaded the South in June 1950. China and

Russia backed the North. The United States and United
Nations backed the South. The result was that the
North was repelled and a demilitarized zone was
created to separate the two Koreas, but tension
continues along the border, no peace treaty was ever
signed, so the two Koreas are technically still at war.
Turkey joined NATO in 1952 as a result of this
conflict. During post-war recovery, South Korea
experienced one of the biggest prayer revivals on earth.
At least 30% of South Koreans converted to
Christianity and the largest born again churches in the
world—one with 800,000 members (*Yoido Full Gospel
Church*)—are in South Korea.

- 1967—This was a landmark year for Israel. **The Six-
Day War** was won in 6 days from 5-10 June. Israel
captured Gaza and the Sinai Peninsula from Egypt, the
West Bank from Jordan, and the Golan Heights from
Syria. Control over Jerusalem was also regained by the
Israelis, though they ceded administration of the
Temple Mount to the Waqf under Jordanian
custodianship. For America, she was in the middle of
her worst war. The **Vietnam War** lasted 19 years from
1955 to 1973 and engulfed Vietnam, Laos and
Cambodia. America entered this war in 1965 to fight
off the communist North from taking over the South.
58,000 Americans perished for the cause. America was
losing, so President Richard Nixon began withdrawing
troops in 1969. The U.S. ceased all combat activity on
15 January 1973. The Communist North won and
reunified the country under communist ideology. This
started the Cambodia-Vietnamese War, which led to
the boat people crisis that brought many Asian
refugees to Australia.

- 1984—The ominous year of **George Orwell's dystopic novel '1984'** (the inverse of 1948) did not actually produce a war. The **Cold War** between the Soviet Union and America (1974-1991) was escalating to a climactic close. (Interestingly, it was George Orwell who coined the term "cold war" in his essay "You and the Atomic Bomb" published in 1945.) President Ronald Reagan pursued "**peace through strength**" in the first term of his presidency, building up the U.S. military to be a powerful deterrent against any would-be enemy daring to make first strike. Some Americans feared "peace through strength" would bring a nuclear arms race that would lead to Armageddon. But Reagan had correctly assessed the Soviet Union. Unlike his predecessors, Reagan did not view the communist country as equal to the United States. He did not even view them as morally legitimate, due to its totalitarian tendencies, and called it an "evil empire" in 1983. He expected it would go bankrupt trying to compete with America on military spending, fighting its war in Afghanistan (dubbed the 'Soviet Vietnam'), and trying to sell oil when his policy successfully reduced the price of oil. After Regan was re-elected in 1984 to a second term, he met with the Soviet General Secretary Mikhail Gorbachev in Geneva in November 1985 and in Reykjavík in October 1986. In a speech on 12 June 1987, Reagan referred to the wall that separated communist East Berlin from free market West Berlin and told the Soviet leader, "Mr. Gorbachev, open this gate...Mr. Gorbachev, tear down this wall!" The wall indeed fell on 9 November 1989, and the Soviet Union dissolved into 15 independent states on 26 December 1991. President Reagan ended and won the Cold War without firing a shot. His faith in God, his eloquence in defending freedom, and his Presidential legacy make him one of the greatest Presidents in American history.

- 2001—**The 9/11 terrorist attack**. On September 11, Muslims from the Islamic terrorist group Al Qaeda hijacked 4 passenger airplanes and flew them into New York's Twin Towers and Washington's Pentagon, killing 2996 people. As passengers in the fourth airplane heard news of the other plane crashes, they understood this was a suicide mission and tried to subdue the terrorists on board. United Airline Flight 93 crashed in a field in Pennsylvania. The leader of the operation became the most common household name for evil: **Osama bin Laden**, often referred to in the news as 'UBL'. Even though 15 out of the 19 hijackers were citizens of Saudi Arabia, President George W. Bush decided to retaliate by going to war against Iraq and Afghanistan. Ten years later, under the presidency of Barack Obama, Osama bin Laden was found hiding in a private compound in Abbottabad, Pakistan. He was shot dead on 2 May 2011.

Islamic terrorist attacks continue to be yearly tragedies, and their frequency has inoculated the population to what used to be intolerable and offensive. In 2016, London's Muslim mayor Sadiq Khan went so far as to claim that terror attacks in London were now "part and parcel of living in a big city".

When acts of terror occurred before 2014, they used to shock us. Decent people blamed the perpetrators and politicians demanded justice. Justice restored peace. Today, the attacks have become so frequent that the media apologizes for the perpetrators. The apologists twist history and claim that terrorism occurs not because terrorists are evil, but because the victims may have criticized Islam or demonized their faith. This adds insult to injury because we are told that terrorists are justified to attack us because of 'Islamophobia'. When did this Islamophobia begin?

Crusades vs Jihads

History records that Islam has subjugated other civilizations for 1400 years, in other words, long before European colonization or America's political existence. Dr. Bill Warner estimated that from 632AD to 1922 (before the modern age of terrorism), Islam launched 548 offensive battles against other civilizations.[6]

By contrast, there were 7-9 main crusades from 1095 to 1291, lasting 196 years. They began as defensive wars to rescue Christians persecuted by Muslim invaders of Christian nations, but some soldiers were ungodly and ended up persecuting Jews and Muslims. The Catholic church (no Protestant was involved) stopped all crusade activity over 700 years ago. Jihad is still ongoing and never-ending.

To understand how long it took for the Crusades to start rescuing Christians in foreign lands, consider the world's passive and slow response to the slaughter of Christians since 9/11:

22 September 2013—"Peshawar Church Bombing". Twin suicide bombings at All Saints Church in Peshawar, Pakistan (killing 127 Christian worshippers and injuring over 250).
26 July 2016—Two ISIS terrorists slit a French priest's throat and held four nuns hostage in a church in Rouen, France.
19 December 2016—"Christmas Market Attack". A Muslim terrorist drove a truck into the Christmas market next to the Kaiser Wilhelm Memorial Church in Berlin (killing 12 and injuring 56).
17 December 2017—"Pre-Christmas Church Bombing" in

Quetta, Pakistan (killing 9 Christian worshippers and injuring 50).

13 May 2018— "2018 Surabaya Bombings". Three churches bombed in Surabaya, Indonesia by Islamists who used children aged 9, 12, 16 and 18 in the attack (killing at least 15 Christians).

27 January 2019—two bomb explosions planted in one church in Jolo, the Philippines (killing 20 Christians and injuring 100s).

21 April 2019—"Sri Lanka Easter Bombings". A series of explosions in three churches and and four hotels during Easter celebration (killing 200 and injuring nearly 500).

In response to continuous atrocities against Christians, no world leader took any action other than a verbal token, "I strongly condemn this act of extremism." Compare this passive reaction to the same leaders' instant and massive response to one shooting at a mosque in Christchurch on 15 March 2019 by a left-wing environmentalist communist.

New Zealand Prime Minister's Jacinda Ardern called for an immediate gun ban (punishing New Zealand's law-abiding citizens), wore a hijab in solidarity with Muslims (even though the hijab is not a symbol of Islam but a symbol of female subjugation in many countries like Iran), and broadcasted on Friday the 'Muslim call to prayer' nationwide (declaring over New Zealand for the first time in its history "There is no god but Allah").

The lack of proportional response to modern killing of Christians is a perfect parallel to how Europe reacted when Medieval Christians were persecuted, beheaded, and driven from their homes from the 7th century to the 11th century. Entire Christian nations like Syria (where believers were first called Christians) were converted to Islam. European Christians passively stood by until the persecution reached a tipping point.

Then the Crusades were initiated. Islamic aggression, not Islamophobia, has been a driving force in the history of Europe.

Muslims invaded Christian Spain in 711 and Islamized the Iberian Peninsula till they were expelled in 1492. Muslims tried to invade Christian France and were repelled at the Battle of Tours in 732. Turkish Muslims tried to invade Western Europe in the Siege of Vienna in 1529. Turkish Muslims arrived at the gates of Vienna again in 1683 but were finally repelled from Europe in the Battle of Vienna. The Ottoman Turks deported, starved and murdered 1.5 million Armenian Christians in a genocidal campaign from 1915 to 1917.

These acts of aggression, violence and terror have nothing to do with poverty, Western colonialism, or American foreign policy. On the contrary, America may have been discovered because of Ottoman Muslim conquest of Bulgaria in 1396 and the Fall of Christian Constantinople in 1453. Christians fled the formerly Christian Byzantine Empire. Forced conversions, massacres, and persecution of Christians deterred European traders from using the ancient trade route to the East. Explorers like Christopher Columbus searched for an alternate trade route. Columbus headed west for Asia and found America. *Persecution of Christians, not Islamophobia*, has been the historical force of European conflicts and mass migration. History dispels many falsehoods and provide context for us to understand the next terrorist act.

- 2018—victory over Islamic terror group ISIS. In 2014, ISIS declared itself a caliphate, seized territories in Iraq and Syria, and terrorized people in the region. On the 17th of November 2017 (yes, two 17's), US military forces retook Raqqah—the last prominent city held by ISIS in Iraq & Syria. This was a critical breakthrough in the global war on terror. Donald Trump was able to accomplish it in less than a year from taking office (on

January 20th), whereas Barack Obama could not do it during his entire second term in office when the terrorist group grew in power. By 2018, ISIS no longer controlled Iraq and Syria. On 20 March 2019, President Trump declared that total victory over ISIS in Syria was within hours. $2 + 0 + 3 + 2 + 0 + 1 + 9 = 17$. Kurdish-led Syrian Democratic Forces (SDF) won the Battle of Baghuz, ending the last stand of ISIS in Syria and declaring final victory.

- 2035—? It will be very close to the 2000th anniversary of Christ's crucifixion.
- 2052—?
- 2069—?
- 2086—? Close to a watch date that appears in Chapters 58 and 708.

ELECTION 2020

The next Presidential election will be on 3 November 2020 which is 17 Cheshvan 5781 on the Hebrew calendar—the same day Noah's Flood began. This, on the surface, is not a good sign, as the flood was destructive, yet it was also cleansing. The election will be controversial for sure, yet it turn into victory for truth seekers and justice lovers. "In the six hundredth year of Noah's life, in the second month, the SEVENTEENTH day of the month, on that day all the fountains of the great deep were broken up, and the windows of heaven were opened" (Genesis 7:11). God's flood to expose and drain away the Deep State Swamp will begin on the 17th.

(Amazingly, despite a Democrat controlled Presidency and Congress, *Roe vWade* was overturned on 24 June 2022. The Church must use this same judicial power to deal with other injustices, not only abortion. The collapse of FTX in November

2022 and Elon Musk's release of the secret Twitter Files in December 2022 are more signs God is exposing corruption and judging the global elites.)

ISRAEL & Jesus

The Israelites left Egypt on the 14th of Nisan and arrived at the Red Sea on the 17th —the day they were miraculously delivered. The Red Sea parted, the Israelites walked through the parted waters, and the Egyptian army followed, only to be destroyed by the closing waters. For Israel, the 17th of Nisan represented the death of their old life and the beginning of a new life by God's saving power. All they had to do was believe God and follow God's representative Moses.

Moses ordered the Israelites to celebrate the 17th of Nisan forever as the Feast of Firstfruits—a feast symbolizing victory and new start. 1600 years later, Jesus Christ (the Messiah) fulfilled this true meaning of this feast by becoming the "firstfruits" of all who would be raised from the dead (1 Corinthians 15:20-23).

For 40 years Israel wandered the desert, surviving on manna which God provided from Heaven. As good as manna was, Israel complained that it was bland and tasteless. One day before they entered the Promised Land, this provision of manna stopped on the 16th of Nisan. Israel entered the Promised Land on the 17th of Nisan and began to eat the new fruits there (Joshua 5:10-12). New life, new tastes, new experiences began on the 17th!

All these 17's point to the greatest victory on earth. Jesus conquered death and hell when He rose from the grave on the 17th of Nisan.

 MARK 16:9
Now when He rose early on the first day of the

week [17th of Nisan], He appeared first to Mary Magdalene, out of whom He had cast seven demons.

Jesus became the Ark of Safety, the Defeater of Satan and the First Fruit from the dead on the 17th. All human history pivots on the victory of this day!

After the ancient Israelites became proud and refused to listen to the prophets who warned them of pending destruction, God had victory over the unbelievers in His own nation on the 17th of Tammuz 586 BC. On this day Nebuchadnezzar's army breached the walls of Jerusalem. The Babylonian siege continued for three weeks until Solomon's Temple was destroyed on the 9th of Av. This three-week summer period (a type of Tribulation) is remembered by a total ban on weddings. Rabbis will not perform marriage ceremonies during this summer period beginning on the 17th of Tammuz.

Even though this tragedy seemed like a defeat, the loss of the Temple proved to the Jews that they could not rely on their pedigree or on external symbols of religion, but must be ready to follow the Messiah for their salvation. This purification of Jewish faith prepared a refined people like Joseph and Mary to welcome the arrival of Messiah into their home and the first Jewish apostles to follow Messiah even unto death. These people no longer looked to the Temple nor the guardians of the Temple (the priests and Pharisees), but to the Creator of the Temple—the Messiah!

God used the breach of the Wall of Jerusalem on the 17th of Tammuz to bring about His plan, to give us some of the best believers who ever lived—Jews who understood the true meaning of faith in God! Today, many people are still impressed by the grandeur of cathedrals, bank buildings and corporate headquarters, but God wants a refined people who understand that none of these things will last like faith in Christ.

17 things cannot separate us from the love of God.[7] Romans

8:35-39 says, "Who shall separate us from the love of Christ? Shall...

1. tribulation, or
2. distress, or
3. persecution, or
4. famine, or
5. nakedness, or
6. peril, or
7. sword? ...Yet in all these things we are more than conquerors through Him who loved us. For I am persuaded that...
8. neither death
9. nor life,
10. nor angels
11. nor principalities
12. nor powers,
13. nor things present
14. nor things to come,
15. nor height
16. nor depth,
17. nor any other created thing, shall be able to separate us from the love of God which is in Christ Jesus our Lord.

The numerical value of the Hebrew word good (*tov*) is 17. There is a wedding tradition of showering the groom with nuts on the sabbath before his wedding, right after he makes his trip up to the Torah (called aliyah) to recite blessings. Why nuts? Jewish rabbis explain this Jewish custom by the fact that the numerical value of the Hebrew word for nut (*egoz*) is the same as that of good (*tov*): 17.

Although counting the numerical values of words and names may seem odd to Gentile Christians today, one must not forget that God tells believers in the book of Revelation to "calculate the number of the beast, for it is the number of a man: His number is 666" (Revelation 13:18). The Apostles were familiar with the proper use of Biblical gematria. It is not to be confused with astrology or kabbalah, which are forbidden practices. Numbers were made by God to point to the things of God. In the Bible, 17 means victory and 17 is good!

18

18 CAN MEAN life or bondage. Jews consider 18 to be the number of life as the numerical value of the Hebrew word life (*hai*)—*het* (8) + *yod* (10) is 18. Man breathes an average of 18 breaths per minute. When man (6) meets God (3), man has life (18). 6 x 3 = 18. Jews often give monetary gifts in multiples of 18. Deuteronomy 17:17 warns any future king of Israel, "Neither shall he multiply wives to himself, that his heart turn not away [from serving the Lord]," but the Scripture did not indicate how many was too many. The Talmud specifies that a Jewish king should take no more than 18 wives and concubines in total.[1]

There are 18 feast days commanded by God in the Torah: 7 days for Passover + 1 for Shavuot + 1 for Yom Teruah + 1 for Yom Kippur + 7 for Sukkot + 1 for Shemini Atzeret. These feast days give us a taste of the life to come.[2]

18 is a significant milestone for many young adults, being the age at which they can be legally married, go to war, drive a car unaccompanied and vote for leaders, depending on which country they live in.

Throughout the Bible, 18 also has a negative meaning, referring to bondage and calamity. Jesus healed a woman whom "Satan has bound" for 18 years (Luke 13:11). 18 people were killed by the collapse of the tower in Siloam (Luke 13:4). In Judges 3:14, the Moabites kept Israel in bondage for 18 years, "So the children of Israel served Eglon the king of Moab eighteen years." In Judges 10:7-8, the Philistines and Ammonites put Israel in bondage for 18 years, "So the anger of the Lord was hot against Israel; and He sold them into the hands of the Philistines and into the hands of the people of Ammon. From that year they harassed and oppressed the children of Israel for eighteen years —all the children of Israel who were on the other side of the Jordan in the land of the Amorites, in Gilead."

The 18th Amendment to the US Constitution prohibited alcoholic drinks. Prohibition created the opposite effect than intended. That usually happens when we try to be more righteous than the Bible requires. Lawmakers make a mistake when they attempt to be stricter than the Bible (which doesn't prohibit alcohol—ask any Jewish rabbi, including Jesus who turned water into wine) or less strict than the Bible (which prohibits pedophilia and sodomy—both of which left-wing activists want legalized). The 18th Amendment forced alcohol sellers and buyers into the black market and increased crime, yielding no benefit. It was bondage. It was repealed by the 21st Amendment.

Psalm 18 is David's song of victory "on the day when the Lord delivered him from the hand of all his enemies, and from the hand of Saul." It is similar to 2 Samuel 22.

The Hallel, a recitation of Psalms 113-118, may be recited 18 times a year:

- On the first day of Passover.
- One the day of Pentecost (Shavuot).

- On the eight days of the Feast of Tabernacles (Sukkot), and
- On the eight days of the Feast of Dedication (Hanukah).

For Jewish children, learning how to pray starts with reciting the *Shema*[3] (which affirms monotheism) and the *Shemoneh Esre* ("The 18" or literally "8 + 10"), originally an 18-point prayer central to Judaism. Jewish adults pray the *Shema* twice a day - evening and morning. Children say it before they go to bed. Torah-observant Jews pray the *Shemoneh Esre* 3 times a day - evening, morning and afternoon - while standing up. For this reason it is also known as the *Amidah* (Standing) and *Tefilah* (The Prayer).

The 18-point prayer is composed of 3 parts: 3 Praises to God, 13 Petitions of God, and 3 Thanksgivings to God. 3 + 13 + 3 = 19. So why do rabbis call it "The 18"? Because an extra, ungracious request against heretics was added in the 2nd century in response to heresies, including what rabbis perceived as the growing threat of Christianity. The name "The 18" reminds us that there should be 18 not 19 points to the proper prayer.

Any prayer template believers choose to follow should serve as a model, a guide or an inspiration, not to be recited mindlessly. That is not called praying to God, but trying to make merit for yourself. Jesus taught us against praying "vain repetitions" which Orthodox Jews were fond of doing. Catholics do the same when they perform the duty of the rosary beads. Easterners do the same and call such repetitions corresponding to prayer beads "mantras". Some repetition is required to develop a habit of prayer, but if we stop there, it is not really prayer.

What Christians now call the "Lord's Prayer"[4] may be a concise version of the *Amida* as it follows the same basic structure of praise, petition, and thanksgiving. The Lord's Prayer is not technically a new covenant prayer as Jesus had not yet died, risen and paid the price for Redemption. As He drew closer to the Cross, Jesus taught new covenant believers to pray in His Name.[5] You can find models of New Testament praying based on using Scriptures for different situations at our ministry website[6].

19

19 IS the number of royalty, gold and faith. There were 19 kings of Israel and 19 kings of Judah. King David had 19 sons: 6 born in Hebron, 4 in Jerusalem by Bathsheba, and 9 others in Jerusalem by other wives. According to 1 Chronicles 3:1-9, daughters and sons of concubines were omitted.

The Golden Number

The royal metal is gold. Gold weighs 19 times heavier than water. Genesis 2:12 says there was gold in the Garden of Eden, "And the gold of that land is good." The Hebrew gematria of "the gold" (*ha zahab*) is 19. The atomic number of gold is 79. You may be asking, "What's the relation between 19 and 79?" They are related on at least two levels.

Genesis 2:8 says, "The Lord God planted a garden eastward in Eden, and there He put the man whom He had formed." He also put the gold (19) in His garden. The Hebrew value for "garden of Yahweh" is 79, the atomic number of gold.[1]

The Gregorian year 2019 is the Hebrew year 5779, or as we

would abbreviate them '19 = '79. You can say 2019 is the "golden year" for the Church. Naturally 2019 means uncommon opportunities for the Church to prosper; spiritually it means many Christians will experience a new level of authority and productivity. 2019 has been a hallmark year for Discover Ministries, when we acquired property to build upon after 19 years of renting many facilities.[2] This book is printed in 2019.

Gold is symbolic of divinity, incorruptibility and justice. Gold is never consumed. Even when it is used in technology, dentistry or medicine, it remains gold. It is a store of value. Every buyer of gold can become a seller of gold. So why are we not using gold as our money like our ancestors did for four thousand years?

Precisely because it is honest money—the only money that has stood the test of time. Fiat money has always been devalued and suffered permanent loss of value. Gold is a standard of financial justice, restricting the appetite of politicians to spend without accountability.

Before paper money, government could only spend the money it collected from its citizens' taxes. It could only pay for wars with gold, so when gold reserves depleted, wars had to end. Gold kept megalomaniacs in check. When paper money was created, it was meant to be a promise to pay gold, not a replacement of gold. After Richard Nixon took paper money off the gold standard in 1971, politicians could spend money they did not have by printing more paper money, thus devaluing the currency, which is an indirect form of taxation. The savers lose their wealth by inflation.

Gold preserves its owners' purchasing power, encouraging people to store it and become savers. Paper money destroys its holders' wealth, encouraging people to spend it and become debtors. It is in the interest of central governments to keep the world off the gold standard, because by the fiat system, spenders plunder the savers.

It is not hard to see that governments, by their over-printing and over-spending, are not only perpetuating global wars, but also leading us towards a financial Armageddon. For the first time in human history, all nations have abandoned gold-backed money and are printing money whose value is based on solely on faith.

The Number of Faith

The number 19 ties together gold, faith, royalty and the end times. As monarchies disappeared in the 1900s, gold and gold-backed currency also disappeared in the 1900s. What has replaced them is faith—a new kind of faith in central governments. Fiat money derives its value from the people's trust in their politicians. The more people believe their government, the less they value gold. The less they trust politicians, the more they hold gold.

Modern people's naive and unquestioning trust in government is directly leading us to the end time scenario predicted in the Bible—a totalitarian tyranny under which people won't be able to buy or sell unless they trust and obey the Anti-Christ. The main thing holding this system from collapsing is global faith in American paper money, and the main thing keeping the US dollar from collapsing is the moral goodness of Americans. When Christian morality is reduced to a minimal influence upon America, evil will rise unchecked, the dollar will collapse, and a digital system based on faith in the Anti-Christ will replace it. The system will continue for a short time before all out chaos, including political imprisonments and murders. Then Christ will appear for those who believe him and refused the Mark of the Beast.

Hebrews chapter 11 commends the outstanding faith of 19 individuals or groups—often called the heroes of faith: 1) Abel, 2) Enoch, 3) Noah, 4) Abraham, 5) Sarah, 6) Isaac, 7) Jacob, 8) Joseph, 9) Moses, 10) Israel crossing the Red Sea, 11) Israel circling the walls of Jericho, 12) Rahab, 13) Gideon, 14) Barak, 15) Samson, 16) Jephthah, 17) David, 18) Samuel, 19) "the prophets"—both men and women, some of whom are identifiable, such as Daniel who stopped the mouths of lions, Isaiah who was sawn in two, John the Baptist who wandered in deserts; others are hard to identify, such as who "escaped the edge of the sword" or "had trial of mockings...scourgings... chains and imprisonment". Many could qualify. Jeremiah would qualify for both. These 19 groups of people are "faith royalty".

THE NUMBER of Time

19 is a master time cycle. It is a prime number of importance to astronomy. The metonic cycle, or the time it takes for the phases of the moon to recur on the same dates, is 19 years. In other words, if one could take a snapshot of the earth, moon and sun in relation to one another, the length of time it would take for us to see the exact same picture again is 19 years! 19 is the number for cosmic cycle.

Our Western calendar is a solar calendar. The Islamic calendar is a lunar calendar. But the Hebrew calendar instituted by God is the only solar-lunar calendar: the months follow the moon; the years follow the sun. While we add a day to our Gentile calendar every 4 years, the Hebrews add a whole month to their calendar 7 times every 19 years!

According to rabbinical understanding, all time is divided into multiples of 7s, and every 7x7 years or 49 years marks a "jubilee". Adam lived for 19 jubilees or 930 years (19 x 49 = 931 - 1 for no year "0" = 930). He was the first royalty on earth. The Book of Jubilees makes 2 interesting comments:

"And he lacked 70 years of 1000 years; for 1000 years are as 1 day in the testimony of the heavens and therefore was it written concerning the tree of knowledge: 'On the day that ye eat thereof ye shall die.' For this reason he did not complete the years of his day; for he died during it."

"For the days of the forefathers of their life were 19 jubilees; and after the Flood they began to grow less than 19 jubilees, and to decrease in jubilees, and to grow old quickly, and to be full of their days by reason of manifold tribulation and the wickedness of their ways, with the exception of Abraham."[3]

THE ROYAL NUMBER

After the glorious days of King David and King Solomon, Israel was divided into north (called Israel, Samaria or Ephraim) and south (called Judah), each with their own succession of kings.

There were 19 Kings of Israel, all of them wicked:

1. Jeroboam
2. Nadab
3. Baasha
4. Elah
5. Zimri
6. Omri (Number 6 established Samaria as capital of Israel and a rival religious center to Jerusalem; the "woman at the well" mentioned this rivalry during her conversation with Jesus in John 4; there was also a division in the northern kingdom during Omri's days, half wanting to follow Tibni, half Omri; Omri fathered a very wicked son named Ahab.)
7. Ahab (husband of idolatress Jezebel)
8. Ahaziah
9. Joram
10. Jehu
11. Jehoahaz
12. Joash
13. Jeroboam II

14. Zechariah
15. Shallum
16. Menahem
17. Pekahiah
18. Pekah
19. Hoshea.

There were 19 Kings of Judah, all descendants of King David. 7 were good, most were bad:

1. Rehobaom
2. Abijah
3. Asa
4. Jehoshaphat
5. Jehoram
6. Ahaziah, x) Queen Athaliah (the wicked daughter of Ahab and Jezebel. The only ruling queen in Judah or Israel, she reigned for 6 years, but is usually excluded from the list of kings)
7. Joash
8. Amaziah
9. Azariah or Uzziah
10. Jotham
11. Ahaz
12. Hezekiah (a leader who brought revival)
13. Manasseh (one of the worst)
14. Amon
15. Josiah (the last good king, he also saw revival)
16. Jehoahaz
17. Jehoiakim
18. Jehoiachin
19. Matthaniah (whose name was changed to Zedekiah by the King of Babylon).

Although there were 19 Kings in both Israel and Judah, their reigns were not of equal length. The northern kings were all wicked and usually died young, were replaced by conspirators or assassinated. The northern kingdom lasted only 207 years until the Assyrian Deportation[4] in 722 BC.

Judah's kings were a mix of good and bad. Some of them chose to follow the example of their father David, others rejected it. Hezekiah avoided the Assyrian Captivity by turning to God and believing Isaiah's two prophecies. Because of godly leadership, Judah was saved by the miraculous defeat of Assyria army when an angel slew 185,000 in one night (2 Kings 19). God could have and would have done the same thing for Israel, but she opted to worship idols and trust her own strength.

The southern kingdom lasted for 393 years until the Babylonian Captivity and destruction of Solomon's Temple in 586 BC. The survivors were deported to Babylon for 70 years, including Ezekiel and Daniel. Only Daniel survived the 70 years.

The stories of Israel and Judah's Kings are recorded in the books of First and Second Kings.[5] They show us how much God cares about families. God wanted fathers to teach their children the Bible because it would cause them to grow up into godly leaders for the nation. Israel failed miserably and that failure started in the kings' homes.

Judah did slightly better—the good kings show us both the blessings of the godly heritage David left his descendants; and also the opportunity children who had bad parents had to *choose God* and redeem their families. Hezekiah and Josiah both had ungodly fathers, but both *chose God* despite of their upbringing and saw revival in their days!

The reasons kings fail can be summarized into two major ones. First, allowing their children to do whatever they wanted without discipline and training. Children need involved parents who model faith and justice. Parents need to communicate to their children what they believe and why they believe it. Parents also need to do what they say. That is justice. They need to deliver swiftly on rewards and punishment, and not renege or delay. Such lessons about God and life are meant to be passed down by godly parents to their children.

Second, allowing their children to marry unbelievers. Ahab of Israel was bad, but he got worse by marrying the manipulative and idolatrous Jezebel. Jehoshaphat of Judah was a godly king, but for political advantage he married his son Jehoram to Athaliah the daughter of Ahab and Jezebel. It cost his grandson's life; Ahaziah the son of Jehoram and Athaliah accompanied the King of Israel to a war he shouldn't have been involved in (2 Kings 9). He did this because the King of Israel was his uncle - his grandfather Ahab's son and his mother's brother. After Ahaziah's death at the tender age of only 23, Jehoshaphat's decision continued to cost Judah 6 years of tyranny under Queen Athaliah who was not even part of the tribe of Judah (2 Kings 11:1-3).

Malachi 2:15 asks the question: why did God make man and woman one? Answer: "That He might seek a godly seed." One of the purposes of marriage is to give children an opportunity to grow up in a God-centered environment. That is why the Holy Spirit commanded Christians not to be "unequally yoked" with unbelievers. One reason Christians should not marry unbelievers is to avoid spiritual conflict and confusion when it's time to raise children. The children of the kings of Israel and Judah are an example for us of what denying a godly heritage can do to a child's life.

Sadly I know Christian parents who are more concerned about their child marrying someone of a particular skin color than marrying a believer. Raising children in an ungodly world is hard enough, you do not want to do your child a disservice by arguing with your spouse whether Jesus Christ is Lord or attending church every week is right. Learn from the 19 kings of Israel and 19 kings of Judah — marry only a mature believer and encourage your children to do the same!

19TH BOOK

The Book of Psalms is the 19th book of the Bible and may map out the prophetic destiny of Israel starting from the 19th century. For instance, Book 19 Psalm 48 seems to allude to the rebirth of Israel in 1948, "Beautiful in elevation, the joy of the whole earth, is Mount Zion [representing Israel]… the city of the great King… the kings assembled, they passed by together. They saw it, and so they marveled [the world marveled that Israel returned to her homeland]… as we have heard, so we have seen in the city of the LORD of hosts, in the city of our God: God will establish it forever."

The most important prophecy in the Bible, other than the coming of the Messiah, is the rebirth of Israel in 1948. It should not be surprising that God would predict it in plain words and in hidden codes. The late J.R. Church believed many of these codes are found in Israel's Psalms. Could Psalms be mapping out God's prophetic plan for Israel? Even the positioning of the book within the Bible may be a macro-clue to the year of Israel's rebirth! Psalms is 19 books from Genesis and 48 books from Revelation!

The notion that God speaks to us not only in plain words, but also in hidden codes and prophetic models is unpopular among some Christian theologians, but not so among Jewish rabbis. They have always taught that there was more to the Bible than the surface text. They believe that the Bible is supernatural, every letter has a meaning, and when Messiah comes, He will reveal the meaning of every letter and even the spaces between the letters! Most Christians today understand that beyond the plain text of the Bible, God also speaks to us through object lessons and messianic metaphors called "types" – such as the Lamb of God, the Feasts of Israel, the story of Ruth and Boaz which parallels Christ and the Gentile Church, etc.

I am not insisting that Psalms is definitely prophetic of Israel's modern events, but let us explore a few more examples before we dismiss the concept.

Book 19 Psalm 42 may correspond to the outbreak of World War II in 1942. Three times the Psalmist wrote that his soul was "cast down". Verse 9 sounds eerily like the cries of the Jews during World War II, "I will say to God my Rock, Why have You forgotten me? Why do I go mourning because of the oppression of the enemy?"

Book 19 Psalm 43 may correspond to the Holocaust: "Vindicate me, O God, and plead my cause against an ungodly nation [Germany?]; Oh, deliver me from the deceitful and unjust man [Adolf Hitler?]." Adolf Hitler deceived the rest of the world while he killed 6 million Jews.

Book 19 Psalm 45 sounds like the end of World War II in 1945: "My heart is overflowing with a good theme… Your arrows [bombs?] are sharp in the heart of the King's enemies; the peoples [Axis powers of Germany, Italy and Japan] fall under You… Instead of Your fathers shall be Your sons [a new Jewish generation assured after the Holocaust], whom You shall make princes in all the earth [many Jews have been among the top leaders of many fields in many countries]."

Book 19 Psalm 46 may be prophetic of 1946, the first full year of peace since World War II: "He makes wars cease to the end of the earth."

Book 19 Psalm 91 is the definitive "Psalm of Protection," often carried and prayed by soldiers at war. It may be prophetic of First Gulf War in 1991, in which the United States won a crushing victory against Saddam Hussein and liberated Kuwait: "You shall not be afraid of the terror by night, nor of the arrow that flies by day, nor of the pestilence [i.e. disease - the US military was very concerned that Saddam would unleash poison gas or biological weapons on them, just as he did on the Kurds] that walks in darkness, nor of the destruction that lays waste at noonday. A thousand may fall at your side, and ten thousand at your right hand; but it shall not come near you [US forces overwhelmed the dictator's military with little casualty, praise the Lord!]."

Since the 19th Book ends on the 150th Psalm, an obvious question is, "Will the world come to an end in 2050 (1900 + 150 = 2050)?" Before we jump to rash conclusions, J.R. Church drew attention to the fact David and Solomon are credited with compiling Psalms 1 to 106, but Ezra is credited with compiling Psalms 107 to 150. Psalms 1 to 106 appear to correspond to prophetic events in chronological order, however the chronology *may* break after Psalm 107. Ezra's Psalms, if we can call them that, look forward to an eternal kingdom under Messiah. No one can set the date when Messiah will come back! I am one who hopes it will be sooner than 2050! But we must work as if Christ may not come back for 100 years, and live as if Christ may return tomorrow.

If the 19th Book of the Bible were really prophetic of events starting from 1900, it would agree with the significance of the number 19 standing for the master time cycle. Whether or not the reader sees the prophetic nature of the 19th Book, the Book of Psalms certainly has many unique features: it is the longest book of the Bible; contains the longest chapter of the Bible (119) and the shortest chapter of the Bible (117); and the middle verses of the Bible (103:1-2): *"Bless the Lord, O my soul; and all that is within me, bless His holy name! Bless the Lord, O my soul, and forget not all His benefits."*[1] Charles Spurgeon once said: "The delightful study of the Psalms has yielded me boundless profit and ever-growing pleasure!"

19 HEALINGS

As I TEACH in churches and seminars, a study of every individual case of sickness and healing in the Bible is extremely helpful to obtaining your own healing. Let me summarize the highlights of my research into healing for you.

There are 19 individual healing stories in the 4 Gospel accounts, not counting all the multitudes of people Jesus healed.[1] Given 19 instances of individual healings, it would be wise to ask, "How were the sick healed?" If we can find out how they got healed, we can find out how we can get healed, because "Jesus Christ is the same yesterday, today and forever" and God never changes (Hebrews 13:8, Malachi 3:6). God is still the same Healer today and He is still healing the same way!

2 CAMPS on Healing

When it comes to healing, there are basically 2 camps: the sovereignty camp and the faith camp. The sovereignty camp holds the view that God can heal, but it's up to Him if He wants to heal you. All you can do is wait and see. If you're healed, it means it was God's will. If you're not healed, it means it must not have been His will. God gets the credit for healing, and God gets the blame for lack of healing.

The faith camp holds the view that healing (like salvation) is always God's will, but whether or not you get healed (or saved) is partly up to you. If you are not healed, it is never God's fault. There's something you either don't know or didn't do. You have a role to play in obtaining forgiveness and healing. God should never be blamed. Your salvation and healing are not all up to God, or else everybody in the world would be saved and healed right now! Each person has a responsibility to cooperate with Him. Responsibility is not a word most people like to hear. Both sides can get very emotionally charged about this subject. Which side is right?

To some extent, both sides are right. They both have merit Scripturally. Sometimes God initiates healing without any faith on the part of the sick; this is called a manifestation or move or gift of the Holy Spirit (1 Corinthians 12:1, 4, 7). Other times the sick initiates healing on their own faith. What would add value to the discussion is counting how many times Jesus approached the sick versus the sick approached Jesus.

Numbers remove emotions out of the debate. We don't need to argue about doctrine if we can count how many times Jesus approached a sick person to heal them (this number points to the sovereignty camp) and how many times the sick approached Jesus for healing (points to the faith camp).

Before I reveal the numbers, I want to reveal the *logos* or logic of divine healing. God heals because sickness is an intruder, a curse of the Fall. Old-time preachers used to say, *"Sickness is the offspring of its mother sin and its father satan."* When we see sickness attack someone, we should all be on the same side—the Healer's side. There is no record of Jesus turning a sick person away and saying what so many modern preachers claim, "Stay sick so that God can teach you a lesson" or "Remain sick for God's glory." On the contrary, people in the New Testament did not give glory to God until they saw the sick was healed.[2] Healing, rather than sickness, brought glory to God.

I believe both sides share more in common with each other than they see. Both sides believe in the sovereignty of God and the importance of faith. But it's a matter of definition. When we say "*God is Sovereign*," we do not mean, "God does whatever He wants." That is not the definition of a sovereign. It is the definition of corruption, tyranny and dictatorship.

A sovereign is a ruler who abides by His own laws. God is sovereign because He always moves in line with His own Word. Once we understand His Word, we understand how God in His sovereignty has chosen to heal. So when we say "God healed sovereignly," we mean He healed by gifts of the Spirit which occur "as He wills." On the other side, when we say "faith," it should be clear we are not referring to "blind faith," which is a caricature of religion made up by Hollywood and anti-theists. No, we are referring to Biblical faith founded upon solid evidence and a thorough knowledge of a good God.

Jesus Approaching the Sick

Out of 19 cases of healing, 7 of them were initiated by Jesus. In other words, Jesus walked up to the sick and healed them without any discernible faith on their part.

238 • THE DIVINE CODE

HEALING INITIATED BY JESUS/ THE SPIRIT	MATT.	MARK	LUKE	JOHN
1. Peter's mother-in-law	8:14-15	1:29-31	4:38-39	
2. Man with withered hand	12:9-13	3:1-5	6:6-10	
3. Deaf and dumb (mute)		7:31-37		
4. Lame man at Pool of Bethesda				5:2-15
5. Man born blind				9:1-7
6. Woman with spirit of infirmity for 18 years			13:10-17	
7. Man with dropsy			14:1-6	

Why did Jesus sovereignly choose to heal these 7 people without faith on their part? By studying we can usually find good reasons why Jesus initiated the healing process.

In the case of the deaf man, he could not hear Jesus. Since faith comes by hearing, this man could not have had any faith. So Jesus approached the deaf, led by the Spirit of God. We can say that most deaf cases must be healed by gifts of the Spirit or the initiation of the Spirit. If the deaf cannot hear, they cannot approach Jesus on their own faith. I have seen 3 deaf children instantly healed in Africa and can tell you that none of them could have heard or understood a word I preached. They were healed by a sovereign move of the Spirit.

Jesus had good reasons to approach others. Peter's mother-in-law was sick in bed and unable to meet Jesus. The lame man in Bethseda was unable to walk. The Lord has compassion on the bed-ridden. I have heard several stories of bed-ridden Christians being visited and healed by the Lord. The lesson seems to be: if you're able-bodied enough to walk and to move, you should not delay to come to Jesus and obtain healing on your own faith!

In the remaining 4 cases where Jesus approached the sick – the man with the withered hand, the man born blind, the crippled woman and the man with dropsy (edema or swollen legs) – we find one commonality in their stories. Jesus deliberately performed these 4 healings *all on the Sabbath!*

The sovereign moves of the Spirit seem to be a divine challenge to the religious attitude of the Pharisees who didn't want Jesus to heal on the Sabbath. He simply ignored religion and proved the religious wrong! Now I would not wait till Saturday to get healed! You can get healed any day of the week!

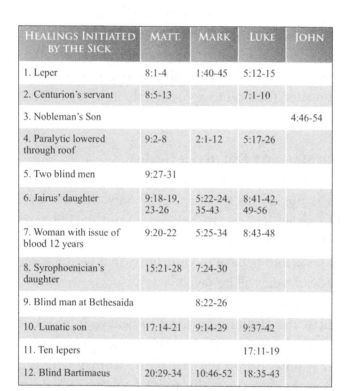

HEALINGS INITIATED BY THE SICK	MATT.	MARK	LUKE	JOHN
1. Leper	8:1-4	1:40-45	5:12-15	
2. Centurion's servant	8:5-13		7:1-10	
3. Nobleman's Son				4:46-54
4. Paralytic lowered through roof	9:2-8	2:1-12	5:17-26	
5. Two blind men	9:27-31			
6. Jairus' daughter	9:18-19, 23-26	5:22-24, 35-43	8:41-42, 49-56	
7. Woman with issue of blood 12 years	9:20-22	5:25-34	8:43-48	
8. Syrophoenician's daughter	15:21-28	7:24-30		
9. Blind man at Bethesaida		8:22-26		
10. Lunatic son	17:14-21	9:14-29	9:37-42	
11. Ten lepers			17:11-19	
12. Blind Bartimaeus	20:29-34	10:46-52	18:35-43	

70% VERSUS 30%

A NUMBER of facts becomes obvious upon glancing at these tables. The majority of sick people were healed through their own faith; the minority of people were healed by waiting for a sovereign move of the Spirit. The ratio of those healed by approaching Jesus versus waiting for Jesus to approach them is 12:7 or 63% by faith versus 37% by gifts of the Spirit.

Since the deaf cannot have faith, the healing of the deaf inflates the 37% of cases healed sovereignly by the Lord. Had he the ability to operate on his own faith, he could also receive healing by faith like the majority can. Removing the deaf case brings the ratio of faith to gifts of the Spirit to 12:6, or 67% healed by faith, and only 33% healed by gifts of the Spirit operating "as He wills" (1 Corinthians 12:11).

In simple terms, 7 out of 10 Christians will be healed by their own faith. Using rounded numbers, we can say: in 70% of cases, the recipient initiated the healing process, while in 30% the recipient waited for God to approach them with healing.

What the Majority Did to Get Healed

You need to understand this: it wasn't all up to Jesus. Your salvation is not all up to Jesus, is it? Salvation requires you to hear the Gospel, choose to believe it, and decide to receive it verbally. Romans 10:9 says, "That if you confess with your mouth the Lord Jesus and believe in your heart that God has raised Him from the dead, you will be saved."

Your healing is not all up to Jesus. Once you hear the truth about Christ the Healer, you need to believe it, speak it and act on it, in order for it to work. Jesus wasn't walking around picking whom He would heal. In the case of the woman with the issue of blood 12 years, Jesus actually turned to the crowd and asked, "Who touched Me?" (Mark 5:31). The woman got healed before Jesus could identify her! Who decided her healing?

There is another insight I want to draw out of the 19 healing cases. It will help you obtain your healing. Out of 12 cases of people who approached Jesus first, the word "faith" is either specifically mentioned or implied in all 12 instances.

To the woman with the issue of blood Jesus said, "YOUR FAITH has made you well. Go in peace, and be healed of your affliction."

To Jairus Jesus said, "Do not be afraid, only BELIEVE."

To the centurion Jesus said, "I have not found so great FAITH, not even in Israel... Go your way, and as you have BELIEVED, so be it done unto you." Isn't it interesting Jesus did not say, "As God wills, so be it done unto you" or "I the Son of God sovereignly choose to heal you"? He could have said that, but Jesus specifically credited the healing to the centurion's own faith.

To two blind men, Jesus asked, "Do you BELIEVE that I am able to do this?" They said to Him, "Yes, Lord." Then He touched their eyes, saying, "According to YOUR FAITH let it be to you." Notice Jesus did not say, "According to MY faith be it done unto you" or "According to the Apostles Peter, James and John's faith, may you be healed." No, your faith matters.

To the Syrophoenician woman Jesus said, "O woman, great is YOUR FAITH! Let it be to you as YOU desire." Why didn't Jesus say, "Let it be to you as GOD desires"? Obviously our desire and our faith have something to do with our healing!

In 12 out of 19 cases, Jesus attributed healing to the recipient's faith. Faith is a key to receiving healing. Too many think, "I will be healed if I really need it, or if I beg God enough, or because I serve God I deserve to get healed." But healing, like salvation, is a gift *by grace through faith*. You cannot deserve to be healed. You cannot beg enough to be healed. You cannot wish to be healed. You cannot say, "But I need it so bad, why hasn't God done anything?" or "O Lord, You know I've served You at church, why don't You heal me?"

It's up to us to study God's Word on healing, trust God is true to His Word, and act according to the Word. I have never failed to receive healing for myself or for my family in this way. Do not trust in your own religious tradition or put it above God's Word.

Do not assume you already know everything there is to know about God's Word.

It is vital to study what the Bible says before accepting other people's opinions, even if they have degrees and PhDs. It's not their body or their health that's on the line, it's mine and my family's, so I cannot trust the best of men's opinions.

LET THE NUMBERS SPEAK HEALING!

What is God trying to teach us through these 19 healing cases? God is clearly showing that in the *majority* of cases (70%), you're going to have to do something about your own healing!

Your volition and your cooperation have much to do with your obtaining a blessing from Jesus. Those who sat passively were *not* healed. Sick people like the woman with the issue of blood and blind Bartimaeus cried and pushed their way through crowds to get to Jesus. They were healed. Despite religious and personal opposition, they believed Jesus, acted on their belief, and obtained their healing.

The statistics tell us: 70% of individuals received healing by approaching Jesus. The remaining 30% waited for God to approach them.

We should put this 30% figure in broader perspective. The reality is healing by gifts of the Spirit was *rare* compared to healing by faith. In 3 ½ years of healing ministry, only 7 cases were reported as initiated by the Lord. In contrast, there were multitudes of cases where innumerable people approached Jesus first for healing.

MATTHEW 21:14
14 Then the blind and the lame CAME TO HIM in the temple, and He healed them.

MATTHEW 14:35

"" 35 And when the men of that place recognized Him, they sent out into all that surrounding region, BROUGHT TO HIM all who were sick,

36 and begged[3] Him that they might only touch the hem of His garment. And as many as touched it were made perfectly well.

"" MARK 3:10 (NIV)

10 For he had healed many, so that those with diseases were PUSHING forward to touch him.

Multitudes of people came to Jesus to obtain healing, and they got it. Not one failed to receive healing! If the number of sick in these multitudes could be counted in our equation, then the percentage of those healed by faith would rise much higher than 70%. It would be safe to say that 80% to as high as 99% of those who got healed did so on their own initiative!

So why be part of the minority (possibly 1%) who are passive about their healing? Isn't it better to be part of the majority who get healed by actively pursuing God? That means reading your Bible, studying healing, and going to a church where the Word of God is demonstrated (people get healed), not just talked about!

SOVEREIGN MANIFESTATIONS

We have established that in the minority of cases, healing can occur without much knowledge or faith. In such cases where the sick did not approach Jesus or didn't even know who Jesus was, gifts of the Spirit were operating. If a sick person gets healed without knowing who Jesus is or without understanding the Word, then their healing could not be based on their own faith. It was a sovereign act of God.

When healing occurs without any faith involved, the Bible calls this a manifestation of 1 of the 9 "gifts of the Spirit" (listed in 1 Corinthians 12:1-11). These supernatural gifts operate through an anointed minister, but are not controlled by the minister, as taught in 1 Corinthians 12:11. Paul said, "But one and the same Spirit works all these things [these 9 gifts], distributing to each one individually AS HE WILLS.

No minister can make the gifts of the Spirit operate at his or her own will. They operate as He wills. A minister simply needs to be open for the Holy Spirit to move. In revival meetings, we often see many people get healed without much Bible knowledge or Bible faith. This clearly is a sovereign manifestation of the Holy Spirit. We also find many of those same people who get healed in revivals will tend to lose their healing shortly after the revival meetings. It's a truism that "if you don't know how you got it, you won't know how to keep it."

When the devil counter-attacks and symptoms recur, those who did not fortify their faith in the Word of God will concede defeat and give up their faith by saying things like, "I guess the Lord didn't heal me." Then of course they're sick again and don't understand why.

They *were* healed by gifts of the Spirit, but they had a responsibility to grow up spiritually. God expects us His children to take hold of His promises based on our own relationship with God, not based on a preacher's relationship with God! The preacher only helps advertise that God is real and His power is real. But then it's up to us to check in with God and get His Word directly into our hearts and minds.

No sick person can force any miracle or gift of the Spirit to operate at their own will. They occur sovereignly "as He wills." But every sick person can come to Jesus on their own initiative and by faith to receive healing. 12 out of 19 New Testament cases prove it.

If you need healing right now, have faith in Christ the Healer, then declare to God, *"I receive my healing from Christ the Healer. I won't wait or worry about it anymore. I will be part of the majority who get healed by approaching Jesus. I will not be the exception! God's Word will not fail. Thank You, Father, for Your Word! Thank You, Jesus, for making me well!"* Then make sure you tell others how God healed you. That gives Jesus all the glory.

19 tells us God wants to heal! It is God's will to heal you!

20

20 IS the number of physical manhood and is associated with war. There are 20 potential opening moves in a chess game, though most of them are not taken because they would quickly lead to the opponent's advantage and your defeat. 20 is the age of military service in ancient Israel. 20 is the minimum age of military service in many modern countries including Japan and Ukraine. 20 is the number of Philistines killed by Jonathan and his armor-bearer in one of the most daring military moves in the Bible.

 1 SAMUEL 14:6

6 Then Jonathan said to the young man who bore his armor, "Come, let us go over to the garrison of these uncircumcised; it may be that the Lord will work for us. For nothing restrains the Lord from saving by many or by few."

13 Then Jonathan climbed up on his hands and feet, and his armor-bearer after him. And they fell

before Jonathan, and his armor-bearer killed them after him.

14 And that first strike, which Jonathan and his armor-bearer made, killed about TWENTY men within as it were half a furrow's length in an acre of land.

15 And there was a panic in the camp, in the field, and among all the people. The garrison and even the raiders trembled, the earth quaked, and it became a very great panic.

Jonathan had faith! He said, "For nothing restrains the Lord from saving by many or by few." Faith does not look at numbers. Our church bought a property in 2019 with not enough money to build, and started a $1.5 million building project with not enough funds in the bank account! We talked to the architect and the builder as if we had no worry in the world. What would make us do that? Faith!

One thing about Bible faith is that it rejoices. If you have a sad faith, unsure faith, or wavering faith, it's not really Bible faith. Don't be presumptuous and buy something you can't afford! Our ministry leaders prayed and knew this property was God's provision. We are still waiting on more financial breakthrough, but we confess as Jonathan did, "For nothing restrains the Lord from saving by many or by few." That means many people may give us little donations, or a handful of people may give us big donations, or one person could underwrite the whole project!

20 is the age at which young men were enlisted into ancient Israel's military. In Numbers 1, the minimum age requirement was repeated 14 times in a single chapter. Many parents may have noticed a significant maturity gap between teenagers and those who hit 20 years of age. Feldhann and Rice offer a scientific explanation:

"Science demonstrates that the frontal lobe of the brain—the area that allows judgment for consequences and control of impulses—doesn't fully develop until after the teen years. So in the absence of a fully functioning frontal lobe, teenage brains rely more on the centers that control emotions—which in effect means they give in much more easily to impulses."[1]

The Bible was way ahead of science: "Take a census of all the congregation of the children of Israel...from TWENTY years old and above — all who are able to go to war in Israel" (Numbers 1:2-3).

Deuteronomy 20 is *the* Torah's chapter on war. Within are instructions for every believer who is facing a test, trial or battle on how to win!

2 Chronicles 20 is *the* Old Testament chapter on how to conduct a successful war campaign. King Jehoshaphat faced an enemy that outnumbered him, but he followed God's strategy for war to victory!

God wants every believer to know that we are all called to battle! Yes, Paul told Timothy we are called to fight the good fight of faith. Eight times in the Book of Revelation we are called to be over-comers.[2] If we are called to be "over-comers," it means we are going to have to "come over" some things! The Bible shows that every time a believer overcomes something, there is always reward waiting! Often when Israel won a victory, they took days to collect all the "spoils"! Great victories are produced out of great battles.

It would behoove every believer to study Deuteronomy chapter 20 and 2 Chronicles chapter 20 to understand how to win a war. Let me list some keys to help you get started.

WAR STRATEGIES FROM DEUTERONOMY 20

1. The priest [minister of God] shall speak to the people God's Word (v. 2).
2. God's Word will eliminate fear (v. 3-4). The teaching of God's Word will always be the foundation of every victory!
3. The officers [leaders] shall speak to the people (v. 5).
4. The fearful must be eliminated out of the camp (v. 8). The Ancient Law of Kings 7:15 elaborates, "If he does not wage war with all his heart and soul, it is considered as if he shed the blood of the entire people."[3] Doubt is destructive and contagious. There is no strength in numbers, only in faith! God reduced Gideon's army of 32,000 to 300 in Judges 7. Gideon asked all the fearful to leave and 22,000 departed. Victory did not depend on numbers, but on the fearless faith of a few!
5. When praying over an important matter, I never ask just anybody to pray with me. I only ask people I can trust—true believers who know their Bibles and are not afraid. I take no comfort in great numbers of people praying, but in the faith of a few believers! *"This is the victory that has overcome the world, even our faith* [not our numbers]" (1 John 5:4).
6. Offers of peace should be extended to human enemies [not to demons who are not open to negotiation; they must be bound or cast out in the Name of Jesus!] (v. 10-12)
7. Victory and spoils are assured (v. 13-15)

WAR STRATEGIES FROM 2 CHRONICLES 20

1. Jehoshaphat sought God's face in prayer (v. 3-5).
2. Jehoshaphat spoke God's Word to the people (v.5-17).
3. God's Word eliminated fear and birthed faith (v. 6-7, 15-17).
4. Jehoshaphat worshipped and appointed worshippers to lead the battle (v. 18-22). *Don't face the devil till you first face God!*
5. The enemies were so confused they began to attack each other (v. 22-24)!
6. Jehoshaphat and his people took 3 days to collect all the spoils (v. 25).
7. The fear of the Lord came upon all their enemies after the victory (v. 29).

2020 is double 20 or double war. Even though 20/20 has a positive connotation of "perfect eyesight", the year 2020 seems to indicate a year of war.

21

21 IS TRIPLE SEVEN, $7 + 7 + 7 = 21$, an important rite of passage in many modern people's lives. In most countries, a 21 year old is a full-fledged adult with all rights and privileges. In America it is the age at which young adults can legally drink. In Australia many graduate a 3-year university course and start a career at the age of 21. Isaac, Abraham's son of promise, was the 21st from Adam.

The demonic "prince of the kingdom of Persia" withstood the angel Gabriel for 21 days, until Michael the archangel came to help him. Then Gabriel was able to deliver the prophetic end time message to Daniel.

It would be no contradiction to extrapolate there is a demonic prince over America, Russia, Europe, China, India, etc., trying to influence the minds of the power brokers of each territory. Believers have the power to pray for our nations in Jesus' Name. The good news is that under the new covenant, we no longer have to wait 21 days to get our prayers answered! No, Colossians 2:15 tells us about Jesus, "Having DISARMED principalities and powers, He made a public spectacle of them, triumphing over them in it."

The Cross made all the difference! Satan has been dethroned and his powers disarmed. He may roar like a lion, but he has been de-fanged and de-clawed! His main power and activity now is to deceive people, but he has no power to hinder our prayer life! Demons are afraid of Christians! James 4:7 says, "...Resist the devil and he will FLEE from you." To flee means he will run as fast as he can when he hears a Christian speak God's Word and use the Name of Jesus! Christians need to understand the authority Jesus gave us in His Name (see Mark 16:17).

21 is the 8th Fibonacci number. The Fibonacci series was discovered by an Italian mathematician *Leonardo* of *Pisa*, the *son* of *Bonaccio* (*filius Bonaccio* was contracted to *Fibonacci*). The sequence starts with 1 and 1 and continues by adding the last two numbers to get the next number: 1, 1, 2, 3, 5, 8, 13, 21, 34, 55, 89, 144, 233, 377, 610, 987, etc. These numbers are frequently recurring in biology, physics, astronomy, art, and the stock market. Most technical analysts of stock charts are aware of the Fibonacci retracements, though they may not know an Intelligent God designed those numbers to reflect His order and have meaning. (See the next Fibonacci number 34 for more on the stock market.)

22

22 IS the number of the Jews, the Bible and end times. There are 22 letters in the Hebrew alef-bet (alphabet). When God says that He created the world by speaking, rabbis hold the view that God literally created by using the 22 letters of the alef-bet. Don't ask me how!

There were 22 heads of mankind from Adam to Jacob. Jacob (or Israel) was the 22nd from Adam. Jacob suffered for 22 years.[1] This is known as the "time of Jacob's trouble" (Jeremiah 30:7).

Joseph suffered for 22 years from the time his brothers threw him down a well to the time they came to buy food from him and bowed down before him.[2] Joseph's dream took 22 years to be fulfilled.

The most important Jewish chapter in the Torah, called the "Akedah" or the story of Abraham enacting the offering up of his son Isaac as a sin-sacrifice, is recorded in Genesis 22.

Israel became a modern nation in a "22" year (1948 = 1+ 9 + 4 + 8 =22). Israel is currently surrounded by 22 Arab states of the Arab League, nearly all of which are hostile to her.[3]

22% of Jews in Israel are strict Torah-observers and Sabbath-keepers who will not ride in a car during Shabbat, according to a study of religious observance in Israel completed by Dr. Yehuda ben Meir of Bar Ilan University.[4]

The *menorah*, a seven-lamp candelabrum, is an eternal symbol of Israel. It was present in Moses' Tabernacle and Solomon's Temple, and is present in every synagogue throughout the world. The Biblical menorah was made of one solid piece of gold with 22 golden bowls for holding oil used to light this golden Lampstand. According to Exodus 25, each bowl had to resemble an almond blossom. The Lord specified 3 almond bowls per menorah branch, plus 4 almond bowls for the center branch. (3 bowls x 6 branches) + (4 bowls x 1 branch) = 22, the number of the Jews.

It is appropriate that 22 is associated with the Light of the Holy. We know Jesus is the "true Light which gives light to every man coming into the world" (John 1:9). The sum of 14 (salvation) + 8 (new beginning) is 22 (the Light of the Jewish Temple, the Light of the World, and the Jewish Messiah).

Psalms 119 (prophetic of 2019) is an acrostic poem divided into 22 sections. Its structure not only tells us it's important to the Jews, the rabbis acknowledge it to be so. 5 Scriptures recited by Jews before the blowing of the *shofar* on *Rosh Hashanah* (aka the Feast of Trumpets) are from Psalm 119 (verses 66, 108, 122, 160, 162). Three more verses from Psalm 119 are recited before the *shema* on the second day of Rosh Hashannah (verses 89, 90, 91). Psalm 119 is significant for being the longest chapter in the Bible.

22 is the number of end times, which by definition is a time when God's dealing with Israel becomes more prominent. This is exactly what we are seeing as the world's attention turns to this little nation in the Middle East. There are 22 chapters in the Book of Revelation, which is a New Testament letter written mainly for the Jews who will be on earth during the time of Tribulation.

Some prophecy teachers have equated the Tribulation with the time of Jacob's Trouble and with Daniel's 70th week. The trouble with this is that the two periods are not of equal length. Daniels' 70th "week" must last a "week" of 7 years. But the "time of Jacob's trouble", literally how long Jacob suffered, lasted 22 years. The patriarch's suffering served as a foreshadow of the Jewish people's suffering during the end times.

Based on my studies, I believe the events of the 7 seals, 7 trumpets and 7 bowls of Revelation fit better in 3 equal periods of three and half years each (3 x 3.5 years = 10.5 or 11 years rounded up) than in 7 years.[5] In other words, the 7 years of Daniel's 70th week belong inside of the 11 years of Revelation, which belong inside the time of Jacob's Trouble. The 70th week is related to but not the same as Jacob's Trouble.

22 is a pattern in the structure of the Bible. There were originally 22 books in the Hebrew Bible as finalized by the High Priest Ezra and the Great Assembly. Jewish Historian Josephus confirmed this by dividing Scripture into 3 parts: 5 books of Torah + 13 Prophetic Books + 4 Hymnal books.

The Christian canon contains 66 books which can be divided into 3 equal parts. Each division would contain 22 books. 66 ÷ 3 = 22.

- 5 Books of the Law + 12 Books of Old Testament History + 5 Books of Wisdom = 22.
- 5 Major Prophets + 12 Minor Prophets + 5 New Testament History = 22.
- All the Epistles (Christian Letters) in the New Testament from Romans to Revelation total 22.

22 is significant to worship. The ancient Hebrews played 2 stringed instruments that are translated in English as the lyre (Hebrew *kinnor*) and harp (*nevel*). The lyre had 10 strings and the harp 12 strings, giving a combination of 22 possible musical

notes, thus corresponding to the 22 letters of the Hebrew alef-bet (Jewish alphabet). If each note corresponds to a Hebrew letter, then playing the right notes in the right sequence can actually be the musical equivalent of speaking out the Scriptures or prophesying!

The Bible indicates that there may be far more going on with music than we naturally understand. In 2 Kings 3:15, the prophet Elisha called for a harpist and "while the harpist was playing, the hand of the Lord came upon Elisha." The right kind of music brought the anointing upon the prophet and enabled him to minister. 1 Chronicles 25:1 tells us that King David and the army captains chose the sons of Asaph, Heman and Jeduthun to "prophesy with harps, stringed instruments, and cymbals." How can one "prophesy" on an instrument? Apparently our vocal cords are not the only means of speaking God's Words. In the ears of angels and devils, our inspired worship may sound like prophetic declarations in the spiritual realm. No wonder worship is so powerful.

Immediately after the 7-day Feast of Tabernacles there is a special one-day celebration called *Simchat Torah* or *Rejoicing in the Torah* on the 22nd of Tishri. On this day Jews who do not normally get to touch the Torah Scroll are given the honor of embracing and dancing with the Torah Scroll. It is customary to stay awake all night to read and learn the Torah. Though God did not command this celebration, it is a beautiful picture of the love for God's Word.

22 is also the number related to man's anatomy. The human head is made of 22 bones: 8 cranial bones and 14 facial bones.[6] There are 22 autosome pairs or non-sex-determining chromosome pairs in the human genome. The final sex-determining chromosome pair — the 23rd pair — determines whether we are born a boy (XY) or a girl (XX).

The suns' magnetic poles reverse about every 11 years,

therefore they return to their original position every 22 years (called the Hale Cycle, see Chapter 11).

Rabbi Jonathan Cahn highlighted in his book *The Paradigm* a parallel between King Ahab and Bill Clinton.[7] Both were influenced by a wicked "queen": Jezebel and Hillary Clinton. Ahab was in power for 22 years. Bill Clinton was in office for 22 years: from 1979-1992 as a two-term Governor of Arkansas, then from 1993-2001 as a two-term President.

Steve Strang in his book *Trump Aftershock* noted the importance of the 22nd Amendment in curbing the political ambition of the powerful. Speaking of Barack Obama, Mr. Strang wrote, "The former president had hinted more than once that if there were enough popular support to mount a challenge to the Twenty-Second Amendment, which limits the president to two terms, he would be willing to run for a third term. He even went as far as telling CNN analyst David Axelrod in December 2016 that he could have beaten Trump if he had been able to run for a third term."[8]

After 22 months of investigation into alleged Trump campaign collusion with Russia, special counsel Robert Mueller submitted his report to Attorney General William Barr on the 22nd of March 2019. There was no collusion. No crime. Federal bureaucracy sympathetic to the Obama administration and Clinton campaign had wasted millions of dollars. The only collusion was between the Democrats and the elite media. Democrats weaponized the government's investigative powers against a sitting President and harassed his family and associates with lawfare (legal warfare). The biased mainstream media peddled the fake news about Donald Trump for 22 months—the number of end times. This type of "legal injustice" is symptomatic of the end times, and one of the reasons Jesus will come back to give justice to the victims of anti-Christ politicians.

It was amazing to witness how Donald Trump took on the intelligence agency, the entire Democrat Party and the hostile media, and won. This type of vindication defined the year 2019 (see Chapter 19 and my video series on Justice)[9].

US national debt hit $22 trillion on 13 February 2019. National debt is the result of Congress spending more money than it receives from the citizens' taxes. The level of government debt is now more than three-quarters of gross national product (GDP). While such staggering debt is usually the sign of an empire's decline, it is not necessarily a sign of the end. The same level of debt was seen during the 2007-2009 recession and the period immediately after WWII.[10] Look out for more patterns of 22 as a confirming sign of the end times!

23

23 IS the total number of chromosome pairs in a human cell.

24 is the number of chromosome pairs in apes, such as gorillas and chimpanzees. This is a big problem to evolutionists who claim that humans evolved from apes. If we did, what happened to the extra chromosome?

Evolutionists frequently get on secular TV to explain the flaws of their theories. Evolutionists now surmise that since apes have 24 chromosome pairs and humans have 23 pairs, then 1 chromosome pair must have fused. They claimed that ape chromosome number 11 and 12 probably fused into human chromosome number 2. On what do they base their assertion?

Before we examine their hypothesis, we first need to know that at the end of each chromosome is a series of repetitive DNA that protects the end of the chromosome from destruction. These protective caps are called *telomeres*. Every chromosome has 2 telomeres, one on each end. So if 2 chromosomes were to fuse (join end-on-end), we would expect to see 3 telomeres, one on each end and one in the middle. Evolutionists viewed human chromosome 2 under a microscope and saw what appeared to be

3 telomeres, two on each end and one in the middle. Voila, they claimed, that proves evolution!

The purveyors of evolution know that the majority of the public has not studied biology. They employ the media in a similar way marketing advertisers do, sending short soundbites and stimulating pictures while leaving out crucial and opposing facts.

The first omission in the telomere argument is that ape telomeres are 24 kilobases long (a kilobase is 1000 base pairs of DNA) whereas human telomeres are 10 kilobases long. Our telomeres differ on *every single* DNA strand, including chromosome number 2! Their argument proved nothing but the old adage, "When you're looking for something, you'll see it everywhere." They are seeing what they *want* to see.

The second omission is the known result of observed fusions: which is, reduced fitness. Biochemist and Neuroscientist Dr. David DeWitt summarized it best when he wrote: "Chromosome fusions can occur but are particularly messy and typically thought to reduce reproductive success due to the resulting monosomy and trisomy in the zygotes [the fertilized eggs] produced by the mating of a normal genotype [the individual with normal genes] and an individual with the fused chromosomes. Many of these types of chromosomal defects are associated with mental retardation."[1]

The third omission is the transmission problem: how would such a fusion (which tends to reduce fitness) get passed on to the entire human population? Dr. DeWitt wrote: "With no known selective advantage it is difficult to see how this fusion would become exclusively characteristic of man... The chance of the same chromosome fusion occurring in two individuals at the same time in the same place such that they just happened to mate with one another to produce viable male and female offspring stretches credulity to breaking point."[2]

Another common argument from evolutionists is that the

human genome is nearly the same as the chimpanzee genome. "We are 98% the same," evolutionists have claimed. There are 2 major problems with this often repeated soundbite.

The first problem is best stated by evolutionist Steve Jones, "Bananas share 50% of our genes, but that doesn't make them half-human."[3] We should expect all of God's creation to share some of similar design because they come from the same Designer. All of Van Gogh's paintings share similar qualities, not because one painting evolved from another, but because they are all from Van Gogh!

A roller-skate and a car both have 4 wheels, but it hardly proves that a car evolved from a roller skate! They share 4 wheels because it's efficient engineering and good design. We may not know the identity of the manufacturer, but we can be certain the 4 wheels could not have arisen by chance or mindless accident. They need an intelligent designer!

Scientists have beliefs just like you and I do. Evolutionary scientists *believe* similarities prove common ancestry. Creation scientists *believe* similarities prove common Creator. What do the most recent DNA studies show? They are, in fact, overturning evolutionary assumptions that organisms with similar features are related!

In 2006, scientists discovered that *bats* and horses share a higher degree of DNA similarity than do *cows* and horses, a finding that was once again contrary to evolutionary thinking.

In 2007, the staunchly evolutionist magazine *The New Scientist* had to admit some key evolutionary ideas are flat wrong: "Don't bother looking at any textbook that's more than a few years old. Chances are that the tree of life you find there will be wrong... These are turbulent times in the world of phylogeny [the study of 'evolutionary relatedness' among organisms], yet there has been one rule that evolutionary biologists felt they could cling to: the amount of complexity in the living world has been on the increase. Now even that is in doubt... The whole concept of a gradualist tree...is wrong.... Some evolutionary biologists now suggest that loss...is the key to understanding evolution... We need to rethink the process of evolution itself."[4]

No matter how many times facts prove them wrong, few evolutionists will abandon their *belief* in evolution because evolution is a worldview. It is the dogma of a religion. Atheism is the religion and evolution is the prophet. Atheism denies God and evolution denies questioning atheism. Evolution works on children; atheism becomes lord over adults. Evolution indoctrinates atheism into children's minds with imaginary pictures, wishful tales, and computer-generated graphics. Without the artists' renditions of still missing "missing links" and fictitious life on other planets, atheism would collapse under the absurdity of its basic tenets of faith: spontaneous universe, spontaneous life, spontaneous improvement, and spontaneous intelligence, none of which has ever been observed.[5] All of these evolutionary dogmas violate observable facts in nature and in our lives, not to mention the Second Law of Thermodynamics (Entropy).[6]

The more scientific explanation is: life was created by Life; design is evidence of a Designer; intelligence was produced by an Intelligence who is communicating with us today through His Son and His written Word – the Bible.

The second problem with the 98% similarity claim is that the figure is highly disputed. You don't need to know much science, just enough math, to know this figure is an exaggeration. Since chimpanzees have 2 extra chromosomes compared to ours, how could we be 98% the same genetically? The chimp genome is about 12% larger than the human genome. This would indicate a *maximum* of 88% DNA similarity from the outset, even if all other genes were identical (but we know they are not; for instance, the human Y chromosome is larger than and extremely different from the chimp's). How was 12% difference accounted for or ignored?

Don't let the evolutionist's use of percentages obscure the magnitude of differences. Let's assume humans and chimps differ by "only" 2%, that may not sound like much until you realize that it represents 60 million mutations (base pair alterations)! If humans and chimps differ by at least 12%, that represents 360 million mutations, all of which have to *add* useful information that gives some evolutionary advantage.

Yet not 1 single genetic mutation has been proven to *add* information to the genome. All known mutations (e.g. super-bug mutations) and natural selection (e.g. population shifts towards light or dark color, big beak or small beak) involves a *loss* of pre-existing information. Let me repeat: there has not been 1 observable instance of new information being added to the genome, a major problem for evolutionists. This fact has not been denied even by Richard Dawkins.[7] Evolutionists would require that something that has never been observed once to occur at least 60 million times flawlessly! Nothing but unholy imagination can bridge the gap between chimps and humans.

The truth is no matter how wide the gap between humans and chimps is found to be – whether 2%, 12% or 20%, most evolutionists will not change their mind because they are emotionally committed to a *belief* that evolution is true. Even if humans were 20% different from chimps, most evolutionists will still shout a victory for Darwin and say, "But we are 80% the same!" The objective question remains: how were millions of new genetic codes added to the genome? Evolutionists have no answer. Creationists have a logical answer.

Humans did not evolve from apes. God created us with 23 chromosomes.

24

24 IS A DOUBLING OF 12. If 12 is the number of earthly government, 24 is the number of heavenly government. There are 24 elders seated around God's throne. There are 24 apostles named in the New Testament (listed below). The 12 tribes of Israel are listed 24 times in the Bible, sometimes by birth order, marching order, inheritance order, prophetic order, etc. (See Chapter 13.)

According to 1 Chronicles 24, there were 24 orders or divisions of priests who rotated their Temple duties during the Old Testament. Priests came from the tribe of Levi, specifically the descendants of Aaron, the brother of Moses. Each division of priests served in the Temple for one week, starting on a Shabbat and ending on the next Shabbat. When all divisions had served their first course, then they repeated the same schedule in a second course. That covered 48 weeks of ministry, but there are 52 weeks in a year. Who served in the other weeks? Due to the number of people present during the Biblical Feasts, all of the orders of priests were present in Jerusalem and served together.

This division of labor no longer exists since the Temple was destroyed in 70 AD.

Most Jews no longer know which tribe they belong to, which presents a problem for verifying the Messiah (who must come from the tribe of Judah and King David's lineage) and the priests (who must be come from the tribe of Levi and Aaron's lineage).

Today, it is assumed that a Jew with the last name *Cohen* or *Kohen* (Hebrew for "priest") is a Levite and descendant of Aaron. The Aaronic priesthood is now dormant because its duty to offer blood sacrifice has been fulfilled by the sacrifice of Yeshua, and the priesthood itself has been superseded by the priesthood of Yeshua, who is a priest after the order of Melchizedek (Hebrews 5:6, 5:10, 6:20, 7:11, 7:15, 7:17).

There are 24 hours in a day. There are 24 books in the Hebrew Bible. They are exactly the same books as the Christian Old Testament, but the Hebrew *Tanak* combines First and Second Samuel, First and Second Kings, First and Second Chronicles, Ezra and Nehemiah, and all 12 Minor Prophets into one book respectively.

The Earth weighs 6×10^{24} kilograms (1 followed by 24 zeros).

We all have 24 ribs. Both male and female have the same number of ribs! Even though God took Eve out of Adam's rib (Genesis 2:21-22), the rib is the *only* bone in the human body that re-grows! Had Eve been taken out of any other bone in Adam's body, Adam would be missing a bone! Given that the only way to know this is through successful surgery, and no civilization had it 6000 years ago, this fact is one of many which point to divine inspiration. The Bible is amazing in its scientific accuracy.

We have 24 vertebrae, divided into three sections of 7 cervical, 12 thoracic, and 5 lumbar vertebrae.

Christian amateur archaeologist Ron Wyatt made a controversial claim that he found the Ark of the Covenant under the site of the Crucifixion. He claimed that the Blood of Christ dripped down from the Cross through an earthquake crack and physically touched the mercy seat (lid of the Ark hidden underground). This would perfectly fulfill the typology of the Day of Atonement and would also explain why Jews can no longer perform the atonement, because it has been accomplished.

How was Ron Wyatt sure that the blood on the mercy seat was Jesus' sinless Blood, and not some other man's blood? He sent a blood sample for DNA testing and the result was that this blood contained only 24 chromosomes, instead of the usual 46 (23 from father, 23 from mother).[1] Unfortunately since his death, there remains no tangible evidence of this blood or the DNA test, but the result is at least genetically plausible.

When God supernaturally fertilized Mary's egg to bring His Son into the world, it is an assumption that He had to contribute 23 chromosomes like a normal father would. It is just as probable that He only had to send one sex-determinant gene, the Y chromosome, or in Hebrew the *yod*. The *yod* is the first letter of the Name of God (YHVH). Mary had the full genome to create another woman descendant, a clone. What God must supply is a Y-chromosome to determine the gender of the baby to be a Son. Mary's 23 chromosomes plus God's single chromosome equals 24, which effectively would have made Him a male genetic version of Mary.

This also makes sense to me in terms of God's desire to send a genuine human substitute who could be touched by the feelings of our infirmities, including our genetic flaws. Had God sent 23 perfect chromosomes into Mary's womb, surely His genetic material would have overridden Mary's, and the progeny would not have been so much human as superhuman with perfect looks, strength and physique. But the Bible says Jesus did not look special from the outside. "He has no form or comeliness; And when we see Him, There is no beauty that we should desire Him" (Isaiah 53:2b). 24 may well be Jesus' unique genetic fingerprint. (See Chapter 316.)

There are 24 apostles named in the New Testament. Most

likely there were many more unnamed (Romans 16:7). Some of them functioned in other offices such as that of prophet or teacher (Acts 13:1). Paul said he was "a preacher, an apostle and a teacher of the Gentiles" (1 Timothy 2:7; 2 Timothy 1:11). Certainly all the New Testament writers qualify as both apostles and prophets (Ephesians 2:20, 3:5). Of the original 12 apostles:

1. **Simon Peter**
2. **Andrew** his brother
3. **James** the son of Zebedee
4. **John** his brother
5. **Philip**
6. **Bartholomew** his brother
7. **James** the son of Alphaeus
8. **Judas** his brother
9. **Matthew** the tax collector (also a son of Alphaeus, perhaps brother to James and Judas)
10. **Simon** Zelotes (tradition[2] says he's also the brother of James and Judas, making possibly 4 brothers from a single family called to be apostles! Alphaeus must have been a very godly father.)
11. **Thomas** Didymus or a Twin (his twin was not an apostle)
12. **Judas** Iscariot (the one who betrayed Jesus). Some theologians teach that the age of healing and miracles has been done away with since the last of the 12 Apostles. However, God continued to call and anoint apostles after the first 12. These continued the Gospel program of preaching, healing and performing miracles in Jesus' Name. God will not take away apostles because He gave the 5-fold ministers as "gifts to men" (Ephesians 4:8-11) and "the gifts and the calling of God are irrevocable" (Romans 11:29). The following 'lesser known' apostles are proof that neither

apostles nor healings and miracles have been done away with:

13. **James** the Lord's half-brother, who was head of the Church in Jerusalem, *not Peter!* (Galatians 1:19, 2:9; James 1:1)

14. **Barnabas** (Acts 13:1-3, 14:4, 14; 1 Corinthians 9:5-6; Galatians 2:9)

15. **Paul** (Galatians 1:1, 2:8; 1 Timothy 2:7; 2 Timothy 1:11)

16. **Andronicus**, a relative of Paul, saved before he was (Romans 16:7)

17. **Junia**, a relative of Paul saved before he was (Romans 16:7)

18. **Apollos**, an eloquent and well-read teacher and apostle (1 Corinthians 4:6-9)

19. **Silas** (1 Thessalonians 1:1, 2:6)

20. **Timothy**, Paul's son in the faith (1 Thessalonians 1:1, 2:6)

21. **Titus** (2 Corinthians 8:23)

22. **Epaphroditus** (Philippians 2:25)

23. **Matthias** (Acts 1:26)

24. **JESUS**, of course, is and will always be the Greatest Apostle or "Sent One" (Hebrews 3:1).

Though you may not know them as "apostles" by their titles, most missionaries and multiple church planters are functioning as living apostles. Since Jesus does not change—He is the same yesterday, today and forever—there is at least one Apostle who continues to heal the sick and work miracles in believers' lives!

25

25 IS the square of 5 (5^2) or 5 x 5. It is a variation on 5, the number of grace, and is connected to grace, forgiveness, and creation. The first day of Creation was most likely Elul 25, placing Adam's birth on Tishri 1 (see Chapter 28). 25 points to Joshua who ruled Israel after Moses for 25 years according to Josephus' *Antiquities* 5.1.29. 25 also points to Jehoiachin's being pardoned, then set free from prison and lifted up above other conquered kings by the King of Babylon on the 25th day of the 12th month (Jeremiah 52:31-34). Some people claim there is no basis for celebrating the 25th day of the 12th month, but for Jehoiachin, it was Christmas in the best sense of the word!

In the Parable of the Sower, Jesus compares Himself to a Sower, the Word of God to a seed, and the listeners to 4 types of soil. When the seed of the Word is sown into the human heart, it meets with 4 different types of soil: the wayside, the stony, the thorny and the good ground. Only the good ground receives the Word of God and bears fruit. 25 is the percentage of hearers who are good ground for the Word of God.

25% helps us have a realistic expectation in ministry. People who expect 100% success are setting themselves up for disappointment. Babe Ruth, one of the greatest baseball players in history, had a batting average of .342. That meant for every 10 balls pitched, Babe Ruth swung the batt 7 times and completely missed! But he only had to hit it those 3 other times to become one of the great sports legends in the world.

Jesus' parable applies to daily life. If a baseball player hits 2.5 out of every 10 balls pitched, his batting average would be a terrific .250! A salesperson who closes 2.5 out of every 10 sales pitches would be one of the top in his or her company. (1 out of 10 would be more realistic!) A Christian who leads to the Lord 2.5 out of every 10 persons he meets would have a level of success matching Jesus'! (Again if 1 out of 10 person you witness to repents and accepts Jesus, it would be superb!)

Jesus told 500 disciples to go wait for the baptism of the Holy Spirit (1 Corinthians 15:6), but how many showed up? Only 120. Those who obeyed Jesus' instruction got filled with the Spirit (Acts 1:15, 2:4). 120 out of 500 represents 24% - just shy of 25%! This is an illustration of the Parable of the Sower.

25 out of 100 is a statistic that appears throughout the Bible. Jesus called 12 disciples, but 3 became His closest friends - Peter, James and John - that's 25%. We sometimes saddle ourselves with unrealistic expectations that only guarantee failure. Then we never step out and take a swing at life due to fear of failure. Even if the best preacher preached a perfect sermon, only 25% will be receptive and responsive to God's Word. 75% will either not remember or not respond positively. The moral of 25 is: we do not need a perfect score to be a tremendous success in life!

AFTERWORD

66 *"Being confident of this very thing, that He who has begun a good work in you will complete it until the day of Jesus Christ." (Philippians 1:6)*

You have just completed 50 chapters in Volume I. Congratulations! There are 58 more chapters in Volume II with amazing facts and anointed revelation. To understand end-time prophecy, these are must-read numbers: '70 Sevens' and 666. To get to know the first person who was raptured—Enoch—you will enjoy chapters 58 and 365. Of course, everyone wants to know how the story ends...the Millennium is contained in Chapter 1000.

If you are ready to begin a relationship with a loving God who is willing to count Christ's sacrifice as payment for your sins, then pray this prayer out loud to ask for forgiveness and receive eternal life:

"Dear Heavenly Father, *I'm lost without You and I'm sorry for all my sins. You said you number the hair on my head; You love me and care for me. Today I believe Jesus Christ is the Son of God. He came and died on the Cross to take away my sins. I believe He rose again on the third day and is able to help me now. I invite Jesus to be my only Savior, my only Lord, now and forever. Amen."*

Welcome to the Family of God! Jesus Christ has cleansed you and reconciled you with God the Father. You can now begin an eternal relationship with God and learn what it means to be in God's Family. Now is a great time for you to read the Bible for yourself, find a good Bible-believing church to attend, and ask the pastor to baptize you! I would love to hear your testimony: care@discover.org.au

NOTES

PREFACE

1. Encyclopedia of Jewish Medical Ethics, Feldheim Publishers, 2003, page 819.

INTRODUCTION

1. Plitcha, Peter, *God's Secret Formula: Deciphering the Riddle of the Universe and the Prime Number Code*, Element Books Ltd, 1998, chapter 17.
2. *The Letters of the Torah*, http://www.aishdas.org/toratemet/en_-pamphlet9.html (14 Oct 2010).

1

1. "Christian" cults are typically cults whose leaders came out of a Christian church background. All Christians cults claim to believe Jesus while denying His Deity and claim to believe the Bible while promoting other religious books (such as the Book of Mormon, the Pearl of Great Price, Watchtower Literature, Awake Magazine).
2. The Bible speaks of 3 heavens. The first heaven is our atmospheric heaven, the second heaven is outer space, the third heaven is the home of Christ, His holy angels and His saints. Our sun and all stars are in the second heaven. Paul said he was caught up to the third heaven (2 Corinthians 12:2).

2

1. Helmenstine, Anne Marie, Ph.D., *What is the Most Abundant Element?* http://chemistry.about.com/cs/howthingswork/f/blabundant.htm (1 Feb 2009).
2. *Babylonian Talmud Sukkah 52a* and *Yerushalmi Talmud Sukka 55b*.
3. We know this 45 day theory is against Scripture because Revelation 11 tells us Elijah as one of the two witnesses will be killed before the 7th trumpet, before the 7 bowl judgments are poured out, before the judgments on Babylon. This most likely puts the end of Elijah's ministry at the mid-point of the Tribulation, around the time the abomination of desolation occurs.

That would separate the ascension of Elijah from the appearance of Messiah by 3 ½ years, not 45 days.

2 DOUBLES

1. *What is the average rate of inflation in the United States?* http://heartsofthe-gods.blogspot.com/2007/07/what-is-average-inflation-rate-in.html (9 February 2009).
2. Population growth rates are not constant, but fluctuate according to fertility and mortality. Couples used to have more children in the past than now. There are 80 more autoimmune diseases now than in the 1970s. Based on current trends, we should estimate population growth rate to have been higher in the past than now. But let us assume the opposite—that there were endless wars and constant incurable diseases in the past. So we opt to use an extremely low growth rate of less than half the current growth rate of 1.2%.
3. Heffner, Dr. John, *World Population Debunks Macroevolution*, http://www.y-outube.com/watch?v=CuJ_-5JZ4xc (19 Oct 2010).
4. *Big Numbers*, http://pages.prodigy.net/jhonig/bignum/indx.html (13 February 2009).
5. Heffner, Dr. John, *ibid*. See also Batten, Don, *Where Are All the People?* http://creation.com/where-are-all-the-people (19 Oct 2010).
6. Morris, Henry, *The Biblical Basis for Modern Science*, part 4, chapter 15. Baker Books, Grand Rapids, Michigan, 1984.
7. Batten, Don, *Where Are All the People?* http://www.answersingene-sis.org/creation/v23/i3/people.asp (13 February 2009).

2 DREAMS

1. *Hagia Sophia might be reverted to a mosque*, Daily Sabah (24 March 2019), https://www.dailysabah.com/politics/2019/03/24/hagia-sophia-might-be-reverted-to-a-mosque-erdogan-says. *Hagia Sophia will be called a mosque*, TRT World (28 March 2019), https://www.trtworld.com/turkey/hagia-sophia-will-be-called-a-mosque-erdogan-25317 (17 April 2019).
2. 2 Corinthians 13:1, Matthew 18:16, Deuteronomy 19:15

3

1. Conner, Kevin, *Interpreting the Symbols and Types*, City Christian Publishing, 1992.

2. http://www.israelnationalnews.com/Articles/Article.aspx/22819, accessed 24 Nov 2018.
3. Similarly, the covenant name of God is made of 4 consonants YHWH which can be vocalized as YaHWeH or JeHoVaH.
4. The entire "out of Africa" theory of human origins rests on the assumption that L0 is the first mtDNA, whereas Dr. Carter statistically shows that mtDNA "R" was more likely Eve's mtDNA. The difference is not in evidence, but how the evidence is explained, i.e. the stories scientists tell. See Carter, Dr Robert, *Mitochondrial Eve and the 3 "Daughters" of Noah DVD*, www.creation.com
5. Kolatch, Alfred, *The Jewish Book of Why*, Jonathan David Publishers, 1981.

3.1415

1. Boatwright, John P, *Proof Pi is Not Given as 3.0 in the Bible* http://home.tele-port.com/~salad/4god/pi.htm (4 Feb 2009).

3.5

1. *Halakim* is plural of *helek*, much as seraphim and cherubim are plurals of seraph and cherub. The word *helek* means "portion".

4

1. In Matthew 1, not counting Mary. Other than the royal mother, women ancestors are not usually named in ancient royal family trees. The mention of these 4 women—a prostitute from Canaan, a Gentile from Moab, an incestuous woman in Israel, and an adulteress in Israel—is purely redemptive. It tells us God is able to restore anyone no matter how dark their past!
2. Human blood types can also be + or –. People with type O– are considered universal donors because they can give blood to any human. People with type AB+ are considered universal recipients because they can receive any blood type. Blood types have nothing to do with personality, but the legend that it does is so popular among the Japanese that they often ask, "What is your blood type?"

   99% of the Chinese have + blood types, yet no one would claim 99% of the Chinese have similar personalities. Cats have 11 blood types, yet no one would claim cats have 11 personalities (9 lives, may be!). The 4 blood types of humans are by God's design, pointing to the Gospel. He wrote 4 Gospels for every type of person. It would not surprise me that the 4 Gospel writers also had 4 different blood types. We won't know till we get to Heaven!

4 ANGELS

1. Ezekiel 1:6,8; 10:21. The only angels with wings are the Cherubim, Seraphim, and Zoas or "living creatures".
2. Leviticus 19:21, 20:6, 20:27; 1 Samuel 28 Saul consulting a medium who calls up a spirit pretending to be the deceased prophet Samuel.
3. Jewish Heritage Online Magazine, *Angels in the Talmud*, http://jhom.-com/topics/angels/talmud_fourangels.htm#5a (12 October 2010).
4. A prayer of the Jews according to *Israel Today* Magazine, April 2005, No. 75, p 12.

4TH COMMANDMENT

1. Exodus 31:13, 17; Ezekiel 20:12, 20.
2. Matthew 11:28-30; Colossians 2:14-17.
3. Matthew 12:8, 24:20; Mark 2:27-28; Luke 6:5.
4. Other European languages retain this custom of counting a week as 8 days and two weeks as 15 days. In French, "in two weeks" is "dans quinze jours" (in 15 days) and "next Sunday" is "dimanche en huit" (literally Sunday in 8).
5. Johnson, Ken, *Ancient Law of Kings*, 2018. Digital.
6. Romans 14; Galatians 4; Colossians 2.

5

1. Samuelian, Thomas, *Armenian Origins*, p 8. http://ararat-center.org/up-load/files/TomasSamuelyan_Origins_2004.pdf (28 Mar 2009).
2. Barton, David, *The Role of Pastors & Christians in Civil Government*, Wall Builder Press, 2016, p. 27-28.

5 GIFTS

1. 1 Kings 17:17-24, 2 Kings 4:18-37, 2 Kings 13:20-25, Matthew 10:18-26, Luke 7:11-16, Jon 11, Acts 9:40, Acts 20:10.

5 LOVE LANGUAGES

1. For further study of the 5 love languages, watch or listen to the 2 DVDs or CDs titled *"Understanding the Father's Love"* at www.discover.org.au/shop.

6

1. According to the Jewish Law of Kings 9.1, God gave Adam these 6 commandments: 1) Abstain from idolatry, 2) Do not commit blasphemy, 3) Do not commit murder, 4) Do not commit fornication, 5) Do not steal, 6) Establish courts of justice. 5 of these are exactly the same as Moses' 10 Commandments. 4 out of 5 precepts of Buddha are exactly the same as Moses' 10 Commandments. See my book "From Buddha to Jesus" to understand the implications of this when comparing Buddhism and Christianity. It is safe to assume that humanity had a common knowledge of these laws since the time of Adam.

2. From which we get the French *eglise*, Spanish *iglesia*, and English *ecclesiastes* (preacher) or *ecclesiastic* (clergyman). The original meaning of this word was the "assembly" or "called out ones" comprised of all men over 30 who owned property. They had to prove themselves by speaking for 6 minutes on the *bema* stone or speaker's platform. They formed the heart of Athenian democracy. God used this Greek concept and applied it directly to His church, calling it the *ecclesia*.

3. *Life Expectancy at Birth*, www.cia.gov/library/publications/the-world-factbook/rankorder/2102rank.html (7 October 2010).

4. Total immediate deaths, excluding post-war deaths from the effects of the atomic bombs, are difficult to determine. Figures vary between 50 to 70 million, so the acceptable average figure is 60 million, a horror to imagine!

5. Both 2 Peter 2:4-5 and Jude 1:6-7 confirm that some fallen angels sinned by having illicit intercourse with women, and for this cause God has cast them into fire. The fact that a class of angels are not loose on the earth with Satan, but are now in confinement, proves they committed a sin besides that of the original rebellion with Satan. Jude 1:7 compares their sin to that of "Sodom and Gomorrah," clearly referring to sexual immorality.

6. Matthew 12:24 or Mark 3:22; Luke 11:15; John 7:20, 8:48, 8:52, 10:20.

7. Matthew 12:38 or Mark 8:11; Matthew 16:1; Matthew 24:3 or Mark 13:4; Luke 11:16; John 2:18; John 6:30.

8. Judges 16:29-30, 1 Samuel 31:4-5, 2 Samuel 17:23, 1 Kings 16:18, Matthew 27:5, Acts 1:18.

9. My near death experience and teaching on suicide are recorded on the DVD *"6 Suicides of the Bible"*. It will help someone you love not to give up!

6TH COMMANDMENT

1. Exodus 20:13; Deuteronomy 5:17; Matthew 5:21; Romans 13:9.

7

1. 1591, 1656, 1787, 1805, 1917, 1935, 1982 according to *A Catalogue of Eclipse Cycles*, www.phys.uu.nl/~vgent/eclipse/eclipsecycles.htm (25 Oct 2010). The next year with 7 eclipses of any kind will be 2038.
2. Rabbi Blech, Benjamin, *The Secrets of Hebrew Words*, Rowman & Littlefield Publishers, Maryland, USA, 1991, 2001. Digital.
3. *Ibid.*
4. Filmer, W.E., *God Counts: A Study in Bible Numbers*, Evangelistic Literature Enterprise, Strathpine QLD, 1984.
5. Isaiah 41:4; 44:6; 48:12; Revelation 1:11, 17; 2:8; 22:13.
6. Panin, Dr. Ivan, *God is a Mathematician*, http://www.bereanpublishers.com/Apologetics/god_is_a_mathematician.htm (17 April 2009).
7. Exodus 15:20, Judges 4:4, 2 Kings 22:14, Nehemiah 6:14, Luke 1:41-45, Luke 1:46-55, Luke 2:36-38.
8. Isaiah's wife in 8:3 and Philip's 4 daughters in Acts 21:9.
9. Smyrna and Philadelphia received no rebuke or condemnation. Sardis and Laodicea received no recognition or commendation. Study the "7 Letters to 7 Churches" in 3 hours by listening to my CDs on the chapters 2 and 3 of the Book of Revelation.
10. Learn the "22 Future Events Predicted by Revelation" in 4 hours or study the entire "Book of Revelation" in 12 hours by watching DVDs available from Discover.org.au/shop.
11. Deuteronomy 18:15-19, John 1:21, John 6:14.
12. Matthew 8:12, 13:42, 13:50, 22:13, 24:15, 25:30; Luke 13:28.
13. Moxham, Steve, *Why Donald Trump Was Elected: God's Appointed President*, https://www.stevemoxham.com/articles/trump-israel-seven.htm (19 April 2019)

7 FEASTS

1. Nisan is the same month as Abib (Exodus 34:18). Both are the 1st month of the sacred calendar and 7th month of the civil calendar. Abib was called Nisan after the Babylonian Captivity (Nehemiah 2:1).
2. Tishri is the same month as Ethanim. Both are the 7th month of the sacred calendar (1 Kings 8:2) and 1st month of the civil calendar.

3. Reinhold, Roy, *Paganism in Christmas*, http://members.aol.com/prophe-cy04/Articles/Christianity/christmas.html (29 September 2004).

7 LAWS OF NOAH

1. Sources include: *The Law of Kings 9, The Ancient Seder Olam 5, Book of Gad the Seer 9, b. Sanhedrin 56a, The Dictionary of Judaism in the Biblical Period "Noahides", Mishneh Torah Kings and Wars 8:11.*
2. Johnson, Ken, *Ancient Law of Kings* 8:11, 2018. Digital.
3. Look for my book "The 7 Laws of Noah" on http://amazon.com/author/newyorktimesbestseller.

8

1. According to both the Bible and the Talmud, Noah and his wife Naamah did not have any more children after the Flood—a failure to obey God's command to repopulate the earth. Rabbis debate over the reasons Noah did not father more children. Two proposals are that Noah was either sodomized or castrated by his grandson Canaan (Ham's son) in the incident of Genesis 9:21-25. Therefore Noah either chose not to bring more children into the wicked world or he was unable to have more children. See https://jbqnew.jewishbible.org/index/books-of-the-bible/genesis/doesnt-noah-children-flood/
2. Genesis 19:23, 2 Samuel 23:4, Psalm 19:4, Psalm 50:1, Jeremiah 8:2, Joel 2:10, Amos 8:9, Luke 21:25.
3. In Biblical times, there was a 7-year cycle of boom and bust which led to the meteoric rise of a man of God named Joseph, who believed God, believed in cycles, and prepared accordingly. The Dust Bowl of the 1930s was also a 7-year drought. The 7-year cycle may have lengthened to 8.6 in more modern times.
4. Armstrong, Martin, *The 8.6 Year Cycle and the Forces of Mother Nature*, http://armstrongeconomics.com/writings (28 Nov 2010).
5. Genesis 17:12, Genesis 21:4, Leviticus 12:3, Luke 1:59, Luke 2:21.
6. *British Journal of Cancer* 19, No. 2, June 1965, p 217-226.
7. 1 Corinthians 3:9, 16, 17; 1 Corinthians 6:19; 2 Corinthians 6:16; Ephesians 2:22; Hebrews 3:6; 1 Peter 2:5.

9

1. Nisan is the start of the calendar, Passover begins at the end of the 2nd week, Pentecost is 7 weeks after Passover, therefore 9 weeks.

2. At least until 24 August 2006, when the International Astronomical Union demoted Pluto to a dwarf planet. This was partially due to the 2005 discovery of the most distant known object in the Solar System, another dwarf planet 27% larger than Pluto called Eris. Both Pluto and Eris have one moon each.
3. Romans 1:24-27, Galatians 5:19, Ephesians 5:3-5, Colossians 3:5. The Greek word for "uncleanness" is *akatharthos* meaning impure in thought and action. The Bible is telling us homosexuality begins with an unchecked thought and unchecked desire. By becoming Christian, the Holy Spirit will empower us to self-control.
4. Besides innumerable healings, signs and wonders not described specifically, such as those in John 2:23, 7:31, 11:47.

10

1. Daniel 1:12 This was an act of faith with a supernatural outcome, because 10 days is not naturally long enough to see the results of a diet.
2. This "Ark" is an ornamental wooden closet or cupboard where Torah scrolls are held in each synagogue. It is supposed to be reminiscent of the original "Ark of the Covenant" which contained the original Ten Commandments. It usually sits against the wall facing Jerusalem or the northern wall.
3. The Book of Jubilees was well known by first-century Jews and Christians, and 15 fragments of the book were found among the Dead Sea Scrolls. It is also known as "Little Genesis" because it gives a condensed version of Genesis 1 to Exodus 12.
4. When God refers to Himself, often the first person plural pronoun "we," "us" or "our" is used (Genesis 1:26, 11:7). Jews cannot understand this since God is One, but they try to explain it away by claiming the plural refers to "greatness" or the "we" refers to God and some of His angels. God does not change the ordinary sense of grammar and we are not to add "angels" to the text when none are referred to. This plurality in the Godhead is easy to understand for the person who believes in the Trinity.
5. Cioccolanti, Steve, *10 Tests of Justice (DVD)*, https://discover.org.au/bookshop/topic/steve-cioccolanti-justice-series.
6. Temporary because they all died afterwards, in contrast with Christ's resurrection that is permanent. He was the first to rise from the dead with a new resurrection body that will never die. We who believe Jesus will be next to be permanently resurrected. The unrighteous dead will be last to be permanently resurrected, then confined eternally in the Lake of Fire (Revelation 20:15, 21:8).

10 DAYS

1. This was Antiochus' birthday. The same day 3 years later marked the restoration of Temple worship in 164 BC The 25th of Kislev is now commemorated by Jews as *Hanukkah* or the winter *Feast of Dedication*. The only mention of this holiday in the Bible is in the New Testament! Jesus celebrated it in John 10:22.
2. *Halley's Bible Handbook*, Zondervan Publishing House, Grand Rapids MI, 1965.
3. The Nicene Creed quoted nowadays is not from the First Council of Nicea in 325 AD, but from the First Council of Constantinople in 381 AD. Both Councils agreed on the Creed; the substantive change by the later Council is an elaboration on the Holy Spirit.

10 COMMANDMENTS

1. The 10 Commandments are based on Exodus 20; Deuteronomy 5, 6:5; Mark 12:30 and Luke 10:27.

10 PERCENT

1. Genesis 18:19, Psalm 33:5, 37:6, 89:14, 97:2, 103:6, Proverbs 21:3, Ecclesiastes 5:8, Isaiah 9:7, 28:17, 32:1, 33:5, 59:9, Amos 5:24.
2. Roy Ngerng, *How Are Taxes Built For The Rich In Singapore?* https://thehearttruths.com/2013/08/23/how-are-taxes-built-for-the-rich-in-singapore/ (2013-08-23).

11 SOLAR CYCLE

1. Solar activity includes sunspots, irradiance and short-wave radiation.
2. *Ireland and Northern European Countries to Benefit from Global Warming*, http://www.finfacts.ie/irelandbusinessnews/publish/article_10008594.shtml (6 August 2010).

13 NEGATIVE

1. Genesis 12:10, 26:1, 41:45; Ruth 1:1; 2 Samuel 21:1; 1 Kings 18:1; 2 Kings 4:38, 7:4, 25:3; Nehemiah 5:3; Jeremiah 14:1; Luke 15:14; Acts 11:28.
2. Judges chapter 12, chapter 20; 2 Samuel 2:1-11, 2:12-3:1, chapters 15-18, chapter 20; 1 Kings chapter 12, 15:7, 15:16-22, 16:8-20, 16:21-22; 2 Kings

chapter 9, chapter 14.

3. Gibeah was the home of King Saul and capital of Israel under his reign.
4. Judges 19-20, total deaths recorded in 19:35, total survivors in 19:47. Both King Saul and Saul of Tarsus descended from one of these 600 survivors. One "Saul" became an apostate king, the other "Saul" became the mighty Apostle Paul. The remnants of this tribe were very important to history. Thank God for those who survived.
5. Samuel recounted this cycle of sin and savior in 1 Samuel 12:9-11.
6. Gideon was also called Jerubbaal, Judges 9:2, 1 Samuel 12:11.
7. Judges 5:16-17 Dan, along with Reuben, Gad (Gilead) and Asher refused to fight with Deborah against the Canaanites.
8. Perhaps uncomfortable with having a serpent as a sign of its tribe, Dan later modified it to an eagle with a serpent in its mouth.

13 POSITIVE

1. According to Stone, Perry, *Breaking the Jewish Code*, p 84.
2. http://time.com/money/4109096/more-millennial-guys-live-at-home-than-women (18 Dec 2018).
3. Samuel Adams and John Adams were second cousins. So Samuel Adams and John Quincy Adams are second cousins once removed.

15

1. The Masoretic text is the authoritative Hebrew and Aramaic text of the Tanakh or Old Testament, copied, punctuated and distributed by a group of Jewish scribes known as the Masoretes who worked between the 7th and 10th centuries AD.
2. Ellicott's Commentary for English Readers, Genesis 33, https://biblehub.com/commentaries/ellicott/genesis/33.htm (7 May 2019).
3. Baumgarten, Albert, *Why Is Esau's Kiss Dotted?*, https://thetorah.com/why-is-esaus-kiss-dotted/ (7 May 2019).
4. The 15 passages where *puncta extraordinaria* appear are: Genesis 16:5, 18:9, 19:33, 33:4, 37:12; Numbers 3:39, 9:10, 21:30, 29:15; Deuteronomy 29:28; 2 Samuel 19:20; Isaiah 44:9; Ezekiel 41:20, 46:22; and Psalms 27:13. As you can see, 10 instances occur in the Torah, 4 in the Prophets, and 1 in the Hagiographa.

17

1. For further study, watch *The Life of Joseph*. This 6-part series will take you through: 1. the Pit (rejection), 2. Potiphar's House (new beginning), 3. Potiphar's Wife (disillusion), 4. the Prison (demotion before promotion), 5. the Palace (dreams come true), and 6. Self-Pity (dealing with the past). https://discover.org.au/bookshop/steve-cioccolanti-the-life-of-joseph-series-dvd

2. I adapted this from Gordon Lindsay's idea in his book *God's Plan of the Ages* published by Christ for the Nations (1988). Some years are off by one year ahead or one year behind, which suggests to me that God may be counting by the Hebrew calendar, which always straddles two Gregorian years. Besides, war is not necessary every 17 years exactly. There will be no war during most of the Millennium and in Heaven (Revelation 20:8, Isaiah 2:4, 4:3).

3. *The Treaty of Paris 1783*, https://en.wikipedia.org/wiki/Treaty_of_Paris_(1783) (18 April 2019).

4. Landon, Fred, *Western Ontario and the American Frontier*, McGill-Queen's Press (1941). p 123.

5. Lindsay, Gordon, *God's Plan of the Ages*, Christ for the Nations (1988), p. 16.

6. Warner, Bill, *Statistical Islam*, https://www.politicalislam.com/trilogy-project/statistical-islam/ (18 April 2019).

7. Lindsay, Gordon, *God's Plan of the Ages*, Christ for the Nations (1988), p. 57-58.

18

1. Solomon violated this rule by taking 700 wives and 300 concubines, and his heart was turned away from serving the Lord the way his father David did.

2. Rabbi Blech, Benjamin, *The Secrets of Hebrew Words*, Rowman & Littlefield Publishers, Maryland, USA, 1991, 2001. Digital.

3. *Shema* comes from the first Hebrew word of Deuteronomy 6:4, "Hear, O Israel, The Lord our God, the Lord is one!" The prayer continues with Deuteronomy 11:13-21 and Numbers 15:37-41.

4. See Matthew 5:5-13 for this model prayer.

5. John 14:13-14, 15:16, 16:23-24, 26, Mark 916:17-18.

6. Use prayer models to pray God's Word on specific needs and get answers: www.discover.org.au/pray.

19

1. Tang, Dafei, *Pekudei—Gold, Silver and Copper*, 11 March 2016, https://blogs. timesofisrael.com/pekudei-gold-silver-and-copper/ (13 April 2019).
2. The story of our ministry property is shared on YouTube: https://youtu.be/ jKLSXPDxTFI. You can claim the book *"A Guide to Making a Will"* for an amount of any donation (plus shipping) towards the building campaign goal of $1.5 million.
3. R.H. Charles translation of *The Book of Jubilees*, 4:30-31, 23:9, Clarendon Press, Oxford, UK, 1913.
4. 2 Kings 17:23-29 Assyria's policy of bringing foreigners into Samaria and encouraging them to inter-marry with the inhabitants of Samaria is partly responsible for the Jews' hatred for the Samaritans. With inter-marriage often came idolatry. See John 4:9 and 8:48 to see the Jews' racism against Samaritans. That is why Jesus' choice of making the "Good Samaritan" the hero of Luke 10 made it a very convicting parable. The Jewish rabbis thought they were good and did not need a Savior, but they failed to obey even the first commandment—love your neighbor! Only the new birth can end racism. Only faith in Christ makes loving our enemies possible.
5. First and Second Chronicles record only the stories of the Kings of Judah, because only they are relevant to the Messianic line. The Messiah must come from the Tribe of Judah and be related to all the kings of Judah. Jesus had such great ancestors as King David, Solomon, Jehoshaphat, Hezekiah and Josiah! He is not only the King of Heaven, but also the rightful heir to the throne of his father David.

19TH BOOK

1. Contrary to popular misconception, the middle verse of the Bible is not Psalm 118:8. Since there is an even number of verses in the Bible (31,102 in KJV), there are 2 middle verses (verses 15,551 and 15,552). See Kizzah, Nic, *King James Bible Statistics*, http://www.biblebelievers.com/believers-org/kjv-stats.html (25 Oct 2010).

19 HEALINGS

1. Matthew 4:23, 9:35, 12,:15, 14:14, 15:30, 19:2; Luke 5:15, 6:17-19, 9. Healing continued after Jesus gave us the same Holy Spirit, as per Acts 5:16 and Mark 16:15-18.
2. Matthew 9:8, 15:31; Mark 2:12; Luke 5:26, 13:13, 17:15; John 11:4; Acts 4:21.

3. Greek *parakaleo*, to urge or implore, not *prosaiteo*, to ask repeatedly or *epaiteo*, to beg. *Parakaleo* shares the same root as *Parakletos*, a title of the Holy Spirit meaning Helper. The Holy Spirit is not a beggar, but One who encourages, urges and implores. The word "begged" should have been translated "requested," but old English used "beg" in the same sense that we still say I "beg your pardon," meaning "I ask you to say it again."

20

1. Feldhann, Shaunti and Rice, Lisa, *For Parents Only*, Multnomah Books, 2007.
2. Revelation 2:7, 11, 17, 26; 3:5, 12, 21; 21:7.
3. Johnson, Ken, *Ancient Law of Kings*, 7:15. Digital.

22

1. 7 years for his wife Leah + 7 years for his second wife Rachel + 6 years under his cheating uncle Laban + 2 years running from his jealous brother Esau.
2. 13 years in Potiphar's house and prison + 7 years in Pharaoh's house during the time of plenty + 2 years of famine before his 10 brothers came to buy food and bow down to him.
3. *Arab World*, https://en.wikipedia.org/wiki/Arab_world. Retrieved 12 March 2019.
4. Kolatch, Afred, *The Jewish Book of Why*, Jonathan David Publishers, 1981. Digital.
5. For more explanation watch my end time DVDs on the Book of Revelation at www.discover.org.au/shop
6. *Definition of Bones in the Head*, http://www.medterms.com/script/main/art.asp?articlekey=8644 (11 Oct 2010). There would be 29 bones in the human head if we counted the 6 auditory ossiciles or tiny bones inside the middle ears.
7. Cahn, Jonathan, *The Paradigm*, Frontline, 2017. Digital.
8. Strang, Stephen, *Trump Aftershock: The President's Seismic Impact on Culture and Faith in America*, Frontline, 2018. Digital.
9. The "Biblical Justice Course" is available on DVDs at www.discover.org.au/bookshop or by streaming at at vimeo.com/stevecioccolanti/vod_pages
10. Chappell, Bill. U.S. *National Debt Hits Record $22 Trillion.* 13 Feb 2019. https://www.npr.org/2019/02/13/694199256/u-s-national-debt-hits-22-trillion-a-new-record-thats-predicted-to-fall

23

1. DeWitt, David, *Chimp Genome Sequences Very Different From Man*, http://creationontheweb.com/images/pdfs/tj/j19_3/j19_3_4-5.pdf (24 March 2009).
2. *Ibid.* (24 March 2009).
3. Weiland, Dr. Carl, *Steve Jones & the 'end of human evolution'*, http://creation.com/steve-jones-and-the-end-of-human-evolution (11 February 2009).
4. The New Scientist, Volume 194, Issue 2608, 16 June 2007, pages 48-51.
5. Sanford, Dr. John, *How Evolution Hurts Science* DVD, by Creation Ministries International.
6. The Second Law of Thermodynamics states that the universe is in decay: that is, everything tends towards disorder or 'entropy'; usable energy is running out; and information does not organize itself but tends to get scrambled. This is in stark contrast to the theory of evolution, which claims that complex order rose out of disorder, intelligible information like DNA appeared by chance, and matter organized itself. Evolutionists irrationally ignore the Second Law of Thermodynamics and claim that this law "does not apply to life." However, Dr. John Ross of Harvard University wrote in *Chemical and Engineering News* (7 July 1980, p. 40), "... there are no known violations of the second law of thermodynamics."
7. *Was Dawkins Stumped?*, www.creationontheweb.com/content/view/5712 (4 March 2009).

24

1. Burleigh, Nina, *The Messiah Cometh*, Newsweek (7 April 2016), https://www.newsweek.com/2016/04/15/hobby-lobby-steve-green-bible-museum-washington-dc-444752.html (2019-03-28).
2. Finnis Dake, *The Dake Annotated Reference Bible*, p 142 of NT.

INDEX

Talmud ★ 2, 6, 70 Sevens, 120
Teeth ★ 32, 366
Telomeres ★ 23
Temple ★ 9 Av, 26, 70 Sevens
Terrorism ★ 11
Test ★ 10, 40, 400
Tetragrammaton ★ 26
Texas ★ 17
Thailand ★ 3, 6, 13 Negative, 150, 193
Thermodynamics, Law of ★ 23
Third Temple ★ 70 Sevens, 120 Cycle, 666
Tibet ★ 193
Time ★ 4, 19, 28, 120 Cycle
Titan ★ 666
Tithe ★ 10 Percent, 136, 666
Tongues ★ 3, 50, 120 Cycle
Trial by jury ★ 7 Laws of Noah
Tribulation ★ 10, 22
Trinity ★ 1, 3, 5, 92
Truth ★ 446
Trump, Donald ★ 2 Dreams, 7, 17, 22, 58
Tuesday ★ 3
Turkey ★ 2 Dreams, 666
U
USA ★ See "America"
V
Vatican ★ 193, 666
Vengeance ★ 77
Victory ★ 17
W
Wandering ★ 38
War ★ 6, 17, 20
Water ★ 3
Wedding ★ 3

BOOKS BY STEVE CIOCCOLANTI

President Trump's Pro-Christian Accomplishments
(Paperback, Kindle or Apple Book)
Trump's Unfinished Business:
10 Prophecies to Save America (Paperback or Ebook)
From Buddha to Jesus
(English, Cambodian, Chinese, French, Indonesian & Thai)
ブッダからイエスへ
(From Buddha to Jesus | Japanese Edition)
30 Days to a New You
(Compact Plan for Personal Growth & Freedom)
30 Días de Transformación Personal (Spanish Edition)
12 Keys to a Good Relationship with God
(Children's Book written with 6-year-old daughter Alexis)
A Guide to Making a Will
(Considering the Church in your legacy)
The Divine Code: A Prophetic Encyclopedia of Numbers,
Vol. 1 & 2 (available as a 2-in-1 set only from Discover.org.au.)

All e-books are available through Amazon.com.

VIDEOS BY STEVE CIOCCOLANTI

7000 Years of Prophecy (1 hour)
End Time Complete Pack (58 hours)
6000 Years of History & Prophecy (3 hours)
4000 Years of History (Old Testament Survey,
12 hours from Creation to Christ. Our #1 Bestseller)
22 Future Events Predicted by Revelation (4 hours)
Jewish vs Christian Dating & Parenting (2 hours)
Where is God During Tragedies? (2 hours)
4 Steps to Enter into Your Call (1 hour)
Why Am I Not There Yet? (1 hour)
Atheists Don't Exists (3 hours)
The Life of Joseph (6 hours)
Defeating Fear (3 hours)
Book of Job (2 hours)
Jezebel (2 hours)

Browse DVDs and CDs at: www.Discover.org.au
Videos-on-demand at: vimeo.com/stevecioccolanti/vod_pages

THE BIBLICAL JUSTICE COURSE

~

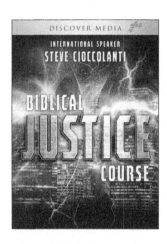

1. The Last Move of God
2. How The Bible Solves Injustice
3. The Key to Reaching Jews in the End-Times
4. How To Curse Like Jesus | The 10th Prayer
5. Raising End Time Kids | Rewards & Punishments That Express God's Justice
6. The Tyranny of Emotions
7. Jesus The Avenger is Coming Soon
8. 10 Tests of Justice | How to Handle People Who Mistreat You
9. When Government Goes Bad | Injustices of Nazis

~

9 DVDs at: www.Discover.org.au/shop

Also available for streaming at: Vimeo.com/stevecioccolanti/vod_pages

ABOUT THE AUTHOR

Steve Cioccolanti, B.A., M.Ed., is a Christian author, a prolific teacher of God's Word and senior pastor of Discover Church in Melbourne, Australia. With over 50 million views, he is one of the most watched Christian YouTubers worldwide and pioneered Online Church before COVID lockdowns. He has authored hundreds of DVDs and five #1 bestselling books on Amazon and Apple.

Pastor Steve has traveled to over 46 counties as a popular speaker, a Biblical tour leader to Israel, Jordan and Saudi Arabia, and a guest on international TV shows, including on Daystar and The Praise the Lord Television Network.

He is currently writing a book, recording a video, blogging a thought or helping someone. To book him for an event or interview, please check his availability at Discover.org.au/invite.

～

Your mentoring doesn't stop with this book! Join Pastor Cioccolanti's online church community at DiscoverChurch.Online. With the power of social media, Pastor Cioccolanti says, *"We can have church anywhere, any time."*

Discover Ministries is the global extension of Discover Church. It exists to glorify God and fulfill Isaiah 11:9, "For the earth shall be full of the knowledge of the Lord as the waters cover the sea."

Your faithful support helps others find life-changing truths. Gift here: Discover.org.au/partner.

facebook.com/discoverministry
twitter.com/cioccolanti
instagram.com/stevecioccolanti
amazon.com/author/newyorktimesbestseller
youtube.com/@discoverministries

Made in United States
North Haven, CT
02 May 2024

52028311R00202